Grounds and Envelopes

Providing a source of vision for the revitalization of ground and envelope as spatial elements that can inform the search for embedded locally specific architectures, this book collects essays and projects that each contribute a particular element to what might constitute an integrated and richly nuanced approach to spatial organization. Projects include the following:

- Paulo Mendes da Rocha: Brazilian Pavilion, Osaka World Expo 1970, Osaka, Japan
- RCR Arquitectes: Marquee at Les Cols Restaurant, Olot, Girona, Spain
- Weiss/Manfredi: Seattle Art Museum: Olympic Sculpture Park, Seattle, Washington, USA
- Peter Eisenman: City of Culture of Galicia, Santiago de Compostela, Spain
- Plasma Studio and Groundlab: Xi'an Horticultural Expo, Longgang, China
- Foreign Office Architects: Yokohama International Port Terminal, Yokohama, Japan
- Nekton Design: Turf City, Reykjavik, Iceland
- Alvaro Siza: Swimming Pool, Leça da Palmeira, Portugal
- Eduardo Souto de Moura: Braga Municipal Stadium, Braga, Portugal
- MVRDV: Villa VPRO, Hilversum, The Netherlands
- Bernard Tschumi: Le Fresnoy Art Centre, Tourcoing, France
- OCEAN: World Centre for Human Concerns, New York City, USA
- R&Sie(n): Spidernethewood, Nîmes, France
- Toyo Ito: Serpentine Pavilion, London, England
- Enric Miralles and Carme Pinós: Olympic Archery Range, Barcelona, Spain
- Kengo Kuma: GC Prostho Museum Research Centre, Aichi Prefecture, Japan
- Cloud 9: MediaTic, Barcelona, Spain
- Diller, Scofidio and Renfro: Blur Building, Swiss National Expo, Yverdon-les-Bains, Switzerland.

With an abundance of built and unbuilt key projects available, it is now possible to outline the contours of a new discourse. This book initiates a new beginning in this direction so that architecture can partake in the creation of heterogeneous space and culturally, socially and environmentally sustainable built environments.

Michael U. Hensel is an architect, researcher, educator and writer. He is currently Professor for Architecture at the Oslo School of Architecture and Design, where he directs the Research Centre for Architecture and Tectonics. He is founding and current chairman of OCEAN – Design Research Association and of SEA – Sustainable Environment Association, and has authored and edited numerous books and journals.

Jeffrey P. Turko is an educator, researcher, and was founding partner of the international award-winning design practice NEKTON DESIGN. Currently he leads the research based practice NEKTON STUDIO and is a Senior Lecturer at the University of Brighton, he is also a registered architect in the Netherlands, an advisory board member of the Research Center for Architecture and Tectonics, and member of OCEAN Design Research Association.

Grounds and Envelopes

Reshaping Architecture and the Built Environment

Michael U. Hensel and Jeffrey P. Turko

LONDON AND NEW YORK

First published 2015
by Routledge
2 Park Square, Milton Park, Abingdon, Oxon OX14 4RN

and by Routledge
711 Third Avenue, New York, NY 10017

Routledge is an imprint of the Taylor & Francis Group, an informa business

© 2015 Michael U. Hensel and Jeffrey P. Turko

The right of Michael U. Hensel and Jeffrey P. Turko to be identified as authors of this work has been asserted by them in accordance with sections 77 and 78 of the Copyright, Designs and Patents Act 1988.

All rights reserved. No part of this book may be reprinted or reproduced or utilized in any form or by any electronic, mechanical, or other means, now known or hereafter invented, including photocopying and recording, or in any information storage or retrieval system, without permission in writing from the publishers.

Trademark notice: Product or corporate names may be trademarks or registered trademarks, and are used only for identification and explanation without intent to infringe.

British Library Cataloguing-in-Publication Data
A catalogue record for this book is available from the British Library

Library of Congress Cataloging-in-Publication Data
Hensel, Michael.
Grounds and envelopes : reshaping architecture and the built environment / Michael U. Hensel and Jeffrey P. Turko.
pages cm
Includes bibliographical references and index.
1. Space (Architecture)   2. Architecture – Environmental aspects.   I. Turko, Jeffrey P.
II. Title.
NA2765.H46 2015
720–dc23   2014032467

ISBN: 978-0-415-63916-3 (hbk)
ISBN: 978-0-415-63917-0 (pbk)
ISBN: 978-1-315-72811-7 (ebk)

Typeset in Avenir
by Servis Filmsetting Ltd, Stockport, Cheshire

Contents

Acknowledgements	x
Foreword: The Crisis of the Object Today by David Leatherbarrow	xi
Foreword: Grounds and Envelopes by Alejandro Zaera-Polo	xiii
Introduction: En route to non-discrete architecture	1
Chapter 01 Space	12
Chapter 02 Grounds	23
Chapter 03 Envelopes	38
Chapter 04 Environments	51
Chapter 05 Locality	63
Thirty projects	82
GROUNDS	83
Project 01 Brazilian Pavilion, Osaka World Expo 1970, Osaka, Japan, 1969 PAULO MENDES DA ROCHA	83
Project 02 MuBE – Brazilian Museum of Sculpture, Sao Paulo, Brazil, 1988 PAULO MENDES DA ROCHA	87
Project 03 Spreebogen – International Urban Planning Competition, Berlin, Germany, 1992 ANDREW ZAGO	94
Project 04 Marquee at Les Cols Restaurant, Olot, Girona, Spain, 2007 to 2011 RCR ARQUITECTES	99
Project 05 Seattle Art Museum: Olympic Sculpture Park, Seattle, Washington, USA, 2001 to 2007 WEISS/MANFREDI	104
Project 06 Meydan – Umraniye Retail Complex & Multiplex, Istanbul, Turkey, 2007 FOREIGN OFFICE ARCHITECTS	111

Project 07 City of Culture of Galicia, Santiago de Compostela, Spain, 1999 to 2012 — 117
PETER EISENMAN

Project 08 Xi'an Horticultural Expo, Longgang, China, 2011 — 125
PLASMA STUDIO AND GROUNDLAB

Project 09 A Thousand Grounds: Spreebogen, Berlin, Germany, 1992 — 132
MICHAEL HENSEL, CHUL KONG, NOPADOL LIMWATANAKUL AND JOHAN BETTUM

Project 10 Yokohama International Port Terminal, Yokohama, Japan, 1995 to 2002 — 138
FOREIGN OFFICE ARCHITECTS

Project 11 Turf City, Reykjavik, Iceland, 2008 — 145
NEKTON DESIGN
JEFFREY PAUL TURKO & GUDJON THOR ERLENDSSON

Project 12 Braga Municipal Stadium, Braga, Portugal, 2003 — 152
EDUARDO SOUTO DE MOURA

Project 13 Swimming Pool, Leça da Palmeira, Portugal, 1966 — 159
ÁLVARO SIZA

Project 14 Asphalt Spot, Tokamashi, Japan, 2003 — 167
R&SIE(N)

Project 15 Geopark Playground, Stavanger, Norway, 2008 — 172
HELEN & HARD

ENVELOPES — 178

Project 16 Villa VPRO, Hilversum, The Netherlands, 1993 to 1997 — 178
MVRDV

Project 17 Palazzo del Cinema, Venice, Italy, 1990 — 184
STEVEN HOLL

Project 18 Le Fresnoy Art Centre, Tourcoing, France, 1991 to 1997   189
BERNARD TSCHUMI

Project 19 World Centre for Human Concerns, New York City, USA, 2001 to 2004   195
OCEAN

Project 20 Wall House, Santiago de Chile, Chile, 2007   200
FAR – FROHN AND ROJAS

Project 21 Three Seaside Second Homes, Norway, 2012   207
JOAKIM HOEN

Project 22 Spidernethewood, Nîmes, France, 2007   212
R&SIE(N)
FRANÇOIS ROCHE, STÉPHANIE LAVAUX, JEAN NAVARRO WITH NICOLAS GREEN

Project 23 Serpentine Pavilion, London, England, 2002   218
TOYO ITO

Project 24 Czech National Library, Prague, Czech Republic, 2006   224
OCEAN AND SCHEFFLER + PARTNER

Project 25 Olympic Archery Range, Barcelona, Spain, 1989 to 1991   230
ENRIC MIRALLES AND CARME PINÓS

Project 26 GC Prostho Museum Research Centre, Torii Matsu Machi, Kasugai-shi, Aichi Prefecture, Japan, 2010   238
KENGO KUMA

Project 27 Endesa Pavilion, Barcelona, Spain, 2011   245
IAAC – INSTITUTE FOR ADVANCED ARCHITECTURE OF CATALONIA

Project 28 Estonian Academy of Arts, Tallinn, Estonia, 2008   253
SEAN LALLY WEATHERS IN COLLABORATION WITH MORRIS ARCHITECTS

Project 29 MediaTic, Barcelona, Spain, 2007 to 2010   258
CLOUD 9

Project 30 Blur Building, Swiss National Expo, Yverdon-les-Bains, Switzerland, 2002   265
DILLER, SCOFIDIO AND RENFRO

Bibliography   270
Author biographies   274
Index   275

We neutralize any and all our misgivings about the inroads of architecture on our lives with lame protests directed at nobody in particular. Part of our troubles result from the tendency to ascribe to architects – or for that matter, to all specialists – exceptional insight into problems of living when, in truth, most of them are concerned with problems of business and prestige.

Bernard Rudofsky

Introducing new measures won't improve the world … changing attitude will.

Albert Schweitzer

To our mothers Betty Ann and Irmgard, our late fathers Paul and Ulrich, our spouses Sarah and Defne and children Felix and Emma, and to our friends. And to all those who share our conviction that architecture can do much better than it presently does.

Acknowledgements

The interests and concerns that underlie the thoughts offered in this book have been with us and at the root of our work and inquiry for quite some time. It all started in the early 1990s when a lot more seemed possible in architecture from both a critical and projective perspective than it may seem today. We embarked upon putting this book together because of the way architecture appears to have developed by giving into profit escalation, formal caprioles and the humongous yet pointless gesturing that marks booming locations where everything seems to go, as well as due to what we perceive as an acute lack of alternative approaches to architectural design that actually deserve this description.

Our endeavour was made possible by the enthusiasm and tireless efforts of Francesca Ford, Commissioning Editor for Architecture books at Routledge, and by the generous contributions of the practices whose works are portrayed here within. Our sincere gratitude belongs to them, as well as to the eminent thinkers whose in- and foresights have had considerable impact upon our approach to the matter at hand. This includes especially David Leatherbarrow who helped us generously with many aspects of this book. Furthermore we would like to thank the OCEAN Design Research Association in the context of which *Grounds and Envelopes* is a key research area, and our friends and collaborators in OCEAN, in particular Pavel Hladik and Søren S. Sørensen, for generously supporting our endeavour. Defne Sunguroğlu Hensel was a key collaborator in developing approaches to notions such as extended thresholds, auxiliary architectures and the analysis of historical projects from a performance perspective. Thanks also go to Sibyl Trigg and Ricardo Rodrigues Ferreira who helped in the redrawing of an ever-evolving list of projects.

We would like to extend our gratitude to our immensely dedicated project editors, at the start Emma Gadsden and subsequently Grace Harrison, and to others in the Routledge team for their committed work.

Last but not least, this book would surely not have seen the light of day without the unwavering support of our families who coped graciously with our different forms of protracted absence while we were immersed in this work. To them belongs our love and to them we dedicate our efforts in working towards a more exciting and relevant architecture, sustainable environment and promising future.

Foreword
THE CRISIS OF THE OBJECT TODAY
DAVID LEATHERBARROW

Crisis: early fifteenth century, from Latinized form of Greek *krisis*, 'turning point in a disease'.
Object: from medieval Latin *objectum*, 'thing put before'; past participle of *obicere*, 'to present, oppose, cast in the way of'.

Grounds and *Envelopes* have emerged today as primary topics of architectural design because there is common consensus that the long-standing obsession with ungrounded and highly stylized or cosmetic objects of design is unsustainable – not in our cities, the natural environment, or our lives. Although this sense of architecture is felt acutely today, there are precedents to the current critique of object-oriented theory and practice.

'Crisis of the Object' is the title of Colin Rowe and Fred Koetter's explanation of why they proposed collage as a way of composing works of architecture and the city. In 1978, when the chapter was printed in *Collage City*, there was a widespread loss of faith in the promise of modern architecture. Although the *Neues Bauen* had arrived, 'the New Jerusalem was not exactly a going concern'. Dispiriting though the realization was, a turning point had been reached; hence the term *crisis*. Their subtitle, 'The predicament of texture', indicated both the topic that concerned them and a hint about the way the crisis could be overcome: architectural and urban collage, in imitation of Picasso's way of putting things together, would lead to a restoration of (urban) texture, and with it the accommodation and expression of the society and culture we desire.

What had led to the crisis? The answer was plain: modern architecture's fixation on *objects*, on self-defined, technological, ahistorical and free-standing works of design, possessed of indestructible perimeters that sheltered partitions and posts, private because insulated, best seen in the round, insensitive to pressures from beyond because they were carefully calibrated for internal effects, practical to some degree but largely aesthetic. A recommendation for overcoming the impasse was implicit in the statement of the problem: 'rather than hoping and waiting for the withering away of the object (while simultaneously manufacturing versions of it in profusion unparalleled), it might be judicious, in most cases, to allow and encourage the object to become digested in a prevalent texture or matrix.' Their account of collage was meant to show how this digesting could occur.

They were not, however, the first to perceive a crisis, nor did they invent the term; it had been used over thirty years earlier by André Breton, whose widely read papers they did not cite but seem to have known. While Breton had spoken of the *crisis of the object* for several years before his lecture in Prague in 1935, his summary argument on that occasion expressed the Surrealist position more clearly than any other. Objects of the kind Rowe and Koetter were to later criticize – objects designed to be used unthinkingly in the fast-paced and highly programmed activities of modern life – were to be replaced by *objects insolites*. This term has been variously translated in attempts to get at Breton's meaning; alternate versions include objects that are unusual, odd, disturbing, or more literally, insolent. Although he was concerned in this talk with the art object in general and the surrealist object in particular, Breton could not prevent himself from noting the (beautifully) disturbing quality of the photomurals depicting micro- and macroscopic images of natural phenomena inside Le Corbusier's recently completed Swiss Pavilion at the *Cité Universitaire* in Paris, a building whose exterior answered 'all the conditions of rationality and coldness anyone could want'. The 'revenge' of the images delighted him. One suspects they delighted Le Corbusier as well. They also provided a clue to some of the characteristics of the objects Breton intended to promote, not art objects in any traditional sense – they had 'had their day' – but more like dream objects or objects of desire, no matter whether they were written, painted or assembled. Oneric and erotic valences did not require the suppression of concrete qualities, nor a certain measure of everydayness; the ready-mades of Man Ray and Marcel Duchamp were no less prosaic than provocative. In the same ways that the hyper-rationalized objects of modern (building) technology were re-qualified by images of animals and fossils on their interiors (likewise rubble walls, vernacular building methods and passive heating and cooling techniques), the hyper-aestheticized objects of traditional art were coupled with things found on the street – Mona Lisa with a moustache. The object's crisis led to its dislocation and disintegration. What had been whole and all of a piece, an autographed work on a gallery wall or a stylized composition on an open site, internally defined and fully coherent in its make-up, entered into relationships with conditions outside itself, conditions that were, oddly enough, both invigorating and unremarkable because they defined the everyday world given to direct experience and perception. The contextualizing term Breton often used is helpful here: he always spoke of the *situation* of the object. Analogous terms in philosophy, typically hyphenated, were *ex-static* perception and *being-in-the-world*. If the *marvellous* were to be reclaimed for art, it would be found in the alleys, gardens and boulevards of the city and the natural world.

In the decades since the *Surrealist Manifestoes* and *Collage City* the architects and architecture which those texts criticized have been re-evaluated. One needn't say the newer accounts are more accurate to admit that they are much more interesting. Anyone who has followed recent scholarship devoted to figures such as Le Corbusier, Adolf Loos, Mies van der Rohe, Marcel Breuer and Richard Neutra, to say nothing about the rereadings of people like Alvar Aalto and Frank Lloyd Wright, will have felt the need to seriously reconsider and probably reject the old idea that the works of modern architecture were intended to be seen 'in the round' because they were conceived as 'isolated objects'. That is simply not true; the opposite was the case. Regardless of whether the wider frame of reference to which their buildings referred is described as the landscape, the city or the (ecological) environment, today's interpretations stress engagement and continuity, not just of views and of 'space', which has always been said to 'flow' from inside to outside, but also with 'exterior' materials, terrain and topography, as well as unplanned uses and forms of behaviour. Of course these kinds of involvement cannot be seen in all of the works of these figures; even less often in the works of the many designers who sought to imitate their solutions. The old criticism of the 'object fetish' is not so much unfounded as misdirected, because it is so generalized. The legacy of the modern tradition is richer, more nuanced than we have been led to believe. Together with the object-oriented works that resulted from poor design, misunderstandings and non-architectural intentions, there were and indeed are a great number of projects that creatively transformed the very landscapes, cities and environments in which they appeared.

This book joins step with the recent studies that show how the better buildings of the modern tradition were *embedded* in the concrete circumstances of their design and construction. This book's opening critique of object-oriented design and theory extends the diagnosis of the crisis of the object presented in earlier accounts by offering interpretations that show the wide range of alternatives produced over recent years.

A number of significant and useful concepts are adduced to guide these interpretations. Most important among them, perhaps, is the idea of a *non-discrete architecture*, which posits that the ground *within* which the building is sited is not merely occupied but inhabited, on not one but many levels, alternately enclosed and open, containing settings and connecting to places beyond the building's assumed limits. In a similar way, the building's enclosing skin, commonly thought of as something disengaged from conditions within and outside its surfaces, is shown instead to be something that spatially intertwines them, variously resisting and allowing the forces of the ambient environment: views, effects of climate and weather, patterns of movement and so on. No less useful is the idea of an *auxiliary architecture*, which accepts the actuality of our built inheritance, problematic though much of it is, and projects ways in which prosthetic elements can enhance its performance, intensify its engagement and increase its relevance. Extensions of familiar terms are also offered: topography, urban ecology, landscape urbanism, mat building and regionalism are recast to explain various aspects of *embedded architecture*. The result is a more workable and refined vocabulary, subtle enough to explain the impressive and inspiring range of projects discussed, without arguing for one or another approach.

The authors believe – and I tend to agree – that now is not the time for strident declarations of the single most important way to move forward. Insights and contributions are arriving from many quarters, varied according to different ways of building, conditions of climate and geography, and of culture. To the degree that the ways of working described in this book may be correlated with the ways of living that we both expect and strive for, this study will help us to see how architecture today maintains its ancient task of discovering and expressing the cultural and natural kinds of order we thought we had lost.

Foreword
GROUNDS AND ENVELOPES
ALEJANDRO ZAERA-POLO

Grounds and envelopes are two forms of the physical environment that have often been treated in opposition within the history of the discipline. In this book they are brought together 'en route to a non-discrete architecture'. For a long time I have been interested in exploring their continuity, and this document is a daring attempt to do this, and a thought-provoking opportunity to theorize about it.

As the Introduction to the book rightly suggests, it is the dichotomy between a physical environment which is understood as a collection of discrete elements and one which is constituted as a continuous milieu, which has become a crucial question for contemporary architects. The authors see these two typologies of the built environment under the scope of the continuum. In that sense they represent a view that was prevalent through the 1990s in the discipline and which I myself supported dutifully. I have since grown slightly more wary about its underlying discourse, and yet I feel as if a long exposure to this theory has now fatally affected my aesthetic tendencies and I would never be able to escape from it, no matter how hard I try.

The authors' own lineage is similar to mine, as we all shared the AA experience in the early 1990s when Jeff Kipnis was preaching against 'collage' and for 'intensive coherence', and everybody was interested in 'the fold' as the right answer to late capitalism. By then I had already been exposed to Koolhaas' 'genericness' and even to Kwinter's Gaia-like tendencies. All the names that keep popping up through the book form a common set of references which I suspect may be useful to the public in understanding the authors' ideological alignments.

Grounds and Envelopes is being published at a time when the borderless euphoria of the 1990s has been tempered by a sequence of global events: September 11 attacks in 2001 and the worldwide credit crisis in 2007 imposed an alternative political background upon the discipline where the free circulation of money, people and goods that had become the prevailing trait of the emergent global economy had floundered. Grounds are now being divided up again with barbed-wire fences and the ubiquitously transparent building envelope – which has become the generic face of globalization – is under threat because the free flow of energy out of the building envelopes is no longer politically correct. New grounds are suddenly full of borders which emerge with inconceivable force, and new envelopes are more prone to insulation than transparency.

In this book, grounds and envelopes become the two sides to the dichotomy between figure and ground that lies at the core of these discussions. In conventional terms, the ground is the seamless, chaotic original milieu: it stands for nature or for public space. It only becomes structured and divided after the envelopes are deployed. The envelopes may be political or climatic or both but they form the artificial demarcation of domains. Grounds have always been politically delimited, and yet their intuitive notion remains primarily continuous. Envelopes are always subdividing the space, and yet they are obviously determining an underlying climatic continuity. We see how these two elements are here mobilized to discuss the question of continuity and discontinuity, part and whole, object and field.

While I do not necessarily agree with the authors in all their appraisals, and I sometimes feel that their quest for a non-discrete architecture is more a desire than a rationally justifiable quality, I feel an inevitable sympathy towards their ideological stance, which revolves around the notion that the processes of the built environment affecting grounds and envelopes are determined by certain forces which transcend the local, and yet are affected by it. Whether we address these oppositions in terms of local/global or smooth/coarse, we are still within the non-discrete paradigm, where the whole does not equal the sum of the parts. The question is, once we draw the line in the sand, how does it affect the constitution of the fields that remain on both sides? Even within the theoretical continuity of space and matter which the authors favour, there is no alternative but to draw the line, to deploy the figures and the individual entities on the field, knowing that they will immediately be incorporated into the constitution of the field. A set of perfectly independent objects has an alternative existence as a field of attachments which may not have a visible translation; the constitution of an envelope will determine the structure of the space it contains. A pile of molecular, discrete bricks may approximate a molar building mass. But also, the accidents on the ground or the microclimatic variations in the atmosphere are able to generate unsurmountable borders in what is otherwise continuous.

A huge domain for thinking and experimentation, the subject addressed by *Grounds and Envelopes* is possibly the most crucial question to answer for the contemporary disciplines of architecture, both in terms of aesthetic and political implications.

Euskadi, August 2014

Introduction
EN ROUTE TO NON-DISCRETE ARCHITECTURE

When we think about space, we have only looked at its containers. As if space itself is invisible, all theory for the production of space is based on an obsessive preoccupation with its opposite: substance and objects, i.e. architecture.
(Koolhaas 2013 [2001]: 5)

Our objective should not be to renounce matter but rather to search for a form of matter other than objects.
(Kuma 2008: 32)

Thus the object – be it a building, a compound site, or an entire urban matrix, insofar as such unities continue to exist at all as functional terms – would be defined now *not by how it appears, but rather by practices*: those it partakes of and those that take place within it. On this reconception, the unitariness of the object would necessarily vanish.
(Kwinter 2001: 14)

This book is intended as a trigger of thought and consideration for all those who take a keen interest in the impact of architecture and the built environment upon our increasingly human-dominated world. Our aim was to explore alternatives to one of today's pronounced yet unaddressed problems: the unquestioned and rampant proliferation of discrete architecture – architecture that thrives on stubbornly maintained artificial dichotomies, that is primarily intended to stand out and is therefore intentionally, explicitly and thoroughly detached from its specific local settings. The consequences that derive from this relentless and unquestioning stance are tangible and mounting: spatially impoverished architectures (disengaged objects) and cities (fast-growing aggregates of disengaged objects that consume a vast amount of ground). When considered from both a detailed and wider perspective, this development seems clearly unsustainable. Therefore we seek to help reignite spatial thinking, discourse and design in architecture, and, more specifically, to search for identifiable traits of what may be called an architecture that is intensively *embedded* in its locally specific settings; in other words, a *non-discrete* architecture that relinquishes the disengaged object as a primary aim for architectural design. Put differently, this effort is driven by the wish to identify alternative approaches to the persistent single-minded predilection, perhaps even mindless infatuation, with the architectural object that places emphasis only on its superficial surface appearances. This dominant yet limited and limiting focus on the architectural object alone comes more often than not hand-in-hand with a general yet pronounced lack of critical analysis and projective thinking, and the routinely spatially disinterested emphasis on form and form generation that has increasingly held reign over the past few decades. We consider this kind of architecture ultimately 'flat' and 'single-sided' as it disengages with spatial organization for the sake of an exclusive emphasis on the distinctive architectural object and a thin threshold that is articulated mainly for exterior visual effect. In order to tackle this problem we aimed to seek out ways in which to overcome today's persistent lack of spatial interest, or even quite possibly its outright evasion, by way of examining the potentials of the key architectural elements, *grounds* and *envelopes*, as the prime initiators of heterogeneous spatial, material and engendering arrangements that can intensely engage their specific local environment. In so doing we examine whether there are ways of spatially and materially articulating architectures that are not primarily predicated on the articulation of discrete architectural objects. However, this book is neither intended as a proclamation of a new avant-garde or style, nor as yet another formulaic recipe book for architectural design or comprehensive outline of everything that is needed to tackle the issues we are addressing. Instead it constitutes an attempt to gather promising thoughts and works en route to non-discrete architectures that can begin to inspire thinking and designing in different ways.

Today, more than ever, ground is simply occupied and envelopes have devolved into spatially disengaged thin skins, whether or not formally elaborated, fashionably styled, patterned, or technologically enhanced. Three of the interrelated and mutually reinforcing drivers of this development are: (1) the deeply entrenched artificial dichotomy that sets the architectural object *against* the ground (figure–ground); (2) the indiscriminate replication of a singular canonic building section (column and slab) and (3) the disjunction of an increasingly uniform spatial and sectional organization from ground, envelope and local setting.

In relation to the first predisposition – the architectural object set against the ground – Peter Eisenman (1992: 424) argued that:

> Traditional architectural theory … assumes that there are two static conditions of object: figure and ground … the terms 'figure/object' and 'ground' are both determinant and all encompassing: they are thought to explain the totality of urbanism. As in most disciplines, though, such all-encompassing totalities have come into question; they are no longer thought to explain the true complexity of phenomena. … What is needed is the possibility of reading figure/object and ground within another frame of reference.

Throughout his work Eisenman pursued various ways of moving away from figure/ground arrangements. During a particular period Eisenman's interest in Piranesi's work led him to experiment with arrangements of interstitial figures in pursuit of what he termed 'figure/figure urbanism' that, instead of giving primacy to ground, rearticulates it as interstitial condition between architectural objects or fragments thereof (Eisenman 2004: 85). In parallel, a number of architects pursued landscape-oriented approaches to architectural design and worked on notions that might be termed 'ground/ground' arrangements in which inhabitable spaces are burrowed within or enveloped by the ground. Yet not in all instances was this done with the intent to overcome the predilection for the discrete architectural object. This is evidenced by Stan Allen's description of key aspects of what he terms 'Landform Buildings'. While for Allen such architectures aim to overcome the opposition between the architectural object and landscape by way of generating 'field-like effects on the scale of buildings', they also 'offer new potentials for the iconic power of the architectural object' (Allen 2011: 34). The quest for field-like spatial organization may therefore be pursued in quite different ways that either reinforce the primacy of the architectural object or, alternatively, seek to diminish it in favour of other spatial, relational and performance-oriented characteristics. It is therefore of vital importance to carefully examine approaches that on first sight appear to share certain characteristics with the search for non-discrete architectures, as similar concepts may be used towards entirely different ends. Approaches that pursue the ceaseless multiplication and intersection of objects in search of a thick expanse of interstitial spaces, and multiple ground approaches that may still be intended to give primacy to the formal expression of idiosyncratic architectural objects, whether in a pronounced or *weak* manner. And when idiosyncrasy remains the primary driving motive the search for alternatives may be rejected as inessential or impracticable. The task at hand is to question this systematically.

In commencing our task we propose grounds and envelopes as potentially correlated spatial devices that can give rise to approaches towards non-discrete architectures for the purpose of a spatially and performatively enriched built environment. As this shift is predicated on grounds and envelopes as a way of staging spatial organization and transitions, it involves careful consideration of the sectional articulation and organization of such architectures, including the way in which these are embedded within their specific local setting.

Today, the sectional articulation of the majority of the new building stock has become increasingly confined to the predictable and uniform modernist column and slab system à la Le Corbusier's Maison Domino principle. Eduardo Torroja (1958: 191) diagnosed that:

> ever since man became infected with the curious mania for piling one dwelling unit on top of another, the floor has been necessary in order to increase the available surface on which to live … to sustain one floor on top of another is, after all, a simple even monotonous problem.

Clearly this monotonous approach is today reigning supreme on a global scale. While from a certain perspective this prevailing diagram was and still is effective in the production of buildings based on considerations specific to spatial and structural efficiency, one may wonder whether any architecture that does not effectively engage in rethinking this type of uniform sectional organization truly warrants the label 'post-modern'. In turn, one may begin to suspect that post-modern architecture entails in the main the fanciful dressing up of buildings that at their core remain thoroughly modern and repetitive in utter disregard for local needs and circumstances, thus disengaging both exterior and interior from its local settings.

Clearly, the column-slab arrangement continues to offer some interesting possibilities. In his seminal book *Delirious New York* Rem Koolhaas (1994: 157) argued in relation to his analysis of the Downtown Athletic Club that:

> Such an architecture is an aleatory form of 'planning' life itself: in the fantastic juxtaposition of its activities, each of the Club's floors is a separate instalment of an infinitely unpredictable intrigue that extols the complete surrender to the definitive instability of life in the Metropolis.

Yet, the disjunction between the stacked floors may either present a great opportunity or a considerable drawback. For each floor the question of its relation to its local setting may be raised: programmatic disjunction between floors does not inevitably and inescapably entail spatial disconnection between floors and setting. Moreover, the stacking of floors and activities may result in juxtapositions that engender unexpected encounters and events, but when subjected to relentless and uncritical deployment it may instead result in the exact contrary: the relinquishment of event for the sake of inflated real-estate profit by way of a tightly controlled narrow scope of predictable lifestyle, retail and consumption patterns. In its careless repetition and in combination with the disjunction of the envelope from the local setting and an indifferent position regarding ground, it often entails a definitive separation between locally specific settings and entirely generic and relentlessly repeated interiors. Likewise, the threshold between inside and outside seems to have decayed into a decorated separator. Kenneth Frampton (1987: 20) commented that:

> As far as architecture is concerned, there seems to be little chance today that large-scale undertakings will yield work of cultural significance. ... The vast size of these works tends to create an overall drive towards optimization, that is, towards the reduction of building to the maximizing of economic criteria and to the adoption of normative plans and construction methods reducing architecture to the provision of an aesthetic skin – the packaging, in fact, of nothing more than a large commodity in order to facilitate marketing.

Yet, it seems obvious that the engagement of ground, section and envelope as spatial devices for social and environmental arrangements that govern possible exchanges may have obvious potentials. As Alejandro Zaera Polo (2008: 79) pointed out:

> A more intricate design of the limit between private and public increases the contact surface between both realms ... a more permeable definition of the property boundary is more likely to accommodate a fluid relationship between private and public in an age when the public realm is increasingly built and managed by private agents. The envelope ... [is] a powerful mechanism of social integration.

However, the envelope in and of itself can hardly provide such possibility. It needs to do so in conjunction with the spatial organization of the spatial and programmatic organization of a given architecture by involving its sectional arrangement in relation to the specific local circumstances within which it is embedded.

Whether intentional or not, contemporary modes of form generation such as parametric architecture seem often to be deployed in such ways that accelerate architecture's acute 'flatness': in this approach ground and envelope are usually fused into a continuous thin skin that establishes a 'total exterior'. The latter frequently lacks the kind of heterogeneous spatial organizations and varied spatial transitions that could accommodate a much wider scope of embeddedness, as well as a locally specific pattern of use and habitation. Its current proponents may argue that parametric design offers a heightened level of integration of design determining variables that are resolved into a consistent formal scheme. Yet, in this, like in any other design approach, success or failure depends on the choice of design criteria and performance and context-related variables and their interrelation, and not on a method of relating and processing data alone. Unfortunately, current parametric design frequently tends to adhere to exclusively formal criteria, developer expectations and superficial lifestyle promises, and hence tends towards entirely predictable space and programme arrangements in the form and format of stacked floors, notwithstanding the hallmark of extravagantly designed lobbies and exteriors. A comprehensive analysis of current 'parametric' architectures swiftly makes this apparent. Moreover, such schemes often largely disregard their immediate and wider settings above and beyond gestural tokens such as extending infrastructural connections or superficial referencing of local typologies. A great number of more elaborate context-related aspects that are dependent on detailed analysis are typically left out of consideration as architects and clients alike frequently deem such analyses unnecessary, unfeasible or even futile, or as architects are unable to undertake and utilize careful analysis in their design process.

Spatially impoverished and disengaged architectures are often made worse by trivial branding exercises related to the shapes of buildings and the patterning of façades. Such architectures are intentionally designed to stand out and to visibly distinguish themselves against their specific context in order to promise the 'new' and the 'next' in lifestyle statement. While these trends may in one way or another satisfy the current economic demands of investors and property developers and the fleeting lifestyle expectations of consumers, they also raise the question as to whether the future of architecture is wholesomely reserved for retail and consumption opportunities and the spectacular yet elusive pseudo-identity. Rem Koolhaas diagnosed that such '*Junkspace* is flamboyant yet unmemorable' (Koolhaas 2013 [2001]: 7). In thinking this through it should strike one as obvious that this trend is in the long term entirely self-defeating: as more and more buildings superficially 'stand out', 'standing out' simply becomes the established canon and *the new generic*, no matter how frenzied or not the next design. Ironically, but logically, current idiosyncratic architecture is claimed into the canon of post-modern architecture by some of its main protagonists. Given that, as discussed above, most of these buildings solely entail extravagant exterior dress-up of entirely modernist column and slab sectional arrangements, they continue to collectively hollow out any consequential and justified application of the term 'post-modern' at least in relation to tangible spatial approaches. Kenneth Frampton succinctly diagnosed this condition as early as 1983: 'so-called post-modern architects are merely feeding the media-society with gratuitous, quietistic images rather than proffering, as they claim, a creative *rappel à l' ordre* after the supposedly proven bankruptcy of the liberative modern project' (Frampton 1983: 19).

Clearly the economic developments of the past few decades have strongly impacted upon architectural production. Economic downturns often confined many challenging and projective architectural schemes to theoretical 'paper architectures' – such works were frequently regarded as utopian and improbable and not necessarily geared towards implementation. Alejandro Zaera Polo, for instance, stated that 'paper architecture has lost its effectiveness as a political vehicle; like utopia, it is restricted to pure representation without the attachments and frictions capable of politicising matters' (Zaera Polo 2008: 77). Economic upturns and hyper-capitalism frequently hastened the design process and instant construction of buildings, thus leading away from in-depth and projective design development and towards idiosyncratic one- or none-liners. This often takes place at such a rate that many architects who had at some stage developed promising approaches during economic downturns left these behind during economic upturns for the questionable benefit of a rushed realization of projects that appear quite strangely simultaneously under- and over-designed: architectures of no relevance, but of lasting consequences past the moment of completion. In addition, a rather problematic outcome of this development is a more cynical division between theory and practice and their associated values by many currently engaged in practice. Due to this tendency unbuilt or so-deemed 'theoretical' projects may receive less attention than they deserve. Inevitably, insistent views end up dogmatically rejecting to look in directions that may offer great potential. Unbuilt projects can still inform projective thinking in potent ways, as some of the examples in this book indicate.

A thorough examination of the conditions resulting from the accelerated proliferation of discrete architectures, as well as the development of feasible alternative approaches to architectural design, has to date effectively not taken place at any significant rate or consequence. Neglecting the development of relevant alternative concepts and approaches has not only left a void in the discourse of spatial organization, but has also exposed a disturbing lack of abysmal proportion of the cultural relevance of current architecture (unless one cynically assumes that culture itself has lost its cultural relevance and that architecture is therefore rather finely attuned to this condition, and, moreover, that it is therefore quite all right for architects to engage in self-satisfied navel gazing and ostentatious posturing in pursuit of fortune, fame and legacy). And so the question arises as to what exactly will be left to architectural design and the built environment when formally excessive yet spatially uniform, 'flat' and discrete architecture will eventually reach its apex and its limit. What might we turn to after the eventual implosion of the singularly visual and blatantly superficial? Will architects lost in pre-fixation chase after yet another style or 'ism' aiming to resurrect yet another incarnation of the recently deceased? Or could this moment be recognized as architecture's eleventh-hour opportunity to consider the options, and might the pursuit of a different paradigm for architecture ensue that actually for once deserves this designation? And if the latter route is chosen how should it be defined and which notions should underpin it?

Peter Eisenman (2004: 104) stated provokingly that:

Three prevailing 'isms' of architecture all involve nostalgia, a malaise involving memory: modernism, a nostalgia for the future; postmodernism, a nostalgia for the past; and contextualism, a nostalgia for the present.

Does this inevitably entail the dismissal of forward-looking discourse that is not exclusively self-referential as fundamentally modernist, attempts in combining heretofore separate pre-existing traits as fundamentally post-modernist, and interest in local setting as fundamentally 'presentist'? Clearly here one needs to choose between either accepting the continuation of entrenched dichotomies and/or hermetic discourses, or, alternatively, to engage in a more substantial rethinking of architectural aims, notions and approaches. A lot would depend on the way in which projective thinking, spatial organization and its purpose, the role of the local, the traits and relational conditions of an alternative architecture, continuity and transformation are defined and employed, and how therefore existing built and unbuilt architectures may be looked at. After all, this effort does not need to start from scratch given the immense repository of knowledge embedded in existing architectures and schemes.

Today there seems to exist a real need for substantial rethinking and reformulation of a wide range of fundamental aspects. Tackling this task at great length would go beyond the limits of this book. Yet, some leads emerge in the selected thoughts and works, and from their potential interrelations and convergences. The use of plural is entirely intentional, as the aim is not to propose a new style for architecture, but instead a multitude of possible trajectories that may lead to articulating non-discrete architectures in different ways. With a number of built and unbuilt projects pointing towards the prospect of non-discrete architectures, it is now possible to glimpse the contours of an altogether different spatial discourse and approach.

Kengo Kuma argued that 'making architecture into an object means distinguishing between its inside and outside and erecting a mass called "inside" in the midst of an "outside"' (Kuma 2008: 77). Continuing from this thought one may expand that the fundamental problem with discrete architecture is that it inevitably locks itself into a whole series of dominant yet fundamentally constraining oppositions, such as object versus context, inside versus outside, and, by extension, natural versus man-made. Therefore, by way of inherently reinforcing such dialectics, discrete architecture may be gridlocked by its own intrinsic logic, restrictions and deficiencies, which now, by way of relentless replication, becomes obvious in so many places where the abundance of fast capital enables it to thrive at an astounding speed and with an incredibly laid-back attitude towards the consequences.

As a precondition to pursuing the notion of non-discrete architecture it is necessary to consider how architectures – as David

Leatherbarrow puts it – participate in 'authored and un-authored conditions', as 'unforeseen influences ... bring about the end of the building's freestanding individuality' (Leatherbarrow 2009: 7). In extending this thought, Leatherbarrow posited what might be the key question: 'to reconsider what it means to establish the actual limits of an architectural setting' (Leatherbarrow 2002: 28). Two propositions are of related interest: (1) Stan Allen suggested a shift from architectural object to 'field' (Allen 1997), and (2) Greg Lynn posited that 'immersion implies that the boundaries between figures and grounds become blurred and envelopes become negotiable' (Lynn 1998 [1994]: 106). Lynn's position implies a spatial approach to grounds and envelopes in consequence of which the discreteness of the architectural object is diminished. Sanford Kwinter expanded that 'design practice and thought are deflected away from the traditional and largely "aesthetically" constituted object and simultaneously reoriented towards a dynamic macro- and microscopic field of interaction' (Kwinter 2001: 21). An architectural setting expanded to the notion of a field of interactions suggests a noteworthy inroad to integrated multi-scalar and performance-oriented notions of architecture and context relations. Already in 1964 Christopher Alexander maintained that architects 'ought to design with a number of nested, overlapped form–context boundaries in mind' (Alexander 1964: 18). This indicates the necessity of a careful reconsideration of the architectural threshold as partaking in the articulation of field conditions, thus not acting as strict separation but instead as concurrently embedded and diversified spatial conditions, and as a means of heterogeneously conditioning space. Clearly we do not propose to rid architecture of its mandate to partition space when needed and to provide discrete spaces wherever required. Quite on the contrary, the aim is to expand the scope of spatial organization so as to be able to challenge constraining dialectics in order to overcome the discrete architectural object as the one and only option to articulate the built environment. There are obvious building programmes that require adequate enclosure for shelter and safety. However, there is an opportunity even in such cases to think of the elements of enclosure as spatially articulated, differentiated and wherever useful as more permeable and with more extended transitions than is typically the case. Such an approach would deliver great potential to a detailed rethinking of the boundary between private and public, man-made and natural, inside and outside, and consequentially reconsidering the entire remit of past and current building typologies. This would entail a significant repositioning of these notions and also a new taxonomy of relations. Clearly, non-discrete architectures, when approached in this manner, do not entail a reduction of creative engagement, but rather a vast expansion. What more in terms of a challenge to architecturally innovate?

No matter which turn these developments may eventually take, both practice and the built environment are likely to be transformed considerably due to the sheer amount of required space and the current onslaught of construction. Encouragingly, though, occasionally works of note continue to appear, which are based on conceptual approaches that point towards non-discrete or embedded architectures. It is not surprising that this is frequently accomplished by a spatial approach to grounds and envelopes. For this reason this book aims to provide a stimulus for the revitalization of the notional and actual elements of grounds and envelopes as vital spatial elements. In so doing, the book collects thoughts and projects, each of which contribute particular elements to what may begin to constitute an integrated and richly nuanced approach to spatial organization and a gradual advancement of non-discrete architectures.

This book is organized into two parts. Part one consists of five chapters which collect theoretical reflections and discussions related to key concepts and potentials that begin to frame the suggested approaches to architectural design.

Chapter 1 addresses questions of spatial organization with emphasis on the role of sectional approaches and arrangements. One of the key questions discussed in this chapter is how to consolidate the need to partition space with the kind of spatial continuity and transitions that enable embedding architectures into their respective context. A current landscape-oriented approach to architectural and urban design is portrayed together with questions as to how continuous space may be locally articulated and particularized, and how this approach can collaborate with another, the traits of whom are multiple envelopes with different degrees of enclosure that can engender spatial transitions and heterogeneous spatial and environmental conditions.

Chapter 2 examines questions pertaining to ground as well as the concepts of multiple and provisional grounds. Although, today, figure–ground arrangements clearly dominate and continue to reinforce the predominance of the discrete architectural object and the deeply entrenched opposition between ground and architectural object, this has not always been so. Throughout architectural history there were many examples that did not position object against ground but, instead, were characterized by their often non-decomposable integration. This chapter seeks to show that ground constitutes a profoundly important element of architecture's relation to its context and in the articulation of its embeddedness within its local settings. Tectonic landscapes constitute a kind of integration of the man-made and aspects of the natural environment, instead of their typical sharp division. Multiple grounds point towards the possibility that ground must not necessarily be thought of as simply occupied and diminished by the footprint of a building, but instead that it can be proliferated through architectural intervention above and beyond simply rehearsing the modernist approach of stacking floors. Provisional grounds indicate that architectures and building operations can be considered and designed to be temporal, either in their material arrangement or by way of engendering a dynamic of use. This is significant, as it is usually assumed that once ground is occupied by construction it will continue to be so for the foreseeable future. The resulting perception of ground, thus lost, often obstructs different ways of thinking about already built-up sites by involuntarily locking their potential futures into a much-reduced range of prejudiced expectations rather than offering new possibilities. As the built environment expands at a fast rate it is of vital importance to open up possibilities by way of design, rather than narrowing them down to a singular and fixed determination.

Chapter 3 focuses on the building envelope(s) and the transition between interior and exterior as extended thresholds. The not so new premise is that thresholds need not inescapably and exclusively divide, but can also connect and be articulated as spatial transitions. More specifically, questions of multiple, articulated and animated envelopes and thick structures and screens are discussed that all share a strong potential as extended thresholds and differentiated spaces. Multiple envelopes engender the staging of transitions from the outermost locations of a setting as field to the innermost locales of a given architecture. Here the notion of *nestedness* finds its perhaps most literal articulation through the spatial and material organization of multiplied and extended thresholds. Articulated and animated envelopes can enrich milieux with information and microclimatic articulation and differentiation. Thick structures and screens deliver specific types of spatial and material articulation to extended threshold conditions. In many instances of relevant architectural examples several of these concepts coincide in the designs. In addition, this chapter examines how existing architectures can be supplemented with what might be called *auxiliary architectures* so as to stage extended threshold conditions in the already existing built environment. The need for this approach is given by the fact that the bulk of existing buildings cannot simply be redesigned and reconstructed in one singular effort and in the short term. Therefore there exists a real need for approaches that can help improve upon the built environment in the interim and as it is at this moment in time.

Moreover, what may be considered auxiliary today may in the future once again become integrated architectural features that stage extended thresholds and transitional spaces as defining elements of new designs.

Chapter 4 focuses on how grounds and envelopes can engage in the generation, provision and modulation of heterogeneous milieux and microclimates in order to deliver a wider scope of provisions for use and habitation in relation to local climate conditions. Inherent in this argument is a preference for solutions that are accomplished primarily through spatial and material organization rather than technological prosthetics. As for landscape-oriented approaches, Stan Allen posited that 'landform buildings can suggest a productive new approach to sustainability and enhanced environmental performance in which architectural form – rather than technological fixes – can play an active role' (Allen 2011: 35). Here some of the most potent capacities of architecture as provision lie dormant at present due to the

INTRODUCTION

1.1 Designed by Minoru Yamasaki, architect of the World Trade Center in New York City, the Pruitt-Igoe project in St. Louis, Missouri (completed in 1954/1955) was an urban housing project for poor families and comprised 33 11-storey buildings. A prime example of a figure–ground arrangement and standard column slab section, it was torn down in the period from 1972 to 1975 due to decay, segregation, poverty, abandonment and crime. Prior to demolition plans were drafted for modifications of the project, which were frequently predicated on an underlying architectural critique pertaining to population density, number of repetitive floors, bland surroundings and shared spaces. Charles Jencks, who proclaimed the demolition 'the day modern architecture died', attributed its failure to modernist visions for society conflicting with actual societal conditions and developments (Jencks 1984). Photography: U.S. Department of Housing and Urban Development, 1972.

dominance of energy-operated technological solutions, which rely upon strict divisions between exterior and interior. Yet, with guidelines for the climatic performance of free-running buildings emerging in many places, there now exists a real opportunity to reignite architecture's spatial and material potential as active boundaries that interact with the local environment. From this position arises the fascinating potential of architecture to underpin efforts related to urban ecology, an interdisciplinary field of study that analyses the relation between species and ecosystems and human-dominated regions and urban environments. Urban ecology today often results in policies and action plans that focus on the larger scales of regions and cities, while the smaller scale effect of architectures remains understudied. We seek to suggest that the scale of a singular architecture can be effective in terms of multi-species provisions and the support of biodiversity in the human-dominated environment. Architecture's capacity to do so is effectively located in the way in which grounds and envelopes are understood, articulated and utilized in providing niches and heterogeneous milieux that respond to questions of ecosystem and multiple species needs.

Chapter 5 seeks to synthesize various aspects of the previous chapters towards what may once again be considered intensely local architectures. This involves a discussion of different approaches to articulating such architectures from a tectonic perspective and the related arrangement of local resources. Giving thus emphasis to the local and referencing a series of historical

1.2 The Barcode project in Oslo constitutes an idiosyncratically dressed version of a standard figure–ground arrangement and standard column slab section. The project has been the focal point of intense public debate. Besides widespread critique focused on the height of the buildings and the way the massing disconnects parts of central Oslo from the fjord, it was criticized that the project caters only for the affluent in the format of branded signature buildings that may lose their intended effect as soon as the next trend hits. Several questions arise from this. Does a superficial exterior surface make a difference to an otherwise bland spatial organization and standard column slab section? What might be said about the surroundings and shared spaces? Do such architectures constitute today's means of exclusion? What will be the urban consequences of a relentless and globally homogeneous replication of such architectures? And will the day arrive when superficial post-modern architecture dies? Photography: Michael Hensel (2013).

architectures in various chapters suggests an inclination towards revitalizing the discussion of the critical regionalism of the 1980s and 1990s. Here the question is which aspects of critical regionalism may be taken forward and how these may be articulated in an approach to locality that is updated, and that takes current circumstances, conditions and developments into consideration. To the latter belongs, among other developments, the latent shift towards locally informed non-standard architectures that are made possible by way of conceptual and technological advances. This chapter concludes with a summary outlook on further inquiries related to the development of intensely local, embedded or non-discrete architectures.

1.3 The Oslo Opera House designed by Snøhetta is best known for its inclined marble-clad public surface that extends on to the top of the building. This surface replaces the area taken up by the building's footprint and offers in its stead a continuous public ground and landscape experience. The other elevations of the building are much less well known and attention demanding, and evoke the image more akin to an industrial shed clad in metal sheet, and that features a largely impermeable perimeter threshold. In this way front- and back-of-house constitute essentially two distinctly different architectures, one with the potential to be continuous with its surroundings, non-discrete, versus another that places the object against the ground. This raises the question as to what criteria to apply to the analysis of buildings with pronounced differences in articulating ground and envelope, and the way they articulate space and address the specific setting along their perimeter. Photography: Michael Hensel (2013).

Part two collects 30 built and unbuilt projects that span a half-century timeline and that are related to specific aspects discussed in part one: 15 projects on the topic of grounds and 15 projects on the topic of envelopes, with some projects addressing both aspects in particularly interesting ways. Each project contributes a specific element to what may eventually characterize and facilitate the next step en route to non-discrete architectures. We have aimed to briefly describe each project, to discuss traits that relate to the themes of the book, to raise further questions and to suggest links between projects that might suggest ways forward. Many more key projects should have been included. At any rate, we sincerely hope that the reader may find stimulating leads for design and is compelled to think further after taking stock of a series of potential inroads to non-discrete architectures.

1
Space

> I have called these settings … discrete, but are they really single or separate? Doesn't the drift or merge of one into another turn them into something other than an ensemble of rooms or settings, into some version of field or landscape? How is one to perceive, to understand, 'rooms within rooms'; does not the annexation of border territories confuse identities by disturbing the integrity or self-sameness of the building's plan, precisely because it integrates it into the surround what one would have thought was properly and pragmatically excluded from it?
>
> (Leatherbarrow 2002: 61)

> Vastness negotiates a middle-ground between the homogeneity of infinite or universal space and the fixed hierarchies of closely articulated space. … Design implications: … extension of free plan to free section, emphasis on residual and interstitial spaces.
>
> (Kipnis 1993: 43)

Architectural discourse on space is a fairly recent affair. The late Peter Collins argued that it emerged initially in the mid-eighteenth century due to the appearance of romantic gardens, 'since here the spaces, although amorphous and unproportionable, clearly had a more positive quality than … flat surfaces' (Collins 2003 [1965]: 285). Intriguingly the relation between space and gardens and, by extension, also landscapes, continually attracted architects. Today it clearly resonates with the interest of many architects in garden and landscape design in search of alternative approaches to architecture and urban design. Bernard Tschumi, for instance, suggested that 'gardens merge the sensual pleasure of space with the pleasure of reason, in a most *useless* manner' (Tschumi 1990 [1977]: 51). For Tschumi, 'uselessness' denoted a positive element of resistance and strength against persistent 'cost/benefit justifications' for architectural design. The Japanese architect Kengo Kuma – who pursues a pronounced shift away from the prevailing emphasis on the architectural object – maintained that 'whereas architecture can be construed as an independent object – as an autonomous figure cut off from the ground – a garden is a continuum, the ground itself'; yet he also cautioned that gardens may be too structured still to accomplish more open spaces and thus 'we must aim for a wilderness rather than a garden' (Kuma 2008: 8–9). In the works of R&Sie(n), for instance, the relation between architecture and closely adjacent flora – whether wild or cultivated – remains a recurrent theme, as exemplified by the Spidernethewood project in Nîmes, Frances (see p. 212), in which architecture and untamed yet partially constrained local vegetation complement one another in providing a continuous, seemingly carved and labyrinthine space. At any rate, the potent interrelation between architecture and garden or landscape offers an interesting starting point en route towards a non-discrete architecture: ground (and ground-facilitated conditions) and space as an interlinked continuum, and, by extension, ground as a potentially space-defining element.

Turning back to the discourse on space, scholars like Collins maintain that the real thrust of the emerging discourse in architecture occurred in the nineteenth century in the German-speaking context:

> its introduction into the history of architectural ideas derives almost entirely from its use by German theorists at this time … we thus find, from the beginning of the nineteenth century a number of writers on aesthetics using the term 'space' in its modern architectural sense.
>
> (Collins 2003 [1965]: 286)

(See e.g. Heinrich Wöfflin 1886, 1894; Adolf von Hildebrand 1893; August Schmarsow 1894.) Yet, according to Collins it was Frank Lloyd Wright who brought the concept of space to bear in architectural works:

> It is probably fair to say that Wölfflin's concept of space would have never achieved its present architectural significance had it not been for the intuitive creative endeavours of Frank Lloyd Wright. It was he who, at the beginning of the century … first exploited the spatial possibilities which had lain dormant since the end of the Baroque, and applied them to buildings appropriate to the new age.
>
> (Collins 2003 [1965]: 286)

David Leatherbarrow located another significant novelty in Frank Lloyd Wright's work: the dissolution of bound space in plan as defined by the planes and corners of walls, in favour of a continuous space that is particularized in section. Wright elaborated the intended condition as 'inside space opening to the outside and the outside coming in' (Wright 1955 [1914]). In furthering his analysis of Wright's work, Leatherbarrow described that 'within such a stratification of slabs or sections of slabs, discrete settings were established by other horizontal elements' (Leatherbarrow 2002: 32). And yet, what Leatherbarrow referred to seems to suggest another kind of 'discreteness', one that is not predicated upon foregrounding the architectural object and its strict delineations and separation from the ground, but instead one that is based on a sectional particularization of a more defined space set within an otherwise continuous space through the sectional manipulation of horizontal planes. Leatherbarrow cautioned, however, that:

> One needs to avoid two alternative conceptions: the abstract space of modernism and the parcelled-out space of schematic historicism. An articulated field or horizon was never intended to be abstract; in fact, it was meant to be concrete, or practically and topographically specific.
> (Leatherbarrow 2002: 22)

In pursuit of the development of this approach, Leatherbarrow discussed related spatial characteristics in the works of Rudolph Schindler, Richard Neutra and others. Eventually Leatherbarrow arrived at rethinking and repositioning the relation between architecture and landscape design by way of suggesting topography as their shared element or interest (Leatherbarrow 2004). What is implied in Leatherbarrow's argument is that the received dialectic between architecture and landscape design could actually be resolved in different and more integrative ways in which both disciplines collaborate on a set of shared tasks without resorting to the entrenched position of opposing and mutually exclusive means, such as assigning ground to the former and the architectural object to the latter while pitching one against the other. Considerations on a different relation between architecture and landscape design also underpin the theory of urbanism known as *landscape urbanism*, which postulates that the city may be better organized through landscape related aspects rather than through architecture. While this could be seen as a critical statement that simply foregrounds architecture's insufficiencies, it could also be understood as a challenging proposition that not only the city but also architecture could adhere to and be informed by specific characteristics and qualities of landscape and thus be rethought. Kengo Kuma, Stan Allen and others have pursued such interest at some length and detail for a while now. This interest in integrating landscape and architecture brought with it a series of significant insights and advances. One development relates to the notion of ground as an extensive thickened, continuous and multiplied surface that can make a multitude of provisions for a wide range of planned and unplanned activities. In examining this development Alex Wall (1999: 233) stated that:

> These works signal a shift of emphasis from the design of enclosed objects to the design and manipulation of larger urban surfaces … this is landscape as active surface, structuring the conditions for new relationships and interactions among the things it supports.

During the 1980s and 1990s a broad range of landscape-inspired projects began to emerge that placed emphasis on landscape and surface. One type of project pursued this thematic through novel approaches to the design of urban parks and includes seminal entries to a series of noteworthy competitions; for instance, Parc de la Villette in Paris (1983) or Downsview Park in Toronto (2000).

Entries to the Parc de la Villette competition included most notably the influential first- and second-prize schemes by Bernard Tschumi and Rem Koolhaas/OMA. Tschumi pursued a scheme based on the superimposition of different organizing systems (lines, points, surfaces and related activities), while Koolhaas proposed parallel bands of disjoint landscape programmes, as if flipping sideward the Downtown Athletics Club with its disjoint floors and related activities, which he had so keenly analysed in *Delirious New York*. Both projects had a tremendous impact on the way not only these practices continued to pursue architectural design, but also on a much broader scope of architects and projects. An increasing number of projects that were not to do with the design of parks began to feature similar characteristics. Juxtaposition of systems and programming that originated in the context of park and landscape design brought spatial characteristics of open landscaped spaces forward into a whole range of architectural projects of various sizes and programmatic complexity.

Nearly two decades later, the Downsview Park competition in Toronto received much attention with expectations running high due to La Villette and other similar high-profile projects. The question was what the next major steps in this direction would be. The finalist entries included Rem Koolhaas/OMA and Bruce Mau's first-prize 'Tree City' scheme, James Corner and Stan Allen's 'Emergent Ecologies', Foreign Office Architects' 'A New Synthetic Landscape' and Bernard Tschumi's 'The Digital and the Coyote'. Again, as in the Parc de la Villette competition, a dominant feature shared by a number of finalist entries was the superimposition systems such as landscape, programme and infrastructure. Some of the finalist teams emphasized formal aspects of ground modulation, while others focused on open-ended time-based processes that addressed city and park relations and interactions, as well as ecological tendencies through which future potentials were intended to unfold. Unlike in the case of La Villette however, several of the entries remained somewhat less tangible, specifically because of the emphasis on open-ended processes and the related absence of finite and final design. However, some commentators embraced this positively. Cary Wolfe, for instance, argued that these schemes constitute 'experiments in how to think anew the relationship between nature and culture' (Wolfe 2010: 203) 'not as questions of substance but as questions of strategy' (Wolfe 2010: 206) and 'a medium associated above all with space now has as its constitutive problem time and temporalization – more specifically, how to temporalize design and the constraints and selections built into it' (Wolfe 2010: 207). This notion clearly resonates with Rem Koolhaas' critique that 'all theory for the production of space is based on an obsessive preoccupation with its opposite: substance and objects, i.e. architecture' (Koolhaas 2013 [2001]: 5). More cautiously one may argue that this may be the case with particular takes on architecture that foreground the discrete and finite object, while field-like conditions may begin to suggest ways of redefining the relation substance and temporality.

Also from the 1990s onwards an increasing number of influential competition entries and speculative projects pursued a strong landscape trait in formal articulation and spatial organization; for instance, OCEAN's 'Nordic Landscape Forum' (1995) and 'Synthetic Landscape' (1995–2000), or RUR's 'Watergarden for Jeff Kipnis' (1997). In parallel an increasing number of noteworthy built landscape or landscaped-inspired projects began to appear over recent decades that engage the actual or constructed ground in correlation with envelopes in the provision of space. These include, for instance, Paulo Mendes da Rocha's designs for the Brazilian Pavilion for the Osaka World Expo (1979) (see p. 83) and the Museum of Sculpture in Sao Paulo (1988) (see p. 87), Enric Miralles and Carme Pinós' designs for the Igualada Cemetery (1985–1994) and the Archery Range for the 1992 Olympics in Barcelona (1989–1991) (see p. 230), as well as FOA's Meydan – Umraniye Retail Complex & Multiplex in Istanbul, Turkey (2007) (see p. 111).

A related key development was the growing interest in continuous surface schemes that operate on ground as a continuous element and provision for activities and events. A momentous precursor to this development was the notion of the *oblique function* developed by Claude Parent and Paul Virilio from the mid-1960s onwards that posited the inclined surface as an enabling device for a wide spectrum of dynamic activities and as inhabitable infrastructure (Parent and Virilio 1996). These radical propositions and related projects such as Claude Parent's Church Sainte-Bernadette du Banlay in Nevers (1961–1963), as well as an increasing awareness of works that was taking shape further afield such as Paulo Mendes da Rocha's projects, underpinned directly or indirectly a large number of continuous surface projects from the 1990s onwards. These included, for instance, OMA's unbuilt Jussieu Library and Yokohama Urban Ring schemes (both 1992), FOA's International Port Terminal in Yokohama (1995–2002) (see p. 138), MVRDV's Villa VPRO (see p. 178), and the Seattle

Art Museum and Olympic Sculpture Park by Weiss/Manfredi (2001–2007) (see p. 104).

A further important advance relates to the compacting of built mass into a thick ground as initiated by the Moroccan CIAM team GAMMA and Team X's sustained efforts in developing the so-called mat-building typology as a 'structuring principle which might be applied to the organisation of the built environment' (Candilis et al. 1964: 2) in which 'architecture and urbanism was coalesced into a continuous entity' (Candilis 1957). Built projects such as the Free University Berlin building (1973) by Candilis, Josic, Woods and Schiedhelm demonstrated one way as to how this typology might be articulated. The renewed interest in this work may be discerned in a number of projects; for instance, OMA's unbuilt scheme for the Agadir Convention Centre (1990) and the Nexus World Housing project in Fukuoka (1991), or more recently Nekton Design's second-prize Turf City project for the redevelopment of Reykjavik airport (2008) (see p. 145) that integrates a version of mat-typology buildings with a series of continuous surfaces for different urban, environmental and agricultural purposes.

Again from the 1990s onwards a number of practices investigated the possibility of extending a landscape-related design approach to the scale of urban planning and into much larger scale continuous and multiple ground arrangements. The intention was to provide planning guidelines for large-scale landscape-based urbanism that could engender the smooth incorporation of similarly motivated and articulated architectural projects. OCEAN UK, for instance, pursued the development of a 'sectional urbanism' that was inspired by Parent and Virilio's *function of the oblique* and geared towards the formulation of 'sectional design policies [that] interrelate strata of urban public activity surfaces, built volume, interiorized public and private space and urban landscape systems' (Hensel and Verebes 1999: 34). This approach was developed in a series of competition schemes, such as the entries to the Lasipalatsi Media Square competition in Helsinki (1996) and the Future Vision for Kyoto for the 21st Century urban design competition (1997). In parallel OCEAN developed a design strategy entitled 'channelling systems' that maps and modulates dynamic landscape and urban processes (Bettum and Hensel 2000) and was deployed in the third phase of their 'Synthetic Landscape' project (1998–1999). Likewise, Jeffrey Turko, developed a series of schemes that integrated landscape and urban programming strategies with extensive continuous surface arrangements for a series of large-scale urban projects such as Urban Anomaly in Oslo, Norway (1999), and as NEKTON Design with the Turf City project (2008) (see p. 145).

Today it seems that the landscape-inspired spatial continuity and qualities these efforts were aiming for are now increasingly interiorized with inclined surfaces relegated back primarily to circulation systems that adhere to the limits of the architectural object and its enclosing envelope. An extended threshold between outside and inside is often not intended or present, and instead interior landscapes are often encapsulated and insulated from the outside. A limited range of retail and consumption activities often colonizes such spaces. Rem Koolhaas' account of 'Junkspace' addressed this problematic in a succinct manner:

(1) Continuity is the essence of Junkspace; it exploits any invention that enables expansion, deploys the infrastructure of the seamless.

(Koolhaas 2013 [2001]: 4)

(2) All architects may unwittingly be working on the same building, so far separate, but with hidden receptors that will eventually make it cohere.

(Koolhaas 2013 [2001]: 5)

(3) The ground is no more. There are too many raw needs to be realised on one plane only. The absolute horizontal has been abandoned. … There is no datum level you always inhabit a sandwich.

(Koolhaas 2013 [2001]: 17, 19)

Koolhaas' critique may well prompt serious suspicions that the notions of spatial continuity, seamlessness and multiplication of ground may have been flawed from the onset or that their profit-oriented exploitation and mindless consumption has corrupted them beyond repair. And yet, the driving motives that bring about 'Junkspace' are rather different from those pursued in a landscape-oriented approach towards non-discrete architectures. While 'Junkspace' thrives on an encapsulated interiorized continuity and seamless interplay between insubstantial styling and consumption, non-discrete architecture opens out and engages the local over time in active participation. While according to Koolhaas 'Junkspace' has architects working on essentially the same context-less interiorized generic space, non-discrete architecture inherently engages architects with the local context-specific environment and its interrelated aspects. While 'Junkspace' constitutes a ground-less spatial sandwich without datum level, non-discrete architecture engages and emphasizes ground in various ways. Its thickened ground is different from the ground-less sandwich of 'Junkspace' in that it foregrounds the positive aspects and potentials of ground and its presence and operates on it. While this may be obvious, if quite general, it is important to understand these differences in the greatest possible detail in order to not accelerate the further spread of 'Junkspace' in spite of all the best intentions. This is not necessarily a question of merely a carefully defined building programme and design brief, but also of a mutual understanding and shared agenda between planners, architects, clients and importantly also the public. An interesting example in this respect is FOA's Meydan – Umraniye Retail Complex & Multiplex in Istanbul, Turkey (2007) (see p. 111), in which retail and consumption is not negated, but at the same time is not so predominant as to preclude or diminish an inherent public and social space agenda engendered by its evident landscape-oriented design approach. In this project architectural volumes are part of an extended landscaped surface that organizes public, social activity, entertainment and retail space in a manner that offers an encouraging alternative to the typical enclosed and difficult-to-access retail environments that increasingly colonize investment-rich cities, while providing substantial surface area that is not assigned to singular activities. Other schemes of the 1990s and early 2000s attempted an integration of landscape surface and urban infrastructural surfaces, such as FOA's Yokohama International Port Terminal (1994–2002) (see p. 138), AAGDG's masterplan for Changliu City with its extensive road-space extension into multiple use and park-landscape activities (1993–1994) (Fig. 1.1), OCEAN's Jyväskylä Music and Art Centre in Finland (2004–2005) (Fig. 1.2) and OCEAN's and Urban Offices' unbuilt Landsc[r]aper Ringbridge project for Düsseldorf, Germany (Fig. 1.3).

Intriguingly, a number of the influential landscape-inspired projects that have emerged over recent decades deployed explicit and innovative sectional design methods. Charles Jencks termed one of the most prominent sectional techniques 'cinematic section', which comprises a large number of serial sections 'that reveal a sequence of varying topography' (Jencks 2013 [1997]: 95). Jencks credited Enric Miralles for first employing this technique in the design of his seminal landscape projects. Specific developments outside of architecture had a significant impact on the interest of intensive sectioning, in particular medical imaging such as X-ray computed tomography that produces serial sectional images of the human body. Throughout the 1990s references to this technology occurred in a wide range of architectural publications. In parallel a discussion of complex geometry began to take shape in the first half of the 1990s. Greg Lynn, one of the proponents of complex geometry in architecture, examined Edmund Husserl's notion of 'an exact yet rigorous' form (Husserl 1939) – as further discussed by Jacques Derrida (Derrida 1989 [1962]) and Gilles Deleuze and Félix Guattari (Deleuze and Guattari 1988 [1980]) - that 'can be described with local precision yet cannot be wholly reduced' (Lynn 1998 [1993]: 84). This implies that such forms cannot be described with a finite number of sections. To tackle this problem Lynn suggested 'a system of serial transections along with their coefficients of size, shape and orientation' (Lynn 1998 [1993]: 86) The project that most prominently made use of the serial sectional technique was FOA's Yokohama International Port Terminal (1994–2002) (see p. 138) (Fig.1.4), with its serial cross- and longitudinal sections that made it possible to articulate the various landscaped levels of the project and to connect them in a seamless manner into what appears to be a thick ground with burrowed ramped connections. Deploying a serial section technique in a similar manner, Jesse Reiser and Nanako Umemoto's unbuilt scheme for the Yokohama International Port Terminal articulated a continuously varied envelope.

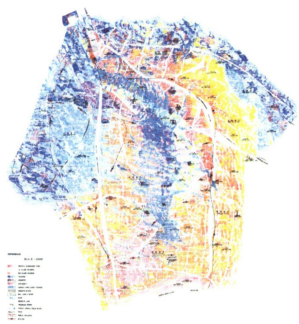

1.1 Chiangliu City masterplan (1993). *Left*: 1/10.000 model showing the extensive road space that is expanded in width and that incorporates multi-use activities and blends with the park-landscape surfaces. *Right*: 1/20.000 masterplan. Copyright: AAGDG 1993–1994.

1.1a Jeffrey P. Turko's Urban Anomaly project (1999) took a tendential approach to traditional master planning. Rather than a fixed vision that might be redundant by its completion, the scheme foregrounds urban tendencies together with prevailing landscape conditions with urban programmes. *Left*: Relational diagrams of the prevailing landscape conditions and urban fabrics of the site in Bjørvika, Olso. *Right*: Timebased maps of densities of programmes. Copyright: Jeffrey Turko.

Other instances of using the section in an innovative manner include, for instance, continuous sections cut along a path of pedestrian movement through a landscape or building. A prime example is OMA's rarely published continuous section through their unbuilt scheme for the Jussieu Library (1992). This sectional approach is still in use, mostly for the purpose of sequencing experiences along specific paths of movement. In various instances sectional strategies have also been used in order to embed a proposed scheme more seamlessly into their specific local setting by way of emphasizing continuity of the ground surface. While a number of these sectional techniques may have evolved from an interest in landscape and thus ground articulation, the interest in complex form focused not only on questions of topography but also on geometry and topology, and was eventually applied to the articulation of the envelope. However, for the latter to gain clear architectural significance a correlated

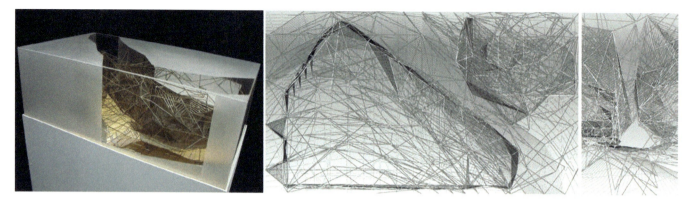

1.2 Phase 2 of OCEAN's scheme for the Jyväskylä Music and Arts Centre in Finland (2004-05) employs the box-in-box section approach to provide an interior urban event space. The different envelopes of the project feature varying degrees of transparency that reveal or veil spaces and enable the visual experience of layered spaces and activities. Copyright: OCEAN Design Research Association.

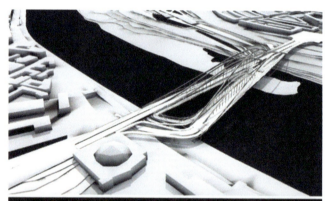

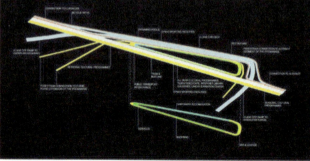

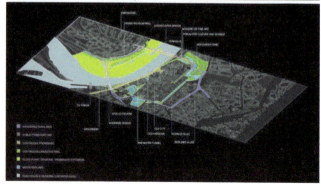

spatial approach was required that addressed, among other questions, the transition from exterior to interior, thus rethinking the articulation of the vertical surface or threshold.

The problem of the building as a 'boxed-in' space, and of 'objectness' and 'discreteness', was thus far discussed as predominately a problem of the dissolution of inner divisions and outer envelopes and a lot of landscape-oriented projects seek to continue along these lines. Thus it would appear that topography singularly emphasizes the question of ground and the various forms of its extension and particularization, and that the building envelope may constitute its antithesis with its emphasis on the vertical threshold. However, both may be extended spatial and topographic elements and there exist interesting built and unbuilt projects that propose envelope designs and methods of partitioning space in such ways that, although seemingly contradictory to the ideally continuous space of landscape-inspired design, may provide a promising inroad towards a useful correlation and, perhaps, an eventual synthesis. What may characterize such projects is an explicitly spatial approach that articulates a differentiated vertically layered sectional space.

In his seminal article 'Towards a New Architecture' the architectural theorist Jeffrey Kipnis outlined criteria for a new architecture that addressed specific sectional characteristics. Kipnis argued that the notion of *vastness* could help overcome the perceived

1.3 The unbuilt Landsc[r]aper Urban Ring Bridge (2000) scheme by OCEAN and Urban Office integrates a new multi-purpose inhabitable bridge for Düsseldorf, Germany, with a looped and integrated infrastructural and landscape scheme for the inner city. Copyright: OCEAN Design Research Association.

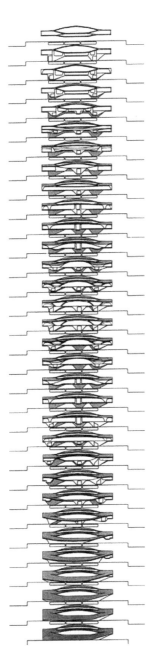

1.4 FOA's iconic serial section for their Yokohama International Port Terminal scheme (1994–2002). Copyright: Foreign Office Architects.

dichotomy between continuous and partitioned space by way of an extended residual or interstitial space that arises out of a particular approach to the sectional articulation of a scheme (Kipnis 1993). With this, the question arises as to what the characteristics of this kind of sectional space are. Peter Eisenman, with whom Kipnis collaborated, derived his particular interest in 'residual' and 'interstitial' space from Piranesi's work and described its sectional aspects as: 'a space between. … It was not left over space, but articulated space, a positive articulation of space that was residual' (Eisenman 2003). In pursuing a similar interest, Bernard Tschumi referred to interstitial space between different enclosures, as 'in-between space' arising from 'boxes inside boxes', which featured in projects such as his Le Fresnoy National Studio for Contemporary Arts in Tourcoing (see p. 189). Likewise, Kipnis referred to this arrangement as 'box-within-box section' (Kipnis 1993: 43). Yet, Kipnis went on to distinguish between two distinctly different approaches that he termed 'InFormation' and 'DeFormation', which both deploy interstitial and residual sectional space in distinctly different ways:

> Both … rely on such devices as box-within-box sections with an emphasis on interstitial and residual spaces. … Yet the tensions between them are pronounced. While DeFormation emphasises the role of new aesthetic form and therefore the visual in the engenderment of new spaces, InFormation de-emphasises the role of aesthetic form in favour of new institutional form, and therefore of programme and events. The event-spaces of new geometries tend to drive the former, while the event-spaces of new technologies occupy the latter.
>
> (Kipnis 1993: 43)

According to Kipnis, 'DeFormationist' schemes include Stephen Holl's unbuilt Palazzo del Cinema for Venice (1990) (see p. 184), AKS Runo's and Robert S. Livesey's entry to the Place Jacques Cartier Event Structure competition in Montreal (1990) and Bahram Shirdel's unbuilt Nara Convention Centre entry (1993). 'InFormationist' examples include Bernard Tschumi's Le Fresnoy Art Centre (1991–1997) (see pp. 189) and Rem Koolhaas/OMA's

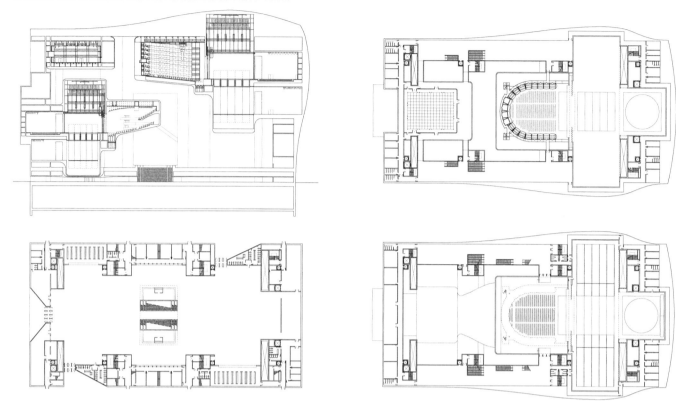

1.5 Section (*top left*) and plans of Jean Novel and Philippe Starck's iconic box-within-a-box scheme for the New National Theatre in Tokyo (1986), showing the volumes of the theatres set within a larger envelope and resulting in extensive residual space. Redrawn by Ricardo Rodrigues Ferreira (2013).

ZKM Centre for Art and Media Karlsruhe (1992). Apart from Kipnis' distinction between DeFormationist and InFormationist approaches to the box-within-box approach, it is useful for the purpose of determining traits of a non-discrete architecture to first draw another distinction between schemes that feature a continuous outer envelope and schemes that feature one or several partially open envelopes that extend the threshold between outside and inside into a spatial zone. The former continue de facto to emphasize and reinforce the architectural object, while the latter begin to suggest diminishing it. This difference between closed and open envelope schemes divides projects quite differently from the InFormation/DeFormation distinction. Closed outer envelope projects include Jean Novel and Philippe Starck's New National Theatre in Tokyo (1986) (Fig. 1.5) and Bahram Shirdel's Nara Convention Centre (1993). Open outer envelope projects include Stephen Holl's Palazzo del Cinema (1990) (see p. 184), Bernard Tschumi's Le Fresnoy Art Centre (1991–1997) (see p. 189), and more recently FOA's Meydan – Umraniye Retail Complex & Multiplex (2007) (see p. 111), Frohn and Rojas' Wall House (2007) (see p. 200) and Joakim Hoen's scheme for three Seaside Second Homes on the Norwegian west coast (2012) (see p. 207).

Needless to say, almost all of these box-within-a-box section projects maintain some emphasis on the architectural object, albeit to different degrees. Yet, all of these designs deserve close attention as to what kind of potential they may reveal vis-à-vis the question of a phased transition from exterior to interior. What is important is the realization that these projects demonstrate a compelling sectional approach that can serve to disperse the common singular separation between an outside and an inside, and perhaps, in so doing, begin to de-emphasize the architectural object and embed it more intensively into its extended setting. Here then the question arises as to how to consolidate the landscape and continuous space approach with that of spatial differentiation and partitioning. An obvious starting point may be located in sectional design approaches that integrate serial sectioning or the continuous sections along trajectories of movement of landscape-oriented designs with the box-within-box sections of multiple envelope projects. Such an approach can enable an intensely correlated articulation of grounds and envelopes and the different kinds of spatial transitions fostered by this procedure. Since the 1990s many projects pursued the search for successful integration, yet remained largely unbuilt at the time; for instance, AAGDG's Chianglu CBD

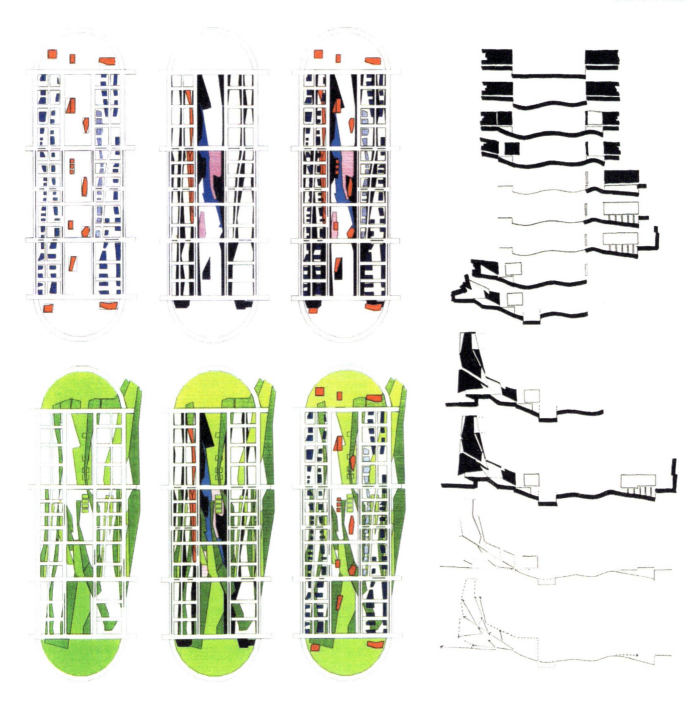

1.6 Plans and principal sectional guidelines of AAGDG's Chianglu CBD masterplan (1993), showing the integration of hard and soft landscape schemes, as well as the gradual transition from more normative massing and building to ground relations, to one that integrates both in section and spatially. Copyright: AAGDG 1993–1994.

masterplan (1993–1994) (Fig. 1.6). Now, recently built projects such as the aforementioned Foreign Office Architect's Meydan – Umraniye Retail Complex & Multiplex (2007) (see p. 111) (Fig. 1.7) successfully demonstrate a first inroad to the integration of continuous surface and box-within-box or multiple envelope approaches.

Furthermore, extended or sequenced threshold conditions may not necessarily be articulated through multiplied building envelopes alone, but, for instance, through relating envelope and local fauna in the production of a continuous space, as demonstrated by R&Sie(n) Spidernethewood project in Nîmes, France (2007) (see p. 212), or by combinations between

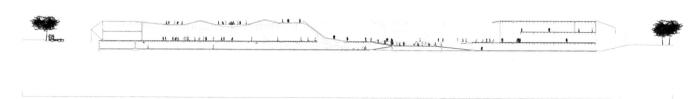

1.7 Section of Foreign Office Architect's Meydan – Umraniye Retail Complex & Multiplex (2007), showing how the landscaped surface of the scheme enfolds interior space and articulates the exterior public landscape. Copyright: Foreign Office Architects.

ground, material layers and plantations as demonstrated by RCR Arquitectes' Marquee at Les Cols Restaurant in Olot, Spain (2007–2011) (see p. 99), or even by envelopes that are entirely dissolved into gradient environmental conditions, as demonstrated by Diller, Scofidio and Renfro's Blur Building in Yverdon-les-Bains (2002) (see p. 265). The exploration of the whole bandwidth of possibilities to spatially and materially articulate non-discrete architectures has at this stage only just begun and it would seem that sectional approaches are likely to remain key to their development. Surely some may feel inclined to argue that in the time of computational design the three-dimensional model has superseded orthogonal projections, such as plan and section, as the locus of design attention and effort. And yet, while this may or may not be so, it should be clear from the above that a sectional approach still has a lot to offer in terms of innovative spatial thinking and organization, as the projects presented in this book persuasively display.

2 Grounds

'Ground' … may be said to have a conceptual potential that one can exploit to suggest new ways of thinking and perhaps also of building.

(Rajchman 1998: 77–78)

Once … the earth is conceived of as a porous mass capable of supporting objects not only on its surface but also burrowing and floating within its mass, then a new sense of ground has been established and a new mobility achieved.

(Lynn 1998 [1994]: 105–106)

For what reason or purpose might 'ground' first have been recognized? And what might the first line that was drawn on the ground have indicated? Was its intent to depict, to instruct, to enable – a count, a pointer or trajectory – or was it to restrict, to divide and to demarcate? While the answer to this question cannot be known, the difference between these two alternatives seems all too clear. They entail two opposed stances towards the ground and its role: continuity and connectivity or delimitation and partition. The struggle between the two alternatives runs through human history and through the history of architecture. In the context of architecture it seems today to be decided in favour of the dominance of the boundary and the division of ground into plots and properties, into public and private, exterior and interior, etc. Thus the line as separator prevails and reinforces the divided and discrete.

Lines drawn on a map can designate a range of items such as topographical features, routes, borders of territories, structures and buildings, or more ephemeral ones such as climate and weather-related data. But there may exist also other lines of an altogether very different notional character and implication. Gilles Deleuze and Félix Guattari described a line 'of variable direction that describes no contour and delimits no form' (Deleuze and Guattari 1988: 499), 'a nomadic absolute, as a local integration moving from part to part and constituting smooth space in an infinite succession of linkages and changes in direction – here the absolute is local, precisely because space is not limited' (Deleuze and Guattari 1988: 494). What does such a line imply in real terms and can such a line coexist with another that delineates identifiable items? Does the delineation of items contradict the possibility of continuity and connectivity? And can their correlation begin to indicate a different attitude towards ground?

When measured surveys of towns became the subject of interest, the method of depiction that was soon established for this purpose became known as *figure–ground* maps that show publicly accessible ground in white as a canvas or backdrop, as it were, for built objects that are depicted as black figures. This type of mapping gained prominence with Giambattista Nolli's map of Rome of 1748 (Fig. 2.1), although this particular map shows publicly accessible space within buildings as open ground and therefore escapes at least in part the strict dualism inherent to common figure–ground maps. As a result, however, the synthetic opposition between open and occupied ground had come to stay, largely due to the fact that the map as a planar projection had gained primacy in the survey and projection of towns and cities. Perspectival views and elevations have played a role for a while (see e.g. Blau and Kaufman 1989), yet sections were always constrained to smaller portions of towns, featuring more recently as typical street profiles in planning and design guidelines. Eventually the figure–ground map underwent a significant expansion in role when it was no longer used merely for the purpose of surveying existing conditions, but, instead, as a projective tool for the planning of new parts of towns. The urban fabric that results from figure–ground maps may be seen as the antithesis of extremely dense settlements where adjacent buildings are connected into a continuous fabric or those that duplicate ground on an extensive scale or are borrowed within it. These settlement types all defy description in a figure–ground manner and require a spatial and sectional description and understanding. Therefore, the increasing reliance on the map and plan as the sole devices for effectively organizing the built environment drastically reduced the possibility for an alternative to figure–ground architecture comprising discrete extruded buildings or blocks to arise. At the same time, however, there also existed striking examples of works that fused architecture and ground in a non-decomposable manner; for example, the types of fortifications known as star fort or *trace italienne*, which

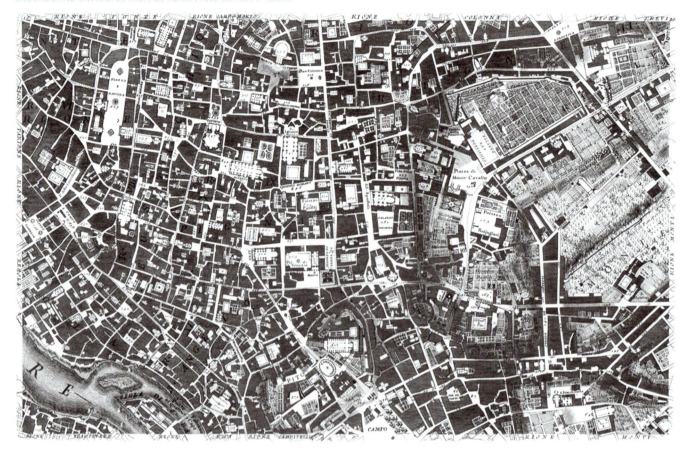

2.1 The excerpt from Giambattista Nolli's map of Rome ('Pianta Grande di Roma', 1748) shows buildings as black pochés and publicly accessible space in white, including publicly accessible interiors.

 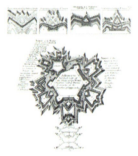

2.2 The star fort or *trace italienne*-style fortification with its intense integration of architecture and shaped terrain form constitutes the opposite of figure–ground relations that set architecture against the ground as a neutral datum. *Left*: Olomaouc bastion fortress (1757), Czech Republic. *Right*: Excerpts from the 'Table of Fortification', *Cyclopedia*, Volume 1, London: Ephraim Chambers.

emerged in fifteenth-century Italy (Fig.2.2). Thus figure–ground arrangements had from the onset of its instrumentalization a clear counterpart.

When landscape urbanism began to take shape from the 1990s onwards, the importance of the map was reaffirmed. Alex Wall stated that 'landscape is the horizontal and continuous surface, the field that is best apprehended in maps and plans. Here, plans are of particular significance because they organize the relationship among parts and activities' (Wall 1999: 247). It comes as a surprise that in the context of landscape urbanism ground is often understood as merely a surface instead of a medium for spatial arrangement, an understanding that in turn limits without any necessity the scope of design-to-surface operations. This renewed commitment to an extensive reliance on maps and plans entailed again that a great range of articulations of the built fabric were effectively taken off the board just when a new chance for rethinking this limitation had presented itself. Why this should have been so is difficult to see. There exists no particular reason to favour means that essentially diminish the full scope of design potentials that arise from things coming together not only 'on' but 'in' or 'of' the ground. Resonating with Deleuze and Guattari's description of the nomadic line, Greg Lynn argued that 'the burrow occupies the earth … as a field of potential spaces, orientations and positions' (Lynn 1998 [1994]: 106). Thus ground may acquire definite spatial attributes. However, in spite of these captivating and design-wise liberating thoughts, architects still elect to operate on the dichotomous relation between figure and ground and the discrete architectural object. Adding to this problem is the current lack of careful analysis of what architectural history may have to offer to inform projective imagination in relation to rethinking ground as a vital spatial element. Anyone who has ever experienced the roof-scape atop of Jerusalem's bazaar will recall a clear image of multiplied ground, a ground that may actually be experienced as one in contrast to the constructed thin horizontal slab that today invariably stands for the multiplication of ground. Throughout architectural history there existed a great number of examples which show how ground and building may enter into different and varied relations that resonate with the notions of thick, multiple and provisional grounds pursued here within.

Yet, prior to examining a number of interesting historical examples it is of importance to recognize that the question of thinking ground differently in terms of a more inclusive approach towards collective use is obviously not simply solved by way of architectural solutions, but must fundamentally be anchored in cultural practices, customs, rights and common sense. Such practices have existed in many places throughout the centuries. One distinct example is the 'freedom to roam' or 'everyman's right', which governs the right of public use of privately owned land and waterways for a number of purposes. Such purposes include moving through, camping temporarily and, more recently, a range of recreational purposes. In such instances it is mandatory to respect the private sphere of the owners and to keep a reasonable distance from private homes. In Norway these rights fall into the category of customary law, which is based on established long-standing patterns of behaviour and standards of local communities, while in Sweden they are today embedded in the country's constitution. Critics of the continued or renewed implementation of such rights argue that these fundamentally undermine ownership. Yet, often, quite a different tendency may be observed with public land being illegally annexed to private land. Be this as it may, throughout architectural history there have been many examples where expansive areas of privately owned land or extensive parcelling was matched with different practices of 'right of way' that helped overcome the stringency of separation and that may serve as examples for similar approaches today. The question is whether such practices may be applicable not only in relation to open landscapes, but also to densely built and populated conditions that offer alternatives to the common figure–ground arrangement and strictly maintained public–private division, in particular when this involves multiple ground schemes that deserve this designation. The examples discussed in the following part all seem to rely on an inherent relation between settlement organization and cultural practices of common use and sense.

A first example that merits inspection is a Neolithic settlement known today as Çatalhöyük. It is located near Konya in Central Anatolia in Turkey, and dates from *circa* 6500 to 5500 BC. With an estimated population of 5,000 to 8,000 inhabitants it was one of the largest Neolithic settlements discovered to date. Charles Gates, Professor of Archaeology and History of Art, argued that 'developments in town planning, architecture, agriculture (including animal husbandry), technology and religion – come together dramatically at Çatalhöyük' (Gates 2003: 24). Gates described the settlement as follows:

> The houses clustered together, their walls touching those of their neighbours. Although small courtyards connected by streets lined the edges of the excavated area, within the cluster courts existed but streets did not. People entered houses from the flat rooftops, descending to the floor by means of ladders. Since the town lay on sloping ground, the height of the roofs varied.
>
> (Gates 2003: 24)

The fact that the buildings were closely clustered together and were entered from the roof indicates that there must have been a common agreement of sorts at work, in that in order to reach any given house it was necessary to move across the roofs of other houses. The aggregation of roof surfaces into a shared elevated ground required a shared understanding in terms of access and use. The elevated new ground was limited by the perimeter of the settlement, a condition due to questions of construction and defensibility, and by trapped courtyards that established inner perimeters. The dense parts of this settlement were therefore not disassociated into discrete figures, even though it consisted of individual units. In addition, there seems to have existed a practice of periodically burning down houses, filling in the ruins and constructing on top of the previous house a new one with the same dimensions. This practice rendered one aspect of ground as gradually accumulating strata and another in consequence as temporal and recurrently reconfigured condition. In this simple example it is possible to glean a number of interrelated conditions that can in today's phrasing be identified as multiple and provisional ground conditions together with common practices that govern its principal collective and individual uses.

A corresponding example in relation to the multiplication of ground is the ancient town of Mardin, one of the oldest settlement areas in Upper Mesopotamia. Mardin is situated on a south-facing mountain slope near the River Tigris from where it overlooks the northern Syrian flat plains. The semi-arid climate entails winter temperatures of down to 0° centigrade with occasional snow, and hot, dry summers with temperatures up to 48° centigrade. The town is characterized by its dense terraced fabric of historical buildings built mainly from locally quarried limestone that are located on a steep slope (Fig. 2.3). Many of the old houses date from the Artuqid dynasty *circa* 1100 to 1400 AD. The buildings are generally introverted and mostly two storeys high, and display a repetitive quasi-modular layout. Interestingly, though, the buildings do not register strongly as discrete architectural objects in the elevation of the town, although they visibly occupy the hillside. Instead they blend into a continuous fabric which itself blends in with the hill. Yet, each architecture effectively participates in the doubling of ground and its three-dimensional maze-like organization in which both the buildings and the compact settlement configuration adhere to the topography of the steeply sloped hill and to the specific local climatic conditions in terms of orientation of the buildings, the density of the built fabric and the more detailed layout of the dwellings. The roof terraces double the ground datum, yet not quite like in Çatalhöyük, where the new datum is somewhat more continuous with no volumes protruding beyond roof level, even though Çatalhöyük's roof-scape was gently stepped due to the lightly sloping terrain (Fig. 2.4). In Mardin, the entrance level of buildings changes in accordance with the steep slope.

The entrance level of a building uphill may thus be located at the same height as the first floor of the directly adjacent building downhill. Pedestrian circulation routes run either along the height lines of the hill between rows of houses or steeply up- and downhill. Frequently terraces and roof terraces are part of the circulation up- and downhill. Locally, buildings bridge over the narrow streets and street junctions, and occasionally display characteristics of burrowed space. Mardin's densely packed and labyrinthine settlement pattern resonates with traditional Arab settlements, albeit in a different spatial arrangement with its own particular characteristics owing to the steep slope of the hill on which the town is situated.

A different type of non-discrete architecture based on ground operations is underground dwellings, which exist in different sizes and complexity in different parts of the world. Often these are still inhabited and can shed light on an interesting interrelation between architecture and cultural practices. One interesting case is the villages on China's semi-arid Huangtu or Loess plateau in the Gansu, Henan, Shanxi and Shaanxi provinces and the Ningxia Hui Autonomous Region. During the 1990s some 30 to 40 million people still lived in underground dwellings known as *yaodong* (house caves) (Fig. 2.7 p. 32) (Fig. 2.8 p. 33), according to Gideon Golany (Golany 1992). According to Golany, *yaodong* dwellings exist in three different types: (1) dwellings dug into loess cliffs on the sides of valleys (cliff cave dwelling); (2) dwellings dug into a flat plain and organized around a sunken courtyard (pit cave dwelling); (3) vaulted dwellings made from stone or brick with one or two storeys above ground that are covered with loess (earth-sheltered dwellings). Golany emphasized that these 'cave dwelling types introduce a variety of forms that are the result of a synthesis among socioeconomic, cultural, traditional, and physical environmental factors including topography and climate' (Golany 1992: 71). Of particular interest are the pit cave dwellings that are organized around sunken courtyards. Bernard Rudofsky brought the astonishing settlements based on the second type to attention in 1964 in the context of his seminal *Architecture without Architects* book and exhibition. For the purpose of illustrating these villages he acquired exceptional aerial black and white photographs taken in the 1930s by the German pilot Wulf-

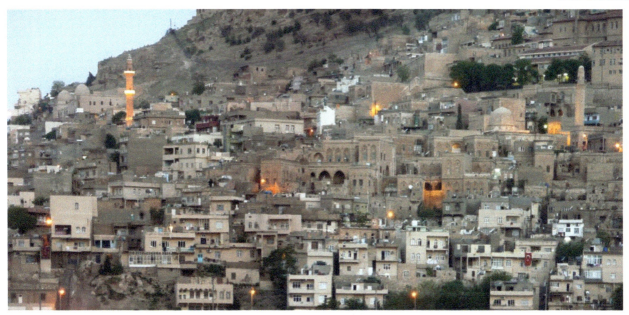

2.3 Views of the old town of Mardin, Turkey, showing the dense, clustered settlement pattern on the steeply sloped hillside. Photography: Nevit Dilmen (2008).

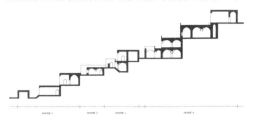

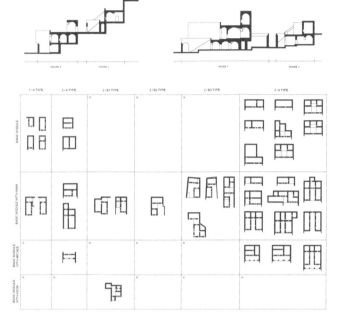

2.4 *Top*: Sections of the old town of Mardin showing the doubling up of the ground. *Bottom*: Typical plan organization of single buildings that make up the dense settlement cluster. Drawn after Füsun Alioğlu, E. (2003). *Mardin – Şehir Dokusu ve Evler* (2nd Edition). Istanbul: Türkiye Ekonomik ve Toplumsal Tarih Vafkı Yayınıdır.

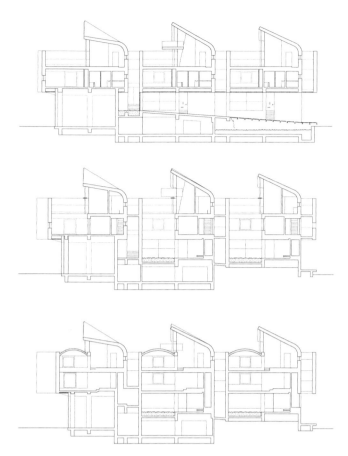

2.4(a) OMA's Nexus World housing project in Fukuoka, Japan (1991) offers an interesting example of a rearticulated mat-building approach and dense sectional settlement pattern within a confined footprint. It is the articulation of the building perimeter, however, that renders the building volume discrete, that is separated from its setting, and finite, in that it cannot easily be extended. Redrawn by Ricardo Rodrigues Ferreira (2014).

Dieter Graf zu Castell. These photos show areas of numerous sunken courtyards that were dug into the soft loess. Rudofsky described the underground dwellings as follows:

> The dark squares in the landscape are pits an eighth of an acre in area, or about the size of a tennis court. Their vertical sides are 25 to 30 feet high. L-shaped staircases lead to the apartments below whose rooms are about 30 feet deep and 15 feet wide, and measure about 15 feet to the top of the vaulted ceiling. They are lighted and aired by openings that give onto the courtyard. The dwellings are clean and free of vermin, warm in winter and cool in summer.
> (Rudofsky 1964: 17–18)

In order to highlight the associated relation to the ground that these settlements suggest, Rudofsky quoted George B. Cressey who stated that 'such land does double duty, with dwellings below and fields upstairs' (Cressey 1955). That this is not entirely correct may be gleaned from the aerial photos that show a wide perimeter of empty ground between the courtyards that is generally void of plantation save for some trees. One of the aerial photos shows that the location of the L-shaped staircases and the trees largely coincide. It is likely that the roots of the trees were meant to help stabilize the soil, while the treetops were thought to diffuse the wind and to prevent the stairway from filling up with airborne dusty silt. Fields, however, were located adjacent to the cleared perimeter of dwellings or settlement clusters. Yet, what is of interest is the space given to the cleared perimeter of the dwellings. The space between dwellings may be due to the necessary distance for construction so that the ground does not become instable or so that the rooms that extend from the courtyards may not intersect. Whatever the reason, the clear space

2.5 Troglodyte Berber pit-cave dwelling, Matmata, Tunisia. Copyright: Dallas & John Heaton/Robert Harding World Imagery/Corbis (2010).

between the dwellings exceeds by far what would be necessary for circulation and constitutes quite an extensive surface where work and gatherings can take place. One of the aerial photos shows the short-cut paths for circulation across the village running diagonally through the chequer pattern of the courtyards. Yet, beyond this there exists currently little accessible information as to what kinds of common practices were associated with the use of the open areas around the dwellings. Clearly though the comprehensive accessibility of the ground is a key feature of this settlement type, as the ground datum is not elevated and thus not constrained by a raised perimeter, as in the case of Çatalhöyük.

Similar to the *yaodong* are the Tunisian cliff-cave and pit-cave dwellings of the Berbers on the Matmata plateau (Figs 2.5 and 2.6). The courtyards of the pit-cave dwellings are typically about 10 metres wide and deep, and offer ample protection from the semi-arid climate of Southern Tunisia and the impact of the adjacent Sahara. Some dwellings consist of multiple courtyards connected by trenches or tunnels. Far more extensive than that are the underground cities of Anatolia in Turkey. In the Nevşehir province some 200 underground cities of significant size have been discovered to date that combine living quarters, refectories, chapels, stables, storage and food-processing rooms, spaces for metallurgic works, ventilation shafts, wells and tunnels for circulation. The largest underground city of the region is Derinkuyu. The city was organized in eight to eleven floors and a depth of around 85 metres. Each room had secured ventilation even when all entry points were closed to prevent raids. Derinkuyu was connected to other similar underground settlements through tunnels. Other large complexes include Kaymaklı and Özkonak. The latter was organized over 10 floors and to a depth of about 40 metres. It is estimated that Özkonak could house up to 60,000 people over shorter periods of time. What these particular examples indicate is that it is entirely conceivable and possible to construct extensively underground and to inhabit such extensive underground settlements if necessary at least for several months at a time.

Yet such extensive burrowed settlements require much more documentation and analyses before they can potentially serve as examples for contemporary design.

Clearly, it would not be of much use to attempt to depict settlements like Çatalhöyük or Mardin or underground settlements as customary figure/ground maps. And curtailing contemporary schemes that use elements of such historical schemes with an

2.6 Troglodyte Berber pit-cave dwelling, Matmata, Tunisia. Copyright: Dallas & John Heaton/Robert Harding World Imagery/Corbis (2010).

arbitrary boundary in plan and drop in section in such ways that would render the new raised ground inaccessible does not make much sense either, as this simply implies a shift of the discrete object and isolated ground to a mega-scale.

The above-cited historical examples resonate in various ways with the labyrinthine North African towns and casbahs that inspired the so-called mat-building typology, which emerged from the research of GAMMA, the Moroccan CIAM group, and which became a central theme in Team X. Eric Mumford elaborated that 'the mat approach shifts the architect's attention from imagery to organization, and from bounded shape-making to the provisional organization of fields of urban activity' (Mumford 2001: 64). Clearly this understanding indicates some of the potential traits of non-discrete architecture.

In its initial phase in the work of GAMMA and Team X the interest that evolved into the mat research involved a detailed examination of local cultural practices and pattern of habitation of local communities, as well as related spatial, material and environmental sensibilities. GAMMA, for instance, met the need to provide large amounts of housing in Morocco with a careful analysis of Berber settlements and dwellings and their specific characteristics. The findings were subsequently translated into a low-rise dense fabric that was therefore to some extent informed by local circumstances and customs.

Yet, in its later stages of development and implementation in other contexts, the initial close relation between cultural practices and local circumstances on the one hand, and the mat typology on the other, seemed to have gradually slipped away. Mat-specific spatial characteristics prevail in the networked, polycentric and circulatory organization of projects like Candilis, Josic and Woods Free University Building in Berlin (1973) or Aldo Van Eyck's orphanage in Amsterdam (1957–1960). George Wagner said about the Free University Building that:

> The building treads a fine and unsteady line between specificity and generality. Understood … as a topography, it is a sort of polyvalent landscape. … As a landscape it possesses no definite ground: each roof is planted to become another level of the garden.
>
> (Wagner 1999: 17)

But the generalized mat approach that was removed from its local specificity so as to make it ready for use in various contexts was subsequently not realigned with local practices. Instead a shift in emphasis occurred. Herman Hertzberger (1996: 2) stated that:

> The architectural 'order' of [Van Eyck's] orphanage provides the lingua franca for a place-by-place interpretation of the demands made by everyday life, to such effect that it convinced me of the need to perceive a building ... as an interweaving of 'competence' and 'performance'.

He followed this commendation with an account of how well the building can accommodate different uses, thus shifting emphasis away from this typology's initial focus of local specificity to the generalization of programmatic flexibility. This broad generalization of the mat building typology without reintegration into locally specific circumstances implied that the main interface with existing conditions was of a circulatory nature and that its spatial organization followed a logic that is internal to the system, yet alien to the context. In so doing, mat buildings of that sort became and remained discrete and detached from their context, thus entirely defeating initial motives and motivations. If this rings all too familiar it is because this identically constitutes the shortcomings and fallacies of most current versions of so-called parametric urbanism.

Thus the mat approach never quite flourished at a more significant scale and fell swiftly out of fashion. Nevertheless, there exists a succession of subsequent projects that attempted to reference it in one way or another, such as OMA's unbuilt Agadir Convention Centre (1990) with its raised volume of courtyard-type hotel rooms, or their Nexus World Housing project in Fukuoka, Japan (1991) with its densely packed courtyard apartments. Yet, as with the generalized mat projects, critical parts of these schemes were not organizationally integrated into their given setting, aside from formal gestures, nor was the suggested elevated ground datum generally accessible as in Çatalhöyük or Mardin, or the Chinese, Northern African or Anatolian underground settlements. Instead the approach had turned into a formal exercise void of the capacities of mat buildings to connect to the surrounding landscape or urban fabric. The raised finite figure based on the square footprint of the Agadir and Nexus World Housing projects makes this immediately clear. The same is true for the sandwiched 'continuous' landscaped space of the Agadir project. With the plinth of the building raised above terrain level, the terrain of this landscape-like level is de facto discontinuous and what remains is simply a formal gesture without effect beyond the visual and the scheme-specific intentions for space use.

In turn, one may begin to wonder whether a mat typology that is made locally specific, in various ways continuous with its setting, and that is designed in relation to practices such as the 'all men's right' may have a better chance of succeeding. Nekton Design's Turf City (see p. 145) incorporated these premises in a scheme for the urban development of the Reykjavik Vatnsmyri domestic airport site. This version of a mat- or field-like urban fabric features a system of public urban surfaces and landscaped surfaces that is designed to sustain local biodiversity. These surfaces are extended over the site and over or through the volume of the buildings that make up the urban fabric in a manner that negotiates the need for spatial enclosure and partitioning with spatial continuity of systems and surfaces within the site and beyond.

The deployment of a similar spatial organization and treatment of ground on a building scale features prominently in Paulo Mendes da Rocha's work, in particular the Brazilian Museum of Sculpture (see p. 87) and the Fernando Millan house, both located in Sao Paulo. Located on inclined terrain, both projects are characterized by continuous surfaces that are extended over and through the building volume and utilize surface materials from the surrounding area to emphasize surface continuity and also feature planting beds with local flora that highlight the landscape character of the tectonic extension of the ground. Perimeters, delineation and discontinuities coexist in these schemes together with extended threshold conditions and multiple grounds assigned to give continuity to different aspects of the local setting.

The discussion thus far may raise the question as to whether an implementation of spatial strategies pertaining to multiple and thick ground necessarily entails applicability only in large-scale projects and settlement organization. This, however, is not the case, as similar strategies may be employed in the design of smaller architectures. This may entail embedding small schemes into the existing landscape so as to maintain spatial and surface continuity, like, for instance, the projects designed and constructed in the context of the SCL33s and SCL68n studios at the Research Centre of Architecture and Tectonics (RCAT) in Oslo: *Las Piedras del Cielo*, a cooking and dining facility set in the Pacific coastal dune landscape in the Open City Ritoque, Chile (2012) , the 2x2 Bathing Platform in Nusfjord, Norway (2013) (Figs 2.9) (for both projects see Chapter 5) and the Sørenga Bridge Event Space (2014) (Figs 2.10). The first two projects provide enclosure by way of small spatial pockets set within structures that smoothly connect to the surrounding landscape surface. An alternative strategy may be based on the design of a constructed landscape where no particular one exists; for instance, Paulo Mendes da Rocha's Brazilian Pavilion for the Osaka Expo 1970 (see p. 83), or RCR Arquitectes Marquee at Les Cols Restaurant (see p. 99). Both projects demonstrate how ground can be engaged in a varied spatial organization in a smaller and more intimate scale. From such projects it is also possible to glean that ground continuity and vertical threshold conditions can coexist without contradiction for as long as a coherent and integrated spatial and sectional scheme informs the design.

The preoccupation of contemporary landscape urbanists with the horizontal surface resonates in various aspects with the afore-discussed historical examples. James Corner (2006: 30–31), for instance, stated that:

> The landscape urbanism project concerns itself with the phenomenon of the horizontal surface, the ground plane, the 'field' of action. … This suggests contemporary interest in surface continuities, where roofs and grounds become one and the same; and this is certainly of great value with regard to conflating separations between landscape and building.

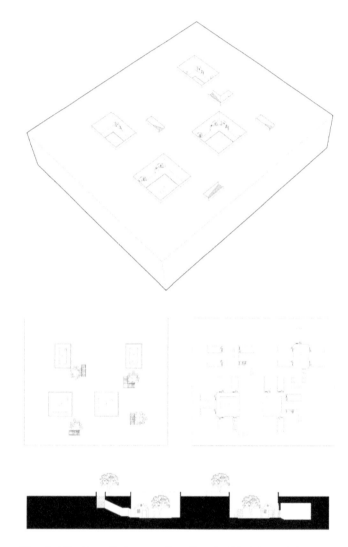

Historical Yoa Dong Underground Dwellings in China's Loess-belt: axonometric view (top), ground plan (centre left) and belowground plan (centre right), and sections (bottom). Copyright: OCEAN | SEA Sustainable Environment Association +RCAT | ACDL Studio 2015.

Yet there is more to this approach, as may be gleaned from Corner's (2006: 30–31) further elaboration:

> However, I would emphasize a second understanding of surface: surface as urban infrastructure. … Unlike architecture, which consumes the potential of a site in order to project, urban infrastructure sows the seeds of future possi-

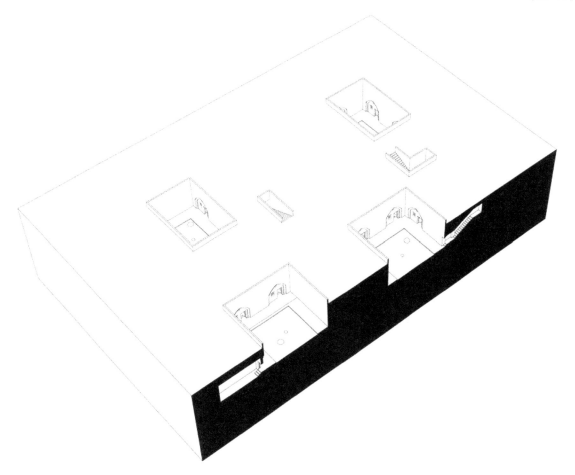

2.8 Sectional axonometric view of historical Yoa Dong Underground Dwellings in China's Loess-belt. Copyright: OCEAN | SEA Sustainable Environment Association + RCAT | ACDL Studio 2015.

bility, staging the ground for both uncertainty and promise. This preparation of surfaces for future appropriation differs from merely formal interest in single surface construction. It is much more strategic, emphasising means over ends and operational logic over compositional design.

However, use and appropriation of ground, rather than mere surface, may be specific to culture and setting. How may this then be related to the question of urban infrastructure? Alex Wall argued that West 8's design for the Schouwburgplein in Rotterdam, for instance, constitutes a thickened equipped and furnished, yet unprogrammed surface that enriches social space by its flexibility of use (Wall 1999). Such a surface does constitute an urban infrastructure. Yet, must flexibility of use and related provisions necessarily be thought of as generic, notwithstanding local conditions and cultural specificity? Is a generalized/generic flexibility of use the only way to instil the provisional character of use which must underlie flexibility? One might think of three alternative approaches that may be employed either separately or jointly:

1 Correlating provision with specific local circumstances, customs and cultural patterns together with continuity and/or multiplication of ground for freely evolving patterns of individual and collective appropriation, as the various historical examples discussed above indicate and demonstrate.

2 Strategically limiting the programmatic scope of a scheme without necessarily limiting ad hoc use and appropriation, while loosely affiliating it with local cultural tendencies and material articulation that foreground provisionality, like, for instance, Helen and Hard's GeoPark project for a playground (see p. 172).

3 Providing a mosaic of programmatically determined areas in close proximity to non-programmed ones, with the former selected at least in parts according to local circumstances, customs and cultural patterns, like, for instance, the schemes for the Spreebogen Governmental Centre by Andrew Zago (see p. 94) and by Hensel, Kong, Limwatanakul and Bettum (see p. 132).

2.9 Views of the 2x2 Bathing Platform project (2013) in Nusfjord, Norway, showing the continuity of the landscaped surface of the project with the surrounding landscape. Copyright: Scarcity and Creativity Studio.

2.10 View of the Sørenga Bridge Event Space (2014) in the wider context of the medieval park of Oslo and the surrounding road and rail spaces and the Barcode project in the background. Copyright: Scarcity and Creativity Studio.

2.11 Various views of the Sørenga Bridge Event Space (2014) as a public landscape. Copyright: Scarcity and Creativity Studio.

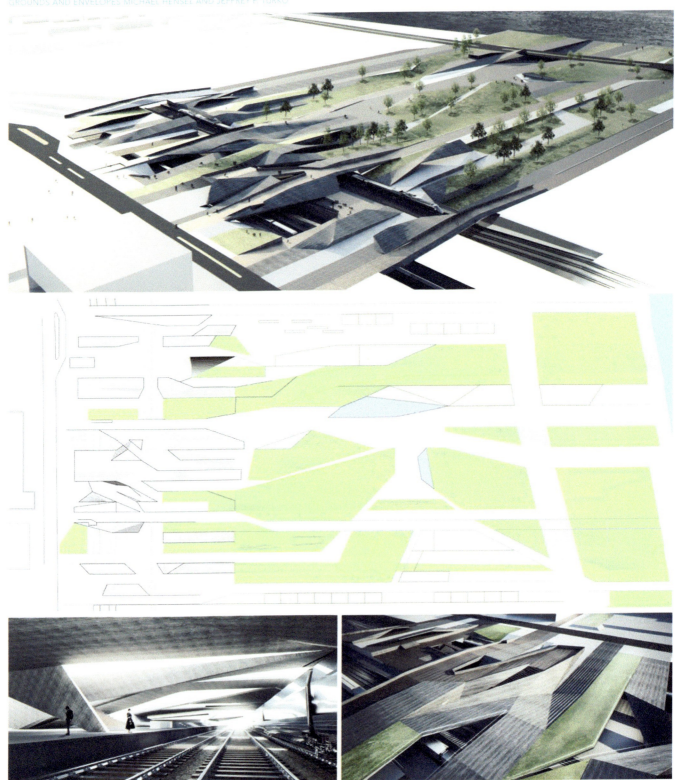

2.12(a) The Station Fabric Patch project by Tom Lea (AA School Diploma Unit 12 2008/2009) rearticulates the existing railway line and ground along the Bío Bío river in Concepcion, Chile into a sectional layering of varied terrains. Top: Bird's-eye view of the scheme, showing the integration of infrastructure and terrain across the site. Middle: Plan of the scheme showing the gradient from urban fabric to landscape. Bottom left: View of railway platform under canopied terrains. Bottom right: Ariel view of terrain bridges crossing over railway line. Copyright: Tom Lea.

2.12(b) The Down River Town project by George Barer (AA School Diploma Unit 12 2009/2010) rearticulates the infrastructural zone of the L.A. river basin into multiple grounds set within the existing terrain and connecting to the existing urban fabric. *Top*: Bird's-eye view of the scheme, showing the integration of landscape and infrastructure across the site. *Centre left:* Plan of the scheme, showing the integration and extension of the surrounding fabrics and grounds into and throughout the scheme. *Centre right:* Cross-section of the scheme. *Bottom*: Longitudinal section along the river bed, showing the variation of landscape, and semi-interior spaces across the scheme. Copyright: George Barer.

The need to render the perception of ground as provisional arises, as we have argued before, from the commonplace assumption that once ground is occupied by construction it will continue to be so. This perception frequently obstructs different ways of thinking about already built-up sites and their transformation over time. With the built environment expanding at a fast rate, it is of vital importance to open up possibilities by way of design, rather than narrowing them down to a singular and fixed determination.

At any rate, our aim was to argue that in order to articulate ground as a vital spatial element above and beyond formal gestures, it is not sufficient to only render ground continuous, to multiply it or to enfold space within it. It is necessary to strive to embed various traits of local specificity, as well as to instil a perception of its provisional character and purpose. In order to make this tangible it is necessary to discuss how this may be possible from a material and construction perspective. This question is addressed further in Chapter 5. Moreover, it is of interest to examine the participation of ground in staging local climate and ecosystems as a way of instilling local specificity and a related alternative take on questions of sustainability. These questions are addressed in Chapter 4.

3 Envelopes

The art of the master-builder entails the creation of space, not the design of façades. A spatial envelope is established by means of walls, through which a space or a series of spaces are manifested.

(Berlage 1908)

Today the practice of architecture seems to be increasingly polarized between, on the one hand, a so-called 'high-tech' approach predicated exclusively on production and, on the other, the provision of a 'compensatory façade' to cover up the harsh realities of this universal system.

(Frampton 1983:17)

Whether architecture and urbanism can or should be critical, projective, progressive, or utopian, and whether speculative architecture can remain an effective practice are still much-debated issues that need to be addressed with respect to a proposal of a *general theory of the building envelope*.

(Zaera Polo 2008: 203)

From the onset we seek to address the building envelope not merely as a material condition, but instead as an extended spatial zone that encompasses all interactions of the physical building envelope with the various conditions and dynamics of its specific setting, be these cultural, environmental or otherwise. The aim is to move away from an understanding of the envelope as an enclosure that merely divides interior and exterior, towards an alternative understanding in which the envelope is understood as an agent in the interaction between different aspects of the local setting and environment, that is spatially articulated and that makes varied provisions for use and habitation. In order to approach this understanding several concepts are discussed: (1) the articulated envelope, such as intricately perforated performative screenwalls, (2) multiple envelopes (whether initially designed as such or arrived at via auxiliary architectures), (3) thick structures that articulate a spatial transition by way of an expansive habitable tectonic, and (4) envelopes that arise out of a deliberate environmental condition and conditioning, such as Yves Klein's Air Architectures, or Diller, Scofidio and Renfro's Blur building.

The case for highly articulated performative envelopes is perhaps best made with the example of screenwalls. Islamic screenwalls in particular have been the renewed subject of interest for a while now, such as the Moghul *jaalis*, perforated stone or lattice screenwalls, or the Arabic *mashrabīyas*, projecting oriel windows clad with wooden latticework. As the late Hassan Fathy pointed out, *mashrabīyas* are characterized by a range of integrated performative capacities: they regulate the passage of light, airflow, temperature and humidity of the air current, as well as visual penetration from the inside and outside. This results from the adjustment of the sizes of the balusters and interstices that make up the latticework. Frequently different parts of these screenwalls provide for different hierarchies of the integrated functions: if, for example, interstices need to be smaller at seating or standing height to reduce glare, the resultant reduction in airflow is compensated for by larger interstices higher up in the latticework. Wooden lattice type screenwalls also display hygroscopic behaviour that may be deployed to modulate the humidity of the air current for the purpose of cooling (see Fathy 1986). As such, screenwalls can therefore provide multi-performative capacity, while at the same not constraining formal articulation. These examples demonstrate in a succinct manner that the insistent dialectic between form and function that still divides architectural camps is no longer useful to uphold.

In addition, it is frequently wrongly assumed that screenwalls are of use only in warm climates. The combination of articulated and multiple envelopes is equally useful to provide semi-sheltered spaces in moderate and cold climates. A number of projects that have in recent times made use of articulated envelopes in combination with multiple envelope arrangements demonstrate this in various ways, such as OCEAN's unbuilt experimental scheme for an apartment block in Cologne (1998) (Fig. 3.1) or Joakim Hoen's unbuilt Seaside Second Homes scheme for the Norwegian west coast (see p. 207). Likewise, the pneumatic façade panels of Cloud 9's MediaTic (see p. 258) with its printed pattern for light and thermal control relates to this approach.

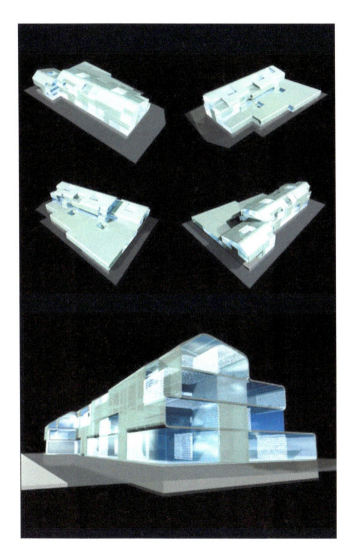

3.1 The axonometric views of OCEAN's unbuilt scheme for an experimental apartment block in Cologne (1998), Germany, show the three different material layers that make up the envelope of the building and that condition heterogeneous interior climate and exposure. Copyright: OCEAN Design Research Association.

This raises the question as to why and how to deploy multiple envelopes.

Throughout architectural history transitional spaces were used between exterior and interior, to help modulate the environment and to provide semi-sheltered spaces for varied use. The arcaded spaces of the Italian Renaissance, for instance, did so and offer an opportunity for reconceptualization. Behling and Behling, for instance, described this type of space as 'the wall becoming habitable shade' (Behling and Behling 2000: 120), thus foregrounding the capacity of such spaces to provide environmental conditions for varied use, similar to the above-discussed Islamic screenwalls, but through spatial organization on the scale of inhabitable space. Interesting historical examples are abundant. The Baghdad Kiosk, for instance, a small two-storey structure dating from 1638/1639 located in the Fourth Courtyard of Istanbul's Topkapı Palace, offers a richly varied space and environmental conditioning (Fig. 3.2). The building is organized on an octagonal footprint with four of the faces recessed. This results in a meandering wall and arcaded space that features semi-sheltered exterior spaces with different orientations and exposure to the sun's path and angle and prevailing wind directions, and at times shaded by the protruding roof. This strategy positions the windows in the protruding corners in a more exposed part of the envelope to gain light for the interior and results in areas of different climatic exposure in the interior, which is organized into four apses occupied by divans. These provide diverse choices of environmental conditions for specific activities relative to the specific preferences of the inhabitants that adapt by way of repositioning within the space. In addition, the arcades could be fully covered by hanging carpets and textile draping, transforming the upper level into exposed or private zones. This textile draping could provide additional visual protection, shading and ventilation. What is surprising is the ratio between the transitional arcaded space and the interior space, which are equal in area. Clearly the transitional space was deemed neither wasteful nor secondary, but instead an essential provision for versatile use.

While such spaces have by and large become rare due to the primacy of the flat and spatially featureless envelope of the age of 'power-operated' architecture and conditioned interiors (Banham 1969), they nevertheless continued to be deployed in some modernist and contemporary schemes. In modernist

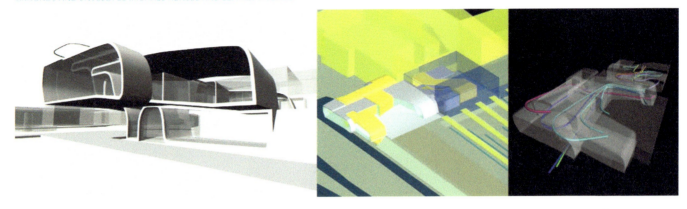

3.1(a) Jeffrey Turko's experimental Anomalous Gallery project (1999), aimed at connecting Oslo's central station to the adjacent harbour front area. The scheme is based on the existing pedestrian circulation pattern in and out of the station and proposes the insertion of a new space into a disused part of the station and its extension beyond the station's perimeter, rendering the perimeter space deep and habitable. *Left*: Perspective showing the Gallery's surfaces that integrate the existing ground and circulation pattern into a new arrangement for a temporal gallery and adjoined spaces for flexible use. *Centre*: Axonometric view of the Gallery's secondary structural envelopes that introduce a new space into Oslo's central station. *Right*: Diagram of the varied paths of circulation through the Gallery and its adjoining spaces. Copyright: Jeffrey P. Turko.

3.2 Baghdad Kiosk (1638–1639) Topkapı Palace, Istanbul, Turkey. *Top*: View of the Bagdad Kiosk from the lowered garden level. *Bottom left*: Serial sectioning of the building volume both in plan and in section. *Bottom right*: airflow analysis showing pressure zones near the envelope due to its articulation and the transitional zone of the arcaded space. The analysis shows that the overhanging roof has a considerable effect on pressure and velocity of airflow. Copyright: Defne Sunguroğlu Hensel.

3.3 Designed by Le Corbusier, the Mill Owners' Association Building in Ahmedabad, completed in 1954, features large louvre walls that are inhabitable and form a transitional zone together with the atrium and circulation system. This type of thick wall plays a key role in the environmental modulation capacity of this largely free-running building and in providing heterogeneous spaces that offer choices for the inhabitants. Photography: Sanyam Bahga (2009).

architecture these types of spaces existed, for instance, in the form of louvre walls, such as those famously deployed by Le Corbusier, in the building of the Mill Owners' Association in Ahmedabad (1954) (Fig. 3.3), or by Henry Clumb's Church of San Martin de Porres (1950) in San Juan, Puerto Rico (for a related analysis see Leatherbarrow 2009). Alan Colquhoun pointed out that the sun breaker, an external louvred wall, 'was more than a technical device; it introduced a new architectural element in the form of a thick permeable wall' (Colquhoun 1989: 187). In extending this argument, David Leatherbarrow argued that modern architecture did not eradicate the architectural boundary as a separation between inside and outside, but instead made this separation subtler, as 'boundaries between spatial interiors and exteriors are not overcome with the adoption of the structural frame, but thickened' (Leatherbarrow 2009: 34).

Likewise, multiple envelopes can stage such spatial transitions from the larger setting to the innermost areas of a given architecture. The deployment of differently articulated envelopes with different kinds and degrees of permeability can, in interaction with the local environment, produce heterogeneous spaces that provide a different model for flexible use. In stark contrast to the largely homogeneously conditioned spaces of power-operated architectures, the heterogeneous conditioning of spaces through multiple envelopes offers choices for the inhabitant. For instance, OCEAN's unbuilt experimental scheme for an apartment block in Cologne (1998) (see fig. 3.1(a)) relinquished space-use allocation (i.e. living room, kitchen, bedroom) in favour of spaces that provide different microclimates, which, in turn, deliver choice and the possibility of adaptive use to the residents. The scheme featured three different envelopes – transparent, veiling (screenwall) and opaque – that are varied in layering order and distance, and that produce different instances of exterior, semi-exterior and interior conditions. Each combination results in a unique range of conditions that change over time due to the dynamics of the local environment. In so doing, this scheme resonates with the aforementioned historical example of the Bagdad Kiosk. Similarly motivated projects include Joakim Hoen's unbuilt Seaside Second Homes scheme for the Norwegian west coast (see p. 207), FAR's Wall House in Chile (see p. 200), Steven Holl's unbuilt scheme for the Venice Cinema Palace (see p. 184), and by extension also R&Sie(n)'s Spidernethewood project in Nîmes, France (see p. 212), which extends spatial articulation and transition by way of both using and constraining the local flora. The latter, however, also shares traits with what might be called deep structures, another potent strategy to articulate an extended threshold. What the deep structure approach entails may be illustrated with the example of the GC Prostho Museum Research Centre designed by Kengo Kuma (see p. 238). A structural lattice of timber profiles is arrayed into a deep sectional space that articulates the most prominent portion of the building. From this is 'carved out' an exhibition space for visitors. The structure itself is visually permeable to a certain extent, as light conditions permit; the rest recedes into an indefinite depth.

In outlining his five points towards a new architecture Jeffrey Kipnis listed a condition he termed 'vastness' which 'negotiates a middle-ground between the homogeneity of infinite or universal space and the fixed hierarchies of closely articulated space. … Design implications: … extension of free plan to free section, emphasis on residual and interstitial spaces' (Kipnis 1993: 43).

In consequence he outlines the box-in-box section, which is constituted by multiple envelopes. Yet, this approach is not reserved to envelopes articulated in one way or another as surfaces; deep structures may equally result in the perception of such a space and its limits. This is made possible when such structures are deep enough to elude full visual access and when some part of the space articulated in this manner recedes into indefinite depth. This indefinite condition articulates an extended threshold that by eluding the perception of finitude destabilizes the perception of definite delineation and territorialization in favour of another space that is more uncertain in terms of its designation. In so doing, both multiple envelopes and deep structures enable what Alejandro Zaera Polo calls 'intricate design of the limit between private and public [that] increases the contact surface between both realms' (Zaera Polo 2008: 79). This condition may render the transitional extended threshold the space of *event*, as discussed by Bernard Tschumi, Jeffrey Kipnis and others. Here residual and interstitial space can unfold its various potentials and subtle provisions.

Yet, the question arises as to how to address in this manner the vast bulk of the built environment that cannot simply be taken down and replaced. What can be done with buildings that will remain for decades? Works like the venerated Church of the Holy Sepulchre in the Old City of Jerusalem, which was built stage after stage over the centuries as new constructions around existing ones, suggest a powerful possibility: it is possible to build layers of envelopes and spaces outward from an existing core, as demonstrated, for instance, by Bernard Tschumi's Le Fresnoy Art Centre in Tourcoing, France (see p. 000). In this example the new roofing over an existing building complex articulates an interstitial space between the existing old roofs and the new roof that is inhabitable.

Such 'auxiliary architectures' (Hensel 2013) can constitute an extensive field of engagement to architecture. Clearly architectural history is rich with such supplementary interventions that may provide varying degrees of shelter.

3.3(a) View of a varied pattern of sunlight generated by a jail, a stone-made Islamic screenwall. Today such screenwalls predominately receive attention due to their ornamental expression of geometric, floral and calligraphic pattern, thus drawing the emphasis to the object. However, screenwalls are multifunctional building elements that prevent views from outside while engendering them from the inside, and that condition airflow, sunlight and thermal impact in a context and time-specific manner. While contemporary building envelopes increasingly feature screenlike layers these are more often than not only considered in exclusively aesthetically and their potential for environmental modulation remains disregarded. Copyright: Michael U. Hensel.

At the former Institute of Lightweight Structures in Stuttgart, Frei Otto and his collaborators invested great effort in charting, for instance, the history of supplementary textile structures.

Numerous publications, such as *Sun and Shade – Toldos, Vela* (Krause-Valdovinos 1984), included research on the Roman vela or sun sails, Spanish toldos and similar convertible sun roofs in Japan. In particular, the latter two are of interest in that they were not part of the initial design of a building. Hamann and Moro (1984: 94) describe the Spanish toldos as follows:

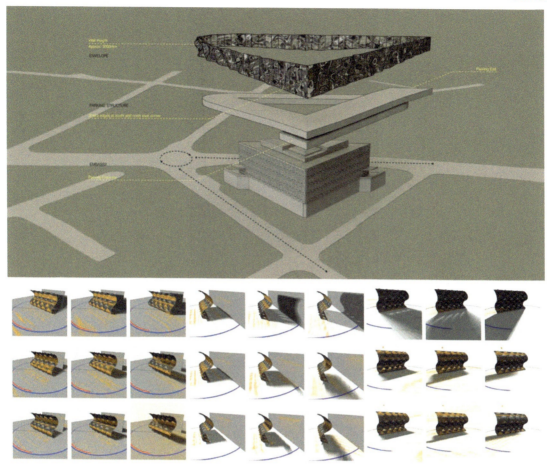

3.3(b) Design for a new perimeter wall for the plot of the American Embassy (Eero Saarinen, 1959) designed by Rikard Jaucis and Joakim Wiig Hoen (2010). The screenwall-like design for the stainless steel perimeter wall aspires to provide both security and a varied visual experience based on varied transparency, light reflection and shading. Copyright: RCAT | ACDL Studio.

Toldos are designed to protect against excessive insolation thereby reducing the heating of the airvolume underneath the toldo, protecting the public against air-borne dust and sometimes against glare. Their space-enclosing and space-creating effect is most impressive.

According to Hamann and Moro, the *cortège toldo* consists of 'individual awning segments which are sewn or thonged together' and are 'suspended from masts and cannot be drawn' (Hamann and Moro 1984: 94), whereas the *street toldo* is 'suspended at guttering height between opposite rows of houses flanking the shopping streets. The street toldo can be extended or drawn using a curtain-type mechanism' (Hamann and Moro 1984: 95). Such awnings are also in use in the Near East and Mediterranean North Africa, parts of Central America and Japan. Therefore existing sun sails are normally either free-standing structures, or suspended between buildings or protrude from a building. In addition, Fritz Lang, collaborator of Frei Otto, described a series of design experiments that add to the pallet of existing ones, including among others so-called 'feather shades' (Lang 1984). When examining the range of different textile auxiliary architectures it is possible to distinguish between the following three types: (1) continuous textile surfaces that cover or enclose a given space, for instance, tents; (2) larger areas covered by arrayed non-varied textile elements, such as toldos that consist of repetitive strips, and (3) arrayed geometrically varied textile elements. Taken together this range of possibilities can enable a great range of combinations and design solutions for auxiliary architectures that are added to the existing built environment so as to provide extended thresholds. Clearly, auxiliary architectures need not be confined to textile material. They can be made from any kind of material system that delivers the desired spatial and environmental conditions.

The benefit in articulating auxiliary architectures as textile systems is that they are lightweight and versatile. Yet, there are also structural implications in that the existing architectures that are to receive auxiliary architectures are not necessarily capable of coping with additional forces. This constitutes therefore one of

3.4 The Luminous Veil textile membrane screenwall at the Izmir University of Economy was designed and assembled by members of OCEAN and students. It modulates the changing light conditions inside the otherwise monotonous corridor space, providing shading during the early hours of the day, while increasing illumination during the late afternoon. Photography: Melih Uçar (2009).

the first and foremost considerations when selecting a material and structural system.

Textile systems may be implemented on a scale and range of provisions akin to screenwalls. One example is the Luminous Veil project designed and implemented by members of the OCEAN Design Research Association with architecture students at the Izmir University of Economics (Fig. 3.4) (see Hensel and Sunguroğlu Hensel 2010). The use of a form-found tension-active textile system articulates the screen as spatial, with the array of individually articulated and rotated textile membranes constituting a deep structure. The Luminous Veil is installed inside of a corridor that needs shading and glare protection during the early hours of the day while at the same time not resulting in a dark space, and illumination during the later hours of the day. The choice of textile was therefore a key decision in this small interior auxiliary intervention.

In a similar manner OCEAN's scheme for the M-Velope project (Fig. 3.5), an unbuilt exterior textile and steel mesh screenwall, addresses questions of views towards and from a gallery space in downtown New York City. Situated in the semi-sheltered space at the entrance of the gallery and adjacent to the primary climate envelope, the screenwall aimed at a nuanced careful modulation of prevailing environmental conditions that impact upon the gallery and its adjacent street space. These conditions include direct and indirect sunlight, solar heat gains and also intense wind gusts. The modulation of these conditions needs to be negotiated with the intended views towards and out of the gallery. The combination of steel frame, mesh and textile elements introduces a conversation between more and less permanent aspects of the scheme, and in so doing facilitates an element of adaptability. This strategy can begin to address different curatorial needs for events related to the gallery, or, alternatively, changes in the pattern of use of the street space.

In the *Las Piedras del Cielo* project (2012) in the Open City in Ritoque, Chile, designed by the Scarcity and Creativity Studio at the Oslo School of Architecture, the textile membrane array is developed into a building scheme (Fig. 3.6). The scheme consists of a timber frame and deck that is articulated as a landscaped surface set within the surrounding dune-landscape. Located above the deck is a membrane roof that consists of nine membranes. Dissolving the roof into an array of membranes helps to dissipate the impact of the seasonally severe wind loads of the Pacific coast. This modestly sized project demonstrates two of the afore-discussed spatial strategies: (1) addressing ground by way of the continuation of the local landscape through the project; and (2) the utilization of different threshold articulations from open to sheltered and to full enclosure. In a similar way the ground and membrane system is used in another project

3.5 *Left and centre*: Rendered views of the M-Velope project as an external screenwall that provides semi-sheltered exterior street space. *Right top*: Expanded axonometric of the structural steel elements, steel mesh and arrayed textile membrane system. *Right centre and bottom*: Analysis of views from the exterior street space to the gallery space and vice versa. Copyright: OCEAN Design Research Association.

3.6 Views of the *Las Piedras del Cielo* project in the Open City Ritoque, designed and constructed by SCL Studio in 2012, showing the project in the Pacific-dune landscape. The timber frames and decking provide both platform and enclosure, while the textile canopy provides an exterior semi-sheltered space with different degrees of exposure to sunlight, wind and rain. Photography: Robin Rakke (2012).

3.7 SCL Studios' project for a new Community Centre in Pumanque, Chile, completed in 2014, features intermediary spaces and spatial pockets, an exterior screenwall that helps modulate the strong impact of sunlight, a roof terrace that extends the ground over the volume – inspired by Villa Malaparte in Capri designed by Adalberto Libera (1937) – and a textile membrane canopy that provides semi-shelter, much like the *Las Piedras del Cielo* project. Photography: Christian Hermansen (2014).

by the Scarcity and Creativity Studio: the Community Centre in Pumanque, Chile (2014) (Fig. 3.7). The scheme offers generous access to the roof terrace that replaces the ground taken up by the footprint of the building. A screenwall is utilized to provide for a transitional space and a membrane canopy provides semi-shelter for the roof terrace. Projects like this demonstrate that it is possible to combine several of the design strategies discussed in this book even in quite modestly sized schemes.

Likewise, such strategies may also be employed for schemes that are larger in size. The Extended Threshold Studio supervised by Søren S. Sørensen and Michael Hensel at the Oslo School of Architecture and Design investigates the theme of auxiliary architectures for use in inner urban public spaces in Oslo, Norway (Fig. 3.8). The design studies tackle specific situations between public activities or retail and exterior public space as an extended threshold that is articulated as textile auxiliary architectures. Integrated computational design and advanced visualization methods and tools, such as Augmented Reality and Virtual Reality, played a key role in the design process as the schemes were not to be built but their local climatic impact and range of provisions was to be analysed and evaluated.

Larger projects offer possibilities to vary the relation between envelope and ground and articulations even more. Diploma Unit 12 at the Architectural Association, supervised by Holger Kehne and Jeffrey Turko, examined the possibility of addressing ground and envelope articulations for large-scale infrastructural projects such as railway stations and freeway borders (Fig. 3.9). Circulation, terrain form, tectonic landscape and varying degrees of shelter and enclosure are amalgamated both at the large scale of the building and at the scale of the individual user. This

approach resonates with Foreign Office Architects' Meydan – Umraniye Retail Complex & Multiplex in Istanbul that features integrated continuous ground and multiple envelope strategies (see p. 111).

While the articulated envelope and multiple envelope strategies entail interaction between material surfaces and local environment, there exists an altogether very different approach, namely the staging of an envelope as a climatic condition engendered by a technical apparatus, yet without a physical enclosure. A useful inroad to this subject is Reyner Banham's (1969: 20) seminal discussion of the campfire:

> Societies who do not build substantial structures tend to group their activities around some central focus – a water hole, a shade tree, a fire, a great teacher – and inhabit a space whose external boundaries are vague, adjustable according to functional need, and rarely regular. The output of heat and light from a campfire is effectively zoned in concentric rings, brightest and hottest close to the fire, coolest and darkest away from it. – But at the same time, the distribution of heat is biased by the wind, and the trail of smoke renders the downwind side of the fire unappetising, so that the concentric zoning is interrupted by other considerations of comfort and need.

This analysis may be applied also to architectures with substantial structures that render their adjacent exterior and interior climates heterogeneous in interaction with the environment and thus offer choices similar to that of the campfire example, such as the aforementioned Bagdad Kiosk. However, it is also possible to adopt a very different approach in which the physical

3.8 The Extended Threshold Studio at the Oslo School of Architecture explored the use of combined cable-net and arrayed membrane systems to articulate semi-sheltered transitional spaces for a number of key public locations in Oslo. This example shows a complex membrane canopy in Vika, Oslo. *Top*: rendered view. *Centre*: Elevations. *Bottom*: Plan. Copyright: The Extended Threshold Studio.

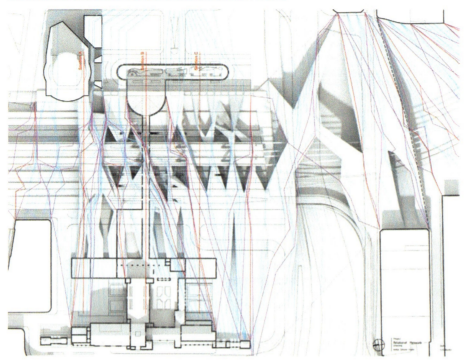

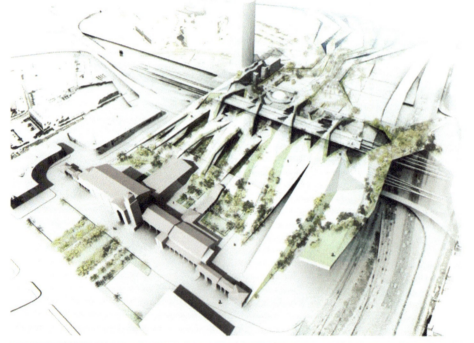

3.9 Re-envisioning Los Angeles project by Mark Chan, AA School Diploma Unit 12 2009/2010 projects a large infrastructural form in which ground is continuous and multiplied to serve in an integrated manner both circulation and landscaping. *Top*: Plan of the new infrastructural bridging surfaces that stitch across the railway lines of Union Station, with an overlay of vectors of visual and material connections from Union Station to Transit Plaza across the expanse of railway lines. *Middle*: Bird's-eye view of the scheme, showing infrastructural surfaces as a new ground that links from Union Station across to Transit Plaza and then on to the edge of the LA river that also forms a new enveloping condition on the undercroft. *Bottom*: Interior views at track level showing the articulated and perforated enveloping conditions that provide ventilation and shading, and integrate and mix the green spaces that inhabit the top surfaces into the interior of the platforms in section. Copyright: Mark Chan (2010).

3.9(a) Oyler Wu Collaborative's Hi Res Lo Rise scheme (2011) suggests an auxiliary architecture as a secondary envelope around an existing building that acts as a screenwall. The steel perforated mesh of the new envelope is designed to reduce the visibility of the unsightly existing façade from passers-by, while enabling views from the interior to the exterior and solar and thermal protection on the interior. For most of the façade the second envelope is much like a standard curtain system except in the centre where the screen, together with a system of bundled structural tubes, culminates in a vertically highly articulated surface that turns into a horizontal canopy. Copyright: Oyler Wu Collaborative.

enclosure is entirely relinquished in favour of environmental event as envelope. Already in the 1950s the artist Yves Klein proposed what he termed 'Air Architecture': 'the idea in space, of using pure energy as a material with which to construct' (Klein 2004 [1958]: 26). Based on this approach, Klein developed a series of schemes for the 'Fire Walls and Fire Fountains' for the Opera in Gelsenkirchen, Germany (1958) or the 'Water and Fire Fountains' in Paris (1959), and set out his approach to 'Immaterial Dwellings': 'in air one builds with air (immaterial-material). In the ground one builds with soil (material-material)' (Klein 2004 [1958]: 28). Like Klein, Diller, Scofidio and Renfro staged the design of their *Blur Building* in Yverdon-les-Bains, Switzerland as a climatic event (see p. 265). Located on Lake Neuchatel, the project uses high-pressure valves to produce a fine mist of water that clouds its physical structures. The cloud of mist in interaction with the wind defines the extent of the project. Visitors literally inhabit this cloud.

Several other projects incorporated in their initial design elements of local environmental manipulation as a way of replacing or augmenting the physical elements of the envelope, such as the Sheats Goldstein Residence by John Lautner, or the Villa VPRO by MVRDV (see p. 178). In both, the use of an air curtain was projected. For the Sheats Goldstein Residence an air curtain was used in the living room which faces out on to the main terrace, thus maintaining spatial continuity. Likewise, the initial scheme for Villa VPRO featured an exterior climate barrier that was to consist merely of an air curtain. However, both schemes finally reverted back to using a glass façade, quite possibly because the technical effort and energy expenditure seemed neither feasible nor sustainable.

With this the question arises as to whether such projects are possible to realize without ultimately relying on an expansive technical apparatus to generate the desired climatic event. Here it is important to bear in mind that evidently all architectures assert measurable impact on their local environment and climate.

One of the preconditions to stage climatic events as part of an architecture is careful consideration of the range of local or microclimatic conditions that are native to a given setting and that may be accomplished in interaction between spatial and material aspects of a project and in interaction with the local climate. Clearly ground in conjunction with water can generate mist and so can an architecture that makes use of this condition. Instrumentalizing this understanding above and beyond what is commonplace today is likely to yield a more complex approach to questions of sustainability. If the question of the envelope is approached in this way, each of the different strategies towards the envelope discussed above, together with related ground strategies, can contribute key aspects towards an embedded non-discrete architecture. Needless to say, such approaches to architectural design clearly defined environmental understanding, objectives and strategies.

4
Environments

The environment must be organised so that its own regeneration and reconstruction does not constantly disrupt its performance.

(Alexander 1964: 3)

In their labour, architectural elements fuse themselves into the latencies of the ambient environment, adopting their capacity for change or movement.

(Leatherbarrow 2009: 37–38)

What comes to the fore are, on the one hand those relations that are smaller than the object, that saturate it and compose it, the 'micro-architectures' for lack of a happier term, and on the other, those relations or systems that are greater or more extensive than the object, that comprehend or envelope it, those 'macro-architectures' of which the 'object', or the level of organization corresponding to the object, is but a relay member or part.

(Kwinter 2001: 14)

Architectures and their specific environments are intricately related in that architectures inevitably interact with their local bio-physical environment (Fig. 4.1). Yet, although architects and vernacular builders have always known this, it is surprising how superficially these interactions are addressed in the bulk of contemporary architecture. The role and potential that grounds and envelopes play in staging interactions with the environment seems obvious. For this reason it is necessary to address the question of local climate and biological environment in the context of this book.

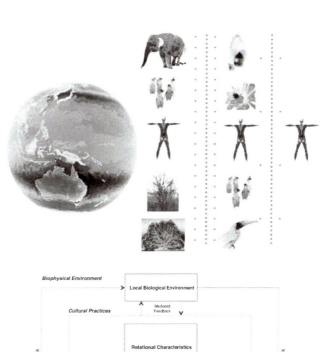

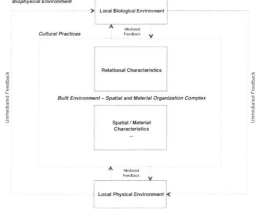

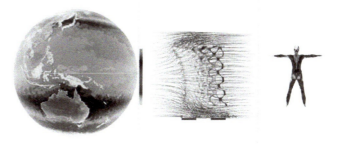

4.1 Performance-oriented Architecture: Four Domains of Agency. *Top*: Architecture + ecology: architecture as niche construction and biodiversity provision underpinning urban ecology efforts. *Centre*: Domains of agency: (1) local biological environment, (2) local physical environment, (3) and (4) spatial and material organization complex and cultural practices. *Bottom*: architecture + local climate: architecture as heterogeneous environmental modulator. Copyright: Michael Hensel (2013).

As Kenneth Frampton (2007 [1987]: 383) pointed out,

> [B]uildings and architecture have an interactive relationship with nature. Nature is not only topography and site, but also climate and light to which architecture is ultimately responsive. ... Built form is necessarily susceptible to an intense interaction with these elements and with time, in its cyclical aspects.

Obvious as this may be, the question is which aspects of architectures are to be considered key in this interaction. In this context Addington *et al.* (2001: 78) contested the usefulness of building typologies as a determinant:

> The parameters that determine energy performance emerge from the specific conditions produced by the interaction of a building with its immediate, and very particular, environmental surroundings. The assumption that these parameters are determined by the type ultimately limits rather than expands the possible solutions: choices regarding the environmental performance of buildings can not be made typologically.

Proceeding from this position it is necessary to look for other traits that are generally present in architectures and that are in their particular articulation specific to their setting. Here, then, the interrelated spatial and material organization of architectures comes to the fore in which grounds and envelopes play a vital role. To commence, four related aspects require consideration: (1) the kinds of interactions that take place between architectures and their specific environments, and the related provisions set out by architectures; (2) the conditions that underlie the exchanges between architectures and environments; (3) the characteristics and extent of the thus modulated environments (above and beyond interiors) and (4) the related key factors for design that can help modulate these exchanges.

One useful inroad into this discussion is reconsidering the boundaries that result from the combined spatial and material organization of architectures, as these directly relate to grounds and envelopes. Michelle Addington and Daniel Schodek (2005: 7) stated:

> for physicists ... the boundary is not a thing, but an action. Environments are understood as energy fields, and the boundary operates as a transitional zone between different states of an energy field. ... Boundaries are therefore, by definition, active zones of mediation rather than of delineation.

In a similar manner the urban climatologist Tim Oke (1987: 33) explicated that:

> for climatic purposes we define the 'active' boundary as a principal plane of climatic activity in a system. This is the level where the majority of the radiant energy is absorbed, reflected and emitted; where the main transformation of energy (e.g. radiant to thermal, sensible to latent) and mass (change of state of water) occur, where precipitation is intercepted; and where the major portion of drag on airflow is exerted.

Oke's work in the expanding field of urban climatology addresses the increasingly complex interaction between urban environments and the atmosphere. In this context the accumulative effect of buildings past a critical threshold comes to the fore, such as the phenomenon of urban heat islands. However, for the design of single architectures it is initially the local and microclimate that are of interest, as these are more immediately accessible and tangible for architects. In this context it seems likely that architects will increasingly need to address questions that are currently still largely outside of the interdisciplinary scope that architects generally engage with. Without engaging local climate specificity architectures will continue to adhere to homogeneous standards that yield material and technological redundancies. Countries like Norway, Chile and so on expand across latitudes and feature significant changes in altitude and terrain form, and thus display considerable differences in local climate even over short distances. Yet, the same homogeneous building codes apply across their

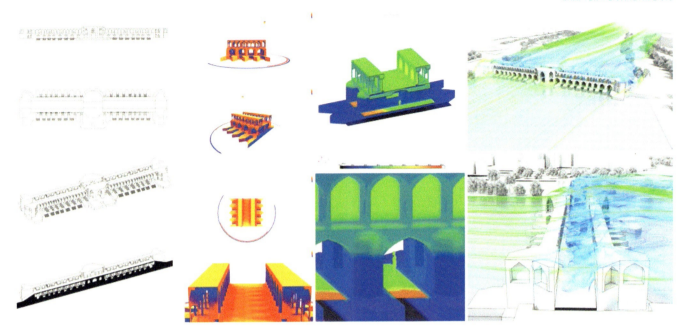

4.2 Khaju Bridge (*pol-e khajoo*) c. 1650 AD, Isfahan.

Left: From top to bottom: (1) elevation; (2) plan; (3) axonometric; (4) axonometric section. *Centre left*: From top to bottom: (1) elevation; (2) axonometric; (3) plan; (4) cross-section of upper level. The analysis shows the likely solar impact on a selected portion of the Khaju Bridge during an average summer afternoon. The arcaded upper level and arched and vaulted spaces of the lower level of the bridge show effective self-shading. *Centre right*: Heat transfer analysis of a selected portion of the bridge.

Top: Selected cross-sectional portion of the bridge. *Bottom*: Close-up view of the lower level arched and vaulted spaces of the bridge. *Right*: Rendered view of the bridge with airflow analysis (CFD) overlay. The analysis suggests that the arched arcaded spaces on the upper level and the arched and vaulted spaces on the lower level allow wind to penetrate the roadway and vaulted space at a lower speed and turbulent flow which circulates the air cooled by evaporation. Copyright: Sustainable Environment Association (2013).

entire territory. The sustainability of this prevailing condition is already beginning to come under question, as may be seen in works like Joakim Hoen's Seaside Second Homes project (see p. 207), which explores variations of a design and building system in response to local terrain and climate differences.

The building envelope plays an obvious role in the interaction between architectures and their environments. How traditional building elements as parts of envelopes may be understood in terms of their diverse environmental modulation capacity for interior spaces may be seen from the discussion of Islamic screenwalls – Moghul *jaalis*, perforated stone or lattice screenwalls – or the Arabic *mashrabīyas*, projecting oriel windows clad with wooden latticework, as analysed by the late Hassan Fathy (Fathy 1986). Yet, the question of environmental performance not only involves the modulation of interior environments, but also the conditioning of adjacent exterior or semi-sheltered spaces of a given architecture as explicit provisions for use (Fig. 4.2). Likewise, surrounding buildings, terrain articulation or vegetation impacts upon the conditioning of such spaces. One project of interest that warrants detailed analysis in this respect is R&Sie(n)'s Spiderinthewood house (see p. 212).

For the purpose of climatically conditioning transitional spaces with envelope-related strategies, auxiliary architectures such as textile membrane systems are of interest (see Chapter 3), since their primary purpose is to provide spaces directly adjacent to pre-existing architectures. Differentiated membrane systems can, for instance, share some properties of foliage of vegetation systems regarding the modulation of microclimate. Oke (1987: 116–117) explained that:

The three-dimensional geometry of a leaf or a canopy layer – are particularly interesting because they have both upper and lower active surfaces. This greatly increases their effective surface area for radiative and convective exchange. … On a plant or tree the leaf is not in isolation, it is intimately linked to its total environmental setting, and the same is true of a plant or tree in a crop or forest. The effects of multiple shading, multiple reflection, long-wave radiation interaction etc. provide important feedbacks not found in the isolated case.

Yet, as Oke cautions, the involved level of complexity confronts microclimatologists with considerable difficulties in analysing and modelling the microclimatic conditions produced by complex vegetation systems. For this reason it is not currently feasible for architects to design such complex interactions. However, first steps may involve the design of less complex auxiliary architectures to gain understanding and skills in this way of working. Complexity may be increased if and when feasible methods are available. Examples like the canopy of the Community Centre in Pumanque, Chile, designed and built by the Scarcity and Creativity Studio (see Chapter 5), and the research of the Extended Threshold Studio into differentiated membrane systems and the development of related integrative design methodologies (Fig. 4.3), are of interest in this context. These works allow both the computational analysis-driven generation of complex designs, as well as the collection of empirical data from the design and built activities. Given the growing impact of the built environment on local climate conditions the objective needs to gradually engage increasingly higher levels of complexity when dealing with multi-directional and multi-scalar interaction that may yield effects, which can end up cascading upwards in scale when going beyond critical thresholds. Yet, for architectural design, the initial focus may need to be confined to the scale of singular architectures and their gradual aggregation into neighbourhoods. This initial focus may serve to gain a better understanding of the interaction of architectures with local climates, but also specific microclimatic conditions. Rosenberg and colleagues (1983: 1) elaborated microclimate as follows:

> Microclimate is the climate near the ground, that is the climate in which plants and animals live. … Whether the surface is bare or vegetated, the greatest diurnal range in temperature experienced at any level occurs there. … Changes in humidity with elevation are greatest near the surface. Very large quantities of energy are exchanged at the surface in the process of evaporation and condensation. Wind speed decreases markedly as the surface is approached and its momentum is transferred to it. Thus it is the great range in environmental conditions near the surface and the rate of these changes with time and elevation that make the microclimate so different from the climate just a few meters above.

Clearly, grounds and envelopes are the locus of such microclimatic modulations. Here a lot can be done to determine the capacity of the built environment to engage and sustain the local physical environment, as well as the local biological environment, ecosystems and biodiversity. Of benefit is the understanding of the interrelation between ground-sustaining local and microclimate and staging vital biotic interactions: 'terrestrial ecosystems consist of both aboveground and belowground subsystems … feedback between these subsystems play a crucial role in regulating community structure and ecosystem functioning' (Bardgett and Wardle 2010: 1). The importance of biotic interactions in the soil and their interaction with above-ground communities are hardly known and rarely considered by architects who design green roofs or façades. Moreover, frequently the 'greening' of architecture consists of non-native species. Yet, gradually an interest in ecosystems is emerging in research-oriented architectural education (Fig. 4.4) and a number of architects go beyond superficial greening, as evidenced by, for instance, the green roof research of Kieran Timberlake that maps the relation between planted species and emergent species over time in a freely evolving manner (Figs 4.5 and 4.6).

Engaging the interaction between architecture and local biological environments raises the question as to how architectures can contribute to maintaining local ecosystems and biodiversity. On larger scales the interdisciplinary field of urban ecology, which analyses the relation between species and ecosystems and human-dominated regions and urban environments, addresses these interactions. This often results in policies and action plans that focus on the larger scales of regions and cities, while the smaller scale effect of singular or smaller ensembles of architectures remains largely understudied. However, the accumulative impact of single architectures can be effective in terms of multi-species provisions and the support of biodiversity in an increasingly human-dominated environment. Architecture's capacity to do so is effectively located in the

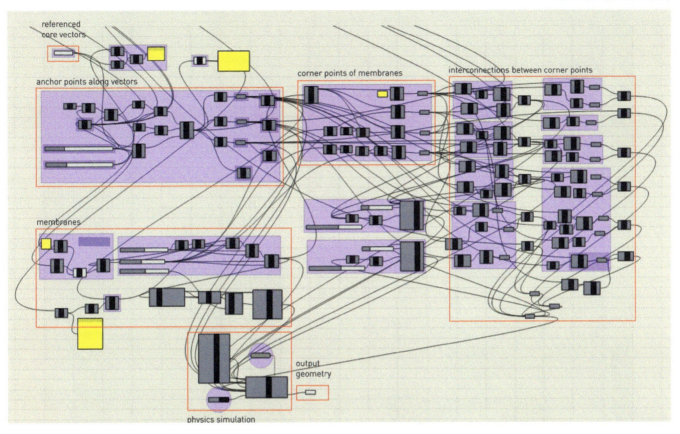

4.3 The Extended Threshold Studio develops computational methods that couple associative modelling, environmental analysis and virtual and augmented reality visualization to generate locally specific auxiliary architectures. This enables designers to prioritize architecture and environment interactions in the design process. Copyright: The Extended Threshold Studio (2012).

way in which grounds and envelopes are understood, articulated and utilized in the provision of heterogeneous milieux that relate to ecosystem and multiple species requirements. For this a much more direct approach is needed that focuses on how architectures can progressively be thought of as embedded in natural processes and therefore can provide for ecosystems by way of mediating the interaction between the abiotic and biotic environment.

4.4 The study of ecology should now be embedded into architectural education and research. The Ecology Workshop conducted at the Department of Architecture at the University of Technology in Sydney in 2008 focused on mapping ecosystems in the Ku-ring-gai National Park, visualizing essential ecological and physiological processes and relating these to different bush-fire survival strategies and morphologies of specific species. This example focuses on an analysis of the habitat, physiology and morphology of the Australian grass-tree [*Xanthorrhoea*]. Copyright: Ecologies Workshop (2008).

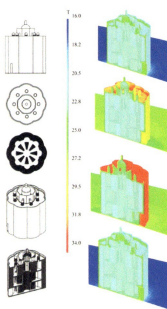
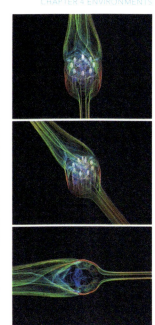

4.5 Architectural history from a performance perspective. How does one design for other species? A detailed and interrelated thermal and airflow analyses of a pigeon tower from the Safavid period located in Isfahan, Iran, shows how a stabile interior climate can be accomplished solely by way of spatial and material organization in correlation with the local climate. These buildings housed up to 10,000 pigeons and served the collection of guano for the purpose of fertilizing fields. Copyright: Sustainable Environment Association (2013).

Ecosystems generate biophysical feedback between living and non-living domains and are sustained by biodiversity, which concerns the extent of genetic, taxonomic and ecological diversity over all spatial and temporal scales (Harper and Hawksworth 1995). Related to the notion of biodiversity is that of geodiversity, which concerns the diversity of earth materials, forms and processes that constitute and shape the abiotic environment. It is generally believed that geology asserts a strong influence on biodiversity (Gray 2004). At any rate, it is of interest to engage the question as to what ground conditions may be required to create a habitat for local species (Fig. 4.7) and how surface areas given over to natural systems may be reconnected in spite of the currently fragmented and interrupted mosaic of land use (Fig. 4.8).

4.6 A researcher surveys a green roof to understand the current state of plant health, the relationship between the original plantings and emergent vegetation, and the trajectories of plant communities and systems in relation to the goals of the green roof, particularly concerning ecological resilience, habitat creation and biodiversity. Copyright: Kieran Timberlake.

Today, ecologists and experts in environmental studies work with different kinds of models to simulate different aspects of ecosystems, abiotic processes or linkages between the two respectively. In this context architectures may be considered as part of the abiotic environment and in so doing its function in the interaction may be defined. To gain an understanding as to how the built environment might interact with the natural environment it is useful to consider current approaches that are specific to other types of human-dominated environments and their relation to the natural environment. One interesting field is agroecosystems management, a field in which experts have begun to hypothesize 'that under conditions of global change, complex agricultural systems are more dependable in production and more sustainable in terms of resource conservation than simple ones' (Vandermeer et al. 1998: 4). In this context 'complex systems' refer to multi-species agroecosystems, while 'simple systems' refer to those tending towards monoculture. In relation to complex systems, Vandermeer et al. distinguish between (1) planned biodiversity, (2) associated biodiversity, and (3) associated components (Fig. 4.9), and elaborated that:

> The planned biodiversity will give rise to an associated biodiversity, the host of weeds and beneficial plants that arrive independently of the farmer's plans, the soil flora and fauna that may respond to particular crops planted, the myriad arthropods that arrive on the farm, etc. Finally, the extra-planned organic resources, plus the planned biodiversity plus the associated biodiversity combine in a complicated fashion to produce the ultimate agroecosystems function, its productivity and sustainability.
>
> (Vandermeer et al. 1998: 6)

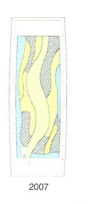  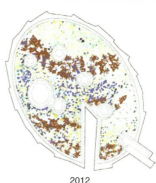

School of Art Gallery, Yale University Atwater Commons, Middlebury College

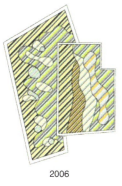  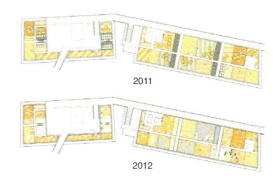

Flora Rose House, Cornell University   Charles David Keeling Apartments, University of California San Diego

4.7 Spatially explicit maps track the evolution and emergence of green roof species over time. Copyright: Kieran Timberlake.

Of interest for architecture is the relation between planned and associated biodiversity in agroecological contexts where 'multi-species cultivation clearly necessitates biodiversity management on the plot-scale. It also, however, requires consideration of its biogeographical context within the surrounding area, requiring recognition of processes operating on various scales' (Vandermeer et al. 1998: 6). Developments in this field can deliver ways of managing the correlation between planned and evolving aspects in ecosystems and their associated biodiversity, and also deliver general models for integrating the various scales involved in human influence and natural processes' interactions. A useful inroad does not therefore necessarily involve highly detailed provisions for the entire scope of biodiversity of a given ecosystem, but, instead, the integration of provisions for planned biodiversity that can help sustain an associated biodiversity and, in turn, sustain the freely evolving one.

This approach may serve to address a central problem in nature conservation. Commonly, ecosystem conservationists consider ecosystems to be in a state of *dynamic equilibrium*, which tends to lead to the protection of species and ecosystems in the condition in which they were found and described. The German zoologist, ecologist and evolutionary scientist Josef Helmut Reichholf criticized this approach as not sufficiently incorporating evolutionary processes and the possibility of natural extinction, since maintained equilibrium entails rigid maintenance of the found condition, and he proposed instead the notion of *stabile disequilibria* (Reichholf 2008).

However, experiments on urban and regional scales are risky and currently not sufficiently matched with experimentation towards multi-species environments on the scale of one or a few buildings. Such experiments would entail an intensely interdisciplinary approach that necessitates the involvement of architects, climatologists and microclimatologists, geologists, botanists, zoologists, ecologists, and also urban ecologists and agroecosystems experts. Non-discrete architectures may provide the spatial and microclimatic niches and extended threshold conditions that are required to negotiate multi-species provisions.

Spatial transitions that generate heterogeneous microclimate can benefit the purpose of species integration of architecture, which may evolve out of the combined study of (1) the ecological

4.8　Reindeer standing on patches of snow to avoid mosquitoes and gadflies. Source: Wikimedia. Photography: Bjørn Christian Tørrissen (2011).

4.9　Wildlife crossing over the Trans-Canada Highway in the Banff National Park in Alberta, Canada. Source: Wikimedia. Photography: Qyd (2006).

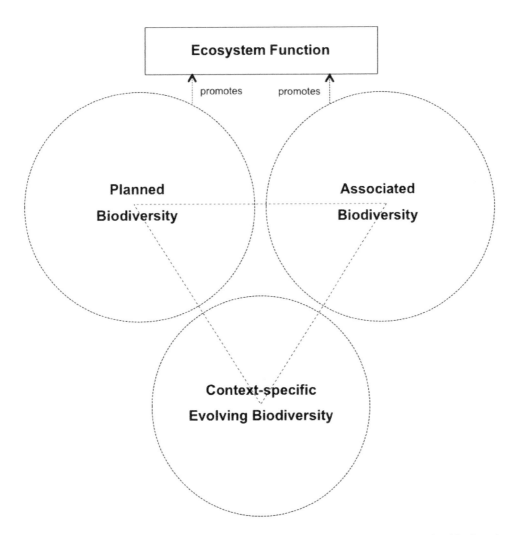

Learning from agroecology. A key consideration of agroecology is the interrelation between designed, associated and freely evolving biodiversity. This entails what species farmers grow, which associated species emerge and how both fit into the context-specific biodiversity, thus maintaining ecosystem function. This field of study provides a promising inroad for defining the relation between architecture and ecology, and a shift towards designing for biodiversity. Modified from Vandeermeer, J. and and Perfecto, I. (1995) *Breakfast of Biodiversity: The truth about rainforest destruction*. Oakland: Food First Books; Altieri, M.A. (1994) 'Biodiversity and Pest Management'. In: *Agroecosystems*. New York: Haworth Press.

niche of a species, (2) conditions characteristic of animal-made shelters, and (3) shelters for different species made by human beings. As for the latter, there exist interesting historical examples of architectures designed to house different animal species. Such projects may serve to indicate potential inroads for contemporary species provisions in architecture. For example, during the Safavid period (1501–1722) of the Persian Empire a special purpose-building type flourished in the Isfahan region, the pigeon towers. The purpose of these up to 20-metre-tall buildings was to provide shelter for pigeons and to collect the pigeon dung as fertilizer for agriculture, in particular for growing melons, as well as for use in Isfahan's tanneries for softening leather. Circular or rectangular in plan with internally buttressed walls, such towers could house up to 10,000 pigeons. Such towers consisted either of a single hollow space or drum, or of an inner drum enclosed by an outer one. Some towers were organized as eight connected drums around a central one, thus increasing the surface area of the interior and hence the number of pigeonholes. Atop of the towers turrets with honeycomb brickwork provided entry and exit points for the pigeons. Human beings accessed the towers normally only once a year to harvest the dung. As analysis shows, the interrelation between thermal mass and effective natural ventilation resulted in an interior climate that seemed suitable for wild pigeons (Fig. 4.10). Structures for the same purpose may be found in Anatolia, such as the often densely clustered half-above and half-below-ground structures. Built on steep slopes, these structures are characterized by a stone-made above-ground tower-like part that is rectangular, square, circular or ellipsoidal in plan and which provides access for the pigeons, and a cave-like rock-hewn underground part that accommodates the nests. A short tunnel and a door from the lower part of the slope provided human access for harvesting the dung. These subterranean spaces are sheltered from the severe Anatolian winter conditions. Of interest for the purpose at hand are also dovecotes that are not free-standing structures, but instead integrated into other buildings. In particular, in the United Kingdom dovecotes were often integrated in the gable wall of barns and farmhouses. This example in particular shows how it is possible to conceive of architectures that serve human beings and other species by way of using the building envelope. The integration of livestock in the same buildings as human beings was common throughout the ages in agricultural societies for obvious purposes. While the reason for doing so might be different today according to context and situation, such an approach might initiate embedded non-anthropocentric architecture that uses its ground and envelope conditions to sustain the local biological environment based on staging a nuanced interaction with the local physical environment.

5
Locality

> There is a paradox: how to become modern and to return to sources; how to revive an old dormant civilisation and take part in universal civilisation.
>
> (Ricoeur 2007 [1965]: 47)

As already discussed in the previous chapters, one of the central problems of architecture today is its global homogenization, a development which exhibits a fundamental indifference to local conditions, culture and climate. This development yields the need to consider both the role of the *local* and the way it may be deployed in contemporary architectural design, and the physical articulation of architectures and the built environment.

The question of the relation between the increasing universalization of architecture and the role of the local is not new. This discussion commenced several decades ago and has a number of different roots and motivations. In 1930 Le Corbusier stated that:

> Architecture is the result of the state of mind of its time. We are facing an event in contemporary thought ... the techniques, the problems raised, like the scientific means to solve them, are universal. Nevertheless, there will be no confusion of regions; for climatic, geographic, topographic conditions, the currents of race and thousands of things still today unknown, will always guide solutions towards forms conditioned by them.
>
> (Le Corbusier 1991 [1930]: 218)

When considering the prevailing contemporary condition, this statement may no longer prove to be true as architectural form today becomes increasingly exchangeable regardless of location.

One of the approaches that addressed this question in response to a perceived shortcoming in modern architecture to address the local is *critical regionalism*. Alan Colquhoun located the origin of the discussion of regionalism in the eighteenth century and pointed out that the understanding which emerged from this development was that 'architecture should be firmly based on specific regional practices based on climate, geography, local materials, and local traditions' (Colquhoun 1996: 141). Yet, Colquhoun succinctly criticized the mismatch of the conditions that underlie this understanding in relation to contemporary conditions:

> One of the intentions of a regionalist approach is the preservation of 'difference'. But difference, which used to be ensured by the co-existence of watertight and autonomous regions of culture, now depends largely on two other phenomena: individualism and the nation-state. ... Designs that emphasise local architecture are no more privileged today than other ways of adapting architecture to the conditions of modernity. The combination of these various ways is the result of the choices of individual architects who are operating from within multiple codes.
>
> (Colquhoun 1996: 152–153)

Colquhoun thus pointed out both a fundamental shift of the conditions from which 'difference' emanates, and a radical change in the grain, manner and distribution of differences; thus he argued that:

> The concept of regionality depends on it being possible to correlate cultural codes with geographical regions. It is based on traditional systems of communication in which climate, geography, craft traditions, and religions are absolutely determining. These determinants are rapidly disappearing and in large parts of the world no longer exist. ... Modern society is polyvalent – that is to say, its codes are generated randomly from within a universal system of rationalisation that, in itself, claims to be 'value free'.
>
> (Colquhoun 1996: 154)

And:

> This, then, is the problem of architecture in the postmodern world. It seems no longer possible to envisage an architecture that has the stable, public meanings that it had when it was connected with the soil and with the regions. How should we define the kinds of architecture that are taking its place?
>
> (Colquhoun 1996: 155)

Several aspects are inherent in Colquhoun's critique that it is useful to examine. The first point concerns the assumed relation between *difference* and *region* that commonly underlies critical regionalism approaches. In this understanding region is defined by a coherent set of traits and similarities. Difference is what distinguishes one region from another along a singular divide. This understanding is inherently problematic.

Can a distinct singular delineation between regions be so readily established, in particular when more than just a small number of characteristics are at stake? Can regions thus be envisaged as 'watertight and autonomous' entities? What one may find more often than not is that when considering a larger number of traits such delineations are never singular, they rarely coincide for all traits and the transitions are often gradual and display hybrid conditions. The obvious shortcoming of this understanding is the simplistic way in which the problem is framed. Addressing this problem requires consideration of what is known in systems thinking as the *boundary problem*: 'the meaning and the validity of professional propositions always depend on boundary judgments as to what "facts" (observations) and "norms" (valuation standards) are to be considered relevant and what others are to be left out or considered less important' (Ulrich 2002: 41). Where the boundaries (plural is intentional) of a given situation are drawn is of vital importance, as this determines how a given situation or problem is understood and therefore which level of complexity is acknowledged and incorporated into a given approach. In the context of architectural design Christopher Alexander advised that architects 'ought always really to design with a number of nested, overlapped form-context boundaries in mind' (Alexander 1964: 18). Kenneth Frampton also acknowledged this problem by stating that 'critical regionalism begs the question as to what are the true limits of a region and what is its institutional status' (Frampton 1987: 380).

In some cases the boundaries between regions may be clearly delineated, for instance, along strongly articulated geographic borders, dramatic changes in resources and related practices, etc. In most cases, however, this seems not to be the case. Vellinga, Oliver and Bridge's *Atlas of Vernacular Architecture of the World* (Vellinga et al. 2007), for instance, which systematically maps materials and resources, structural systems and technologies, building forms and types, services and functions, symbolism and so on, shows this clearly.

Hence, although the following will surely draw the criticism of some expert regionalists and historians, one might consider a different understanding of either a laterally fluid model of regions as displaying in many instances multiple overlapped boundaries that frequently generate hybrid solutions, or, alternatively, a bottom-up approach which commences from a specific location that displays particular combinations of traits.

Even though in the view of Frampton 'it would be foolishly restrictive if we conceive of region only in terms of locality and climate, etc., although these factors are surely critical to the constitution and expressivity of local form' (Frampton 1987: 380), his list of local conditions for design is rather abbreviated. A more inclusive approach may then render an entirely local approach more promising.

In the context of this argument Frampton cautioned that the institutional role of a region includes two critical aspects: that of a '"school" of local culture' and 'the cultivation of a client in a profound sense' (Frampton 1987: 380). Yet, local schools of thought can emerge from succinct approaches to the question of locality, even though such schools may not be located in the same area as the works, nor do all works necessarily need to be in one area that constitutes this locale. This take would aid in moving forward from a position in which individualism is rampant and largely disinterested in the local for the sake of superficial idiosyncrasy, towards another position in which schools of thought arise from common interests and shared approaches.

A key example of a locally based school of thought and related projects that are locally placed is the School of Architecture and Design in Valparaiso and the related work that comprises the Open City in Ritoque, Chile. Here the question is pursued as to what the architecture of this region should be without narrowing down this effort to the search for a singular identity. Another approach is that of the Scarcity and Creativity Studio at the Oslo School of Architecture and Design, which operates in different locations based on an approach to develop architectures that feature rearticulated local traits and engage conditions.

These approaches to develop schools of thought around questions of the local can lead away from a rigid understanding of regional autonomy that preserves differences, to one that rearticulates difference. Such an understanding yields the need for a more acute and detailed analysis of locations based on an understanding that defining traits are neither necessarily stabile over time nor entirely identical with adjacent locations, and therefore not easily transposable or compatible. Likewise, it would seem necessary to enable different concurrent schools of thought in order to prevent homogenization and stagnation. The driver of differences in local architectures may thus be shifted from individual expression to a pluralism of schools of thought. Clearly there is also a possible downside to this approach, when, for instance, policies are enforced that dictate style as a common denominator. The result of such policies is frequently a superficial externally more unified appearance to the same universal articulation of the space and section of the building stock. Another point of caution is that the logic of the vernacular cannot be equated with the logic of designed architecture. It is the trait of design to seek out in one way or another novel solutions according to a rather different logic, new concerns or needs and a contemporary *modus operandi*. Having already examined questions of spatial organization, grounds, envelopes and their potential interactions with their specific settings we may extend the discussion to questions of local tectonics.

In his seminal essay from 1983 entitled 'Towards a Critical Regionalism: Six Points for an Architecture of Resistance', Kenneth Frampton stated that the objective of critical regionalism 'is to mediate the impact of universal civilisation with elements derived indirectly from the peculiarities of a particular place' (Frampton 1983: 21). Regarding the indirect use of peculiarities of a particular place, Frampton argued that the architecture 'may find its governing inspiration in such things as the range and quality of the local light, or in a tectonic derived from a peculiar structural mode, or in the topography of a given site' (Frampton 1983: 21). Yet, regarding the impact of universal civilization, Frampton cautioned against an approach that exclusively emphasizes optimized technology, as this can limit designs:

> either to the manipulation of elements predetermined by the imperatives of production, or to a kind of 'superficial masking' and thus lead to on the one hand, a so-called 'high-tech' approach predicated exclusively upon production and, on the other, the provision of a 'compensatory façade' to cover up the harsh realities of this universal system.
>
> (Frampton 1983: 17)

The concerns thus expressed seem today equally acute as in 1983. From this the question arises the need to set forth, if tentatively, theoretical conceptual frameworks and design approaches and methods that may be deployed to arrive at the kind of mediation Frampton calls for, in search of spatially more enriched and locally more specific architectures. Yet, it is important to resist both resorting to a formulaic approach that considers a finite set of traits for every location and/or to consider a too reduced or generic set of local conditions as factors that influence the design. Activating the local will require to some extent starting from basic questions and considerations, while also seeking to determine what the scope of still existing local conditions, sensibilities and practices really are.

In *The Four Elements of Architecture* (1851), Gottfried Semper distinguished between *tectonics* and *stereotomics*. In reference to Semper, Kenneth Frampton (1996: 5) elaborated these elements as two

> fundamental procedures: the tectonics of the frame, in which lightweight, linear components are assembled so as to encompass a spatial matrix, and the stereotomics of the earthwork, wherein mass and volume are conjointly formed through the repetitious piling up of heavy elements.

Moreover, Frampton, in accordance with Semper, emphasized that 'according to climate, custom, and available material the respective roles played by tectonics and stereotomics vary considerably' (Frampton 1996: 6). Thus, when tectonics are discussed, stereotomics must also be considered, and, moreover, in the definition of Semper and Frampton tectonics and stereotomics have in the past inherently been locally specific.

The current trend towards the homogenization of architecture on a global scale suggests reviewing the relation between tectonics and stereotomics relative to local settings with the focus placed on their context-specific performative capacities. The characteristic of a globalized architecture is the typical erasure of terrain articulation in favour of a flattened site, the use of a large amount of reinforced concrete for foundations, basements and the core of buildings, and frequently frames and envelopes made from steel and glass, as well as a technical apparatus for the climatization of the interior. The design process is subjected to and constrained by technical standards and optimization in particular in medium- to large-sized projects. Kenneth Frampton pointed out that:

> These works tend to create an overall drive towards optimization, that is, towards the reduction of building to the maximizing of economic criteria and to the adoption of normative plans and construction methods reducing architecture to the provision of an aesthetic skin – the packaging, in fact, of nothing more than a large commodity in order to facilitate its marketing.
>
> (Frampton 1987: 376)

A first step, then, in addressing this problematic may be to release the constraint of the normative from the parts of schemes that are increasingly subjected to it. One interesting starting point is the 2003/2004 Non-standard Architectures exhibition mounted by the Centre Pompidou in Paris, which foregrounded the capacity of computer-aided design, production and industrialization of architecture with the aim to showcase 'the generalization of singularity, within a new order: the non-standard' (www.designboom.com/contemporary/nonstandard.html). This development was portrayed by a number of built and unbuilt projects by some of the key proponents of digital methods and techniques since the early 1990s. In the context of the exhibition and the related discourse at the time, the formal potential of what are essentially idiosyncratic architectures was foregrounded. However, non-standard architectures may be subjected to particularization to local conditions, just as any other architecture, yet it can facilitate a wide scope of variation in formal articulation, spatial organization and materialization within one defined design system. Thus, an informed non-standard architecture may arise that may have significant implications in terms of application in everyday architecture and the larger built environment.

One example of such an informed non-standard approach is the unbuilt Seaside Second Homes project by Joakim Hoen (see p. 207). However, efforts to engender approaches that seek to overcome the constraints of globalized architecture need also to address localities that do not have access to the technologies that facilitate the feasible industrial production of non-standard solutions. In this case focus must be placed on a design approach that considers local conditions of scarcity, viability, labour and skill that may be tapped into in order to articulate an innovative, intensely local architecture. At any rate, the pursuit of such approaches requires a systematic approach to spatial and material organization and tectonics/stereotomics, in conjunction with the performative capacities of a given scheme and its interactions with the local environment, as well as the provisions that result from this interaction that provide for local practices of using space and their expansion in scope over time.

Kenneth Frampton restated the four elements of architecture, which Semper had proposed as quintessential historical elements of architecture, as (1) earthwork, (2) the hearth, (3) framework/roof and (4) lightweight enclosing membrane (Frampton 1996: 5). Moreover, as mentioned before, Frampton maintained in accordance with Semper that:

> According to climate, custom, and available material the respective roles played by tectonic and stereotomic form vary considerably, so that the primal dwelling passes from a condition in which the earthwork is reduced to point foundations … to a situation in which stereotomic walls are extended horizontally to become floors and roofs.
>
> (Frampton 1996: 6)

A first interesting inroad towards developing a contemporary approach to intensely local architectures may be found in experimental small-scale projects that are designed and constructed in contexts that are for various reasons less subjected to the constraints of globalized architecture. What seems obvious is that the implications for experimenting and elaborating alternative approaches to tectonics and stereotomics are today entirely different in relation to the size of project. While medium and large projects have their own specific logic and set of constraints and are currently frequently driven by considerations that are largely prohibitive to experimentation, it is the small-scale projects that offer a broad scope of possibilities. This is further enhanced if small projects by way of their design brief are assigned as experimental and when these are undertaken in research-oriented environments.

In the context of the Scarcity and Creativity Studio at the Oslo School of Architecture, such projects are developed and constructed for different challenging locations. Typically, these projects are designed and constructed within one semester with a construction time of one month.

Designed and constructed in 2013, the 2x2 Bathing Platform is located north of the Arctic Circle in Nusfjord, a well-preserved historical Norwegian fishing hamlet with a natural harbour and traditional timber buildings set within the rocky shoreline of the Lofoten archipelago. The project faces the sea in a south-eastern direction towards the Westfjord in the direction of Bodø, and integrates a sundeck with various bathing facilities, including a sauna and a hot tub (Fig. 5.1). Two traditional timber buildings define the north-western perimeter of the project (Fig. 5.2). The site is an undulating granite shore that slopes from the existing buildings towards the sea and forms a trough in its centre that is filled with large rocks. Particular attention was placed on the integration of the project into the existing landscape, as well as its capacity to withstand the onslaught of North Atlantic winter storms and waves. A grid of point foundations consisting of steel pins that are directly set into the rock to minimize ground impact supports the substructure of the project. With the explicit reduction of ground impact and terrain preservation, the project follows a key strategic trait of traditional Norwegian architecture.

The tectonic of the project is not defined by skilled and refined joining, but instead by a coordinated design and assembly logic that considers the internal seams of the platform wherever it changes in slope and the external edges wherever it meets the surrounding landscape. The platform also articulates the enclosure for a transitional semi-sheltered space and sauna. It is in parts articulated as stepped seating to double up as spectator seats during musical and theatrical events on site (Fig. 5.3) and articulated in a screenwall-like manner by alternating the 2x2" timber profiles with spacers to render the platform visually permeable (Fig. 5.3). In this project, ground and envelope are co-articulated and continuous with the wider landscape. This fusion of architecture and landscape utilizes tectonics and omits stereotomics in search of a literal middle ground between architecture and landscape.

In 2012 the Scarcity and Creativity Studio designed and constructed several projects for the Open City in Ritoque (Chile) (Fig. 5.7 p. 73, Fig. 5.8 p. 74), itself a seminal showcase of architectural and tectonic experimentation and research. One of these small projects is named *Las Piedrad del Cielo* and serves the purpose of food preparation, communal outdoor eating and nature observation. The project is situated in the Pacific coastal dune landscape of the Open City facing a river estuary and wetlands that are a bird sanctuary (Fig. 5.4). The project consists of a landscaped deck with an enclosed space for a small kitchen (Fig. 5.5) and a textile membrane canopy that provides some shelter from the strong impact of the sun. The landscaped deck provides a sitting surface that forms a horseshoe in plan (Fig. 5.6). Located in the centre of the horseshoe in the sand of the dune is a fireplace. The timber frame of the deck and the canopy are structurally integrated and require only relatively small point foundations. However, each of the point foundations is subjected to different and often combined load cases that also change with the direction and impact of horizontal wind forces and the resulting uplift. For this reason and to keep each point foundation as small as possible, it was necessary to undergo detailed structural analysis and calculation. The canopy is subjected to the impact of gale-force winds during the winter season (Fig. 5.6) and the whole structure also to earthquake impact, which is, however, moderated due to the sandy

5.1 View of the 2x2 Bathing Platform (2013) facing south-west towards the west fjord and showing its relation to the wider landscape. Copyright: Scarcity and Creativity Studio.

5.2 View of the 2x2 Bathing Platform (2013) showing its relation to the local terrain and adjacent buildings. While the project includes an enclosed space for a sauna it is not articulated as an architectural object, but instead as a tectonic landscape. Copyright: Scarcity and Creativity Studio.

5.3　Close-up views from above and below the screenwall-like surface of the 2x2 Bathing Platform (2013). Copyright: Scarcity and Creativity Studio.

5.4 Views of Las Piedras del Cielo (2012) in the coastal dune landscape of the Open City in Ritoque, Chile. Copyright: Scarcity and Creativity Studio.

ground. The provision for communal outdoor eating combined with nature observation constitutes a reflection on the common lunch which constitutes an important event in the weekly lives of the members of the Open City. The project does so, however, by externalizing this event and giving it a less formal setting with seating provided by the articulated deck that extends the landscape, which offers the opportunity to either sit in a circle with the fireplace in the centre, or on smaller and more intimate surface areas facing outward towards the dune landscape.

In 2014 the Scarcity and Creativity Studio designed and constructed a new community centre for Pumanque, a town that was devastated by the 27 February 2010 earthquake that damaged most of the town's buildings. Like the *Las Piedrad del Cielo* project the community centre consists of a timber structure and a textile membrane canopy (Fig. 5.9). The project features two multi-purpose rooms, a semi-sheltered transitional space, a roof terrace accessible through multiple stairways and a canopy that partly shelters the roof terrace (Fig. 5.10). The massing of the single-storey building reflects that of the single-storey buildings in town. A second floor is a luxury available to only a few in Pumanque. However, while most buildings have a slanted roof, the Community Centre has a roof terrace that is inspired by Villa Malaparte in Capri designed by Adalberto Libera (1937). Yet, while Villa Malaparte articulates a continuous relation with

5.5 Close-up views of Las Piedras del Cielo (2012) showing the enclosure for the kitchen formed by the landscaped platform of the project. Copyright: Scarcity and Creativity Studio.

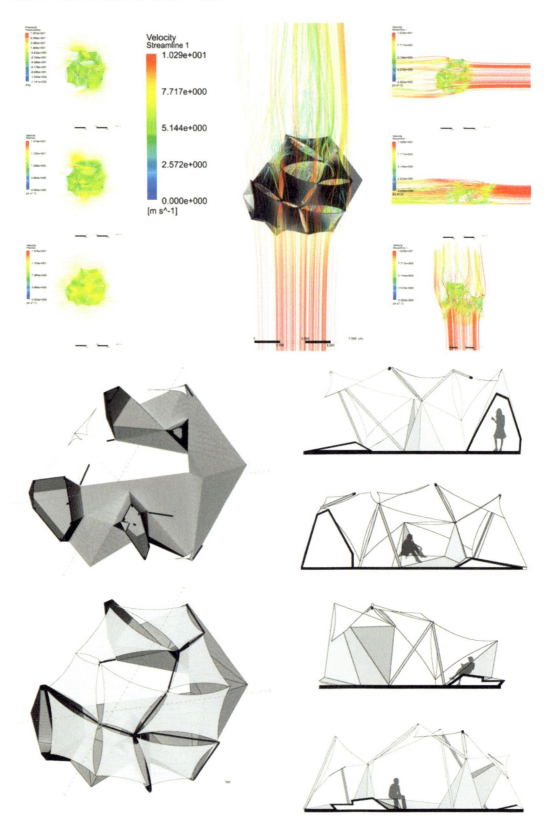

5.6 Top: Airflow analysis of Las Piedras del Cielo (2012) showing air pressure acting on the membranes and velocity of airflow under and above the canopy. Copyright: Scarcity and Creativity Studio. Bottom: plans and sections of Las Piedras del Cielo (2012). The sections reveal the enclosed spaces formed by the landscapes platform. Copyright: Scarcity and Creativity Studio.

5.7 Top: View of the lower coastal dune zone of the Open City in Ritoque Chile. Center and Bottom: Views of the Compass Card Lodge in the Open City Ritoque, Chile (1998) designed by David Luza Building Workshop. The building is integrated in the coastal dune landscape and consists of a group of single rooms each of which face the open landscape in a specific manner, and a shared kitchen and bathroom. Copyright: Michael U. Hensel

5.8 Views of the amphitheatre in Open City Ritoque, Chile (1976-2002) designed by Juan Ignacio Baixas, Jorge Sánchez, and Juan Purcell. the rocky outcrop upon which it sits through a mainly stereoto-mic approach, the Community Centre does so predominately through a tectonic one that mediates between the surrounding buildings and the wider landscape.

the rocky outcrop upon which it sits through a mainly stereotomic approach, the Community Centre does so predominately through a tectonic one that mediates between the surrounding buildings and the wider landscape. The roof terrace replaces the ground that is taken up by the building volume at a raised level and is accessible by way of several stairways (Fig. 5.12). This strategy reflects the terrain form of the hills that flank the town, yet unlike the 2x2 Bathing Platform the community centre does so not as a landform building, but instead as a clearly defined architectural volume that corresponds with the surrounding buildings. An exterior screenwall provides for varied semi-sheltered and carefully modulated interior conditions. The screenwall is made from 2x2" profiles using spacers to produce interstices, similar to the 2x2 Bathing Platform (Fig. 5.10 p. 77). Typically, traditional screenwalls are characterized by high-level craftsmanship that result in intricate ornamentation and performance, including regulating views, thermal and light impact, airflow, etc. The screenwall of the Community Centre derives its apparent intricacy not from high-level craftsmanship, but instead from a design strategy based on a simple assembly procedure. Three different panels were designed for the screenwall. Through rotation these result in six different patterns that are placed in a non-repetitive manner.

The project required a large number of point foundations to support the timber building, as well as the canopy columns and tension cables. However, ground impact was minimized as much as possible. The textile membrane canopy was developed as a rearticulation of the colonnaded walkways that are directly adjacent to the houses in Pumanque, and provides similarly shading of the spaces adjacent to the building (Fig. 5.13) and reduces direct sunlight impact on the interior spaces. On the roof terrace the canopy provides shading and some shelter from rain. The placement and articulation of the volume of the building responds to the location of the existing trees on site that in conjunction with the building and habitable exterior spatial pockets in the envelope provide sheltered intimate outdoor spaces (Fig. 5.11). The main entrance to the project is centrally located between two interior spaces and sheltered by the screenwall and a bridge that connects the two parts of the roof terrace. This space can serve as an extension to the two interior spaces, combining them

5.9 Views of the Community Centre in Pumanque (2014), Chile, showing the building volume enclosed by a timber screenwall and the membrane canopy. Copyright: Scarcity and Creativity Studio.

5.10 Community Centre in Pumanque (2014). *Top*: View of the roof terrace and membrane canopy of the Community Centre. *Bottom*: View of the backyard of the Community Centre and the exterior spaces sheltered by the membrane canopy. Copyright: Scarcity and Creativity Studio.

5.11 Community Centre in Pumanque (2014). Top: The existing trees on site shelter the backyard of the buildings towards the wider surroundings and provide shading for the area adjacent to the building. Bottom: Alcove-like spatial pockets in the exterior envelope of the building that provides sheltered seating. Copyright: Scarcity and Creativity Studio..

5.12 Community Centre in Pumanque (2014). View of the main stairs to the roof terrace. In the background a secondary staircase may be seen. Copyright: Scarcity and Creativity Studio.

into one large space. Overall the project reflects on a number of themes discussed by Christopher Alexander and colleagues in their seminal book *A Pattern Language* (Alexander et al. 1977), including entrance transition, staircase as stage, quiet backs, tree places, connected play, adventure playground and indoor sunlight. The tectonic elements or envelopes of the project – screenwall, climate envelope and canopy – enter into varied relations with one another and other space-defining elements, such as existing trees and perimeter wall of the site, so as to provide a variety of spaces that range from fully sheltered to fully exposed and from collective to intimate. Added plantation is intended to further articulate spatial transitions and interaction between the architecture and the surroundings, in particular along the front façade of the building. In its layered spatial organization and tectonic articulation the Community Centre resonates on a comparable scale with FAR's Wall House (see p. 200).

5.13 Shading analysis of the canopy of the Community Centre in Pumanque, for 21 December (*top*) and 21 June (*bottom*), overlay of three times a day: 10 a.m. (green), 12 noon (purple) and 3 p.m. (red). Copyright: Scarcity and Creativity Studio.

5.14 The development of locally specific tectonic systems is frequently accomplished by way of rigorous iterative processes that combine design generation and analysis. Experimental analogue scaled models (top), full-scale installations (centre) and pilot projects (bottom) play a key role in this process.

5.14(a) Oyler Wu Collaborative's temporary *NETSCAPE* SCI-Arc Graduation Pavilion (2011) is an experimental architecture that offers shelter from seasonally specific intense solar and thermal impact enhanced by the large asphalt surface on which the project is located. The project is a light structure consisting of a steel frame, nets and textile louvres. In its articulation of the textile louvres the scheme resonates with the traditional Spanish toldos that are spanned between buildings to shade the pedestrian spaces beneath. Yet, by articulating an independent architecture the approach becomes more readily adaptable to specific local conditions. It will be interesting to see how this approach will develop in response to locally available material, manufacturing, craftsmanship, and spatial and tectonic specificity. Copyright: Oyler Wu Collaborative.

Yet, while the scheme integrates the existing trees into the scheme it does not do so with R&Sie(n)'s Spidernethewood project (see p. 212). The latter utilizes the existing vegetation in its location by way of pruning along a precisely defined interface constituted by netting, which results in a space that is highly co-defined by architecture and vegetation.

The questions that arise from the above concern the transferability of the light tectonic approaches that articulate these small-scale projects into larger ones. Current practice foregrounds much more the use of heavy stereotomic measures, which may even be justifiable in many cases. Yet, it would seem that the vast amounts of constructions today are governed by considerations that prevent different tectonic approaches from being pursued and implemented. As the legacy of the prevailing ways begins to become apparent, the question is whether amplified fatalism will prevail or whether the opportunity for different approaches will be recognized and engaged.

Grounds and envelopes
THIRTY PROJECTS

Thirty selected projects are portrayed in this part of the book. These projects adopt a variety of different approaches to the questions of grounds and envelopes. Half of these projects address the question of ground while the other half addresses the question of envelope. Some projects even combine interesting approaches to both ground and envelope. The different ground-related projects address questions of continuous, multiple and provisional grounds. They often either accentuate existing terrain conditions such as slopes or embankments and incorporate landscape features as an integral part of the architecture, or, in cases where terrain articulation has already been erased by human intervention, construct new grounds and tectonic landscapes. The envelope-related projects demonstrate how the multiplication of envelopes and/or the deepening of the threshold between exterior and interior can offer transitional and interstitial spaces that provide a broader range of environmental conditions and habitational potential. None of the selected projects coherently and decisively embodies the various aspects and traits of intensely local and embedded architectures that are addressed in the reflections of the first half of the book. Nor is it the intention that this initial discussion reflects and contains a definitive set of traits that could be used as some sort of handbook for design. On the contrary, each thought and each project is an invitation to critically reflect and to boldly project further. It is an invitation to neither let architectural discourse exhaust itself in specialist deliberations, nor to allow it to become entirely insubstantial. After all, architecture co-defines how one dwells, relates to, interacts with and transforms our shared environment: it is one key factor in the rapid changes that our world undergoes and in which architecture plays a central role, whether one wants it or not. Thus architects and clients alike cannot reasonably deny responsibility. However, for architecture to be exciting, relevant and responsible, doom and gloom seem not to be the best approach; instead one may look forward optimistically fuelled by the fact that there are indeed many projects that are worth looking at carefully and that can contribute en route to non-discrete architectures.

Grounds

PROJECT 1
BRAZILIAN PAVILION
Osaka World Expo 1970, Osaka, Japan, 1969
Paulo Mendes da Rocha

World Expos and similar high-profile venues appear not to be the first places that come to mind when searching for projects that may be considered to be non-discrete architecture. What one associates instead with such events are highly idiosyncratic architectural projects designed to stand out even in a dense context of a large ensemble of similarly expressive objects. In so doing, World Expos tend to more and more resemble today's urban condition in booming locations: increasing amounts of eccentric architectures that accumulate to a fabric of folly, yet one that is built to last. The Brazilian Pavilion, designed by Paulo Mendes da Rocha for the Osaka World Expo 1970 located in Osaka, Japan, is one of the few unexpected exceptions to this engrained pattern in that it withdraws from the cacophony of eccentric objects and instead engages a continuous if constructed ground condition in the articulation of space and an extended threshold condition. There is almost no real object to behold. The plot for the pavilion was located along the northwestern perimeter of the Expo site and close to the Monorail station, the Expo's main mode of transport. Given this location, the site could be thought of as both an entry to the Expo beyond and an experience en route.

The project constituted, in the words of da Rocha, 'a reflection, in the realm of architecture, on the relationship between nature and construction' (da Rocha 2007: 74). However, instead of insisting on foregrounding the opposition between nature and construction, the project presents an attempt towards their explicit integration by way of a constructed landscape with architectural features and a spatially articulated thick ground. A concrete canopy with glassed bands covered a constructed undulating landscape. Beneath the landscape surface and connected by ramps, a small theatre, exhibition space and utilities were located. Landscape surface, ramps and below-ground surfaces in the burrowed space were articulated as a seamless transition with no real terminal locations and instead a continuously extended threshold. The sections were key to the development of a continuous yet particularized space that featured different characteristics: compressed and locally grounded by the combination of the landscape and sheltering canopy, and burrowed space set within a thick ground. The combination of shelter and burrow and the spatial transition and fusion via the continuous landscape surface is of specific interest, as through these means the entire project constitutes an extended threshold in which surfaces that have some sort of enveloping function step back and are unassuming, and no architectural object is discernible except for the canopy. In addition, the glassed bands in the canopy enabled shifting bands of sunlight that animated the constructed and continuous landscape surface beneath.

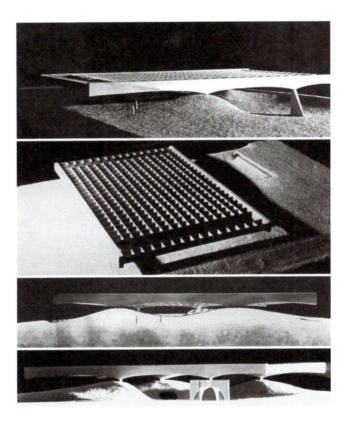

1.1 Four views of a scaled model of the Brazilian Pavilion. The way the model is made evidences that the ground is thought of as continuous and as actual ground and not as object. The canopy constitutes the only object-like architectural element but does not amount to a built volume. The project is accessible along its entire perimeter. Copyright: Paulo Mendes da Rocha.

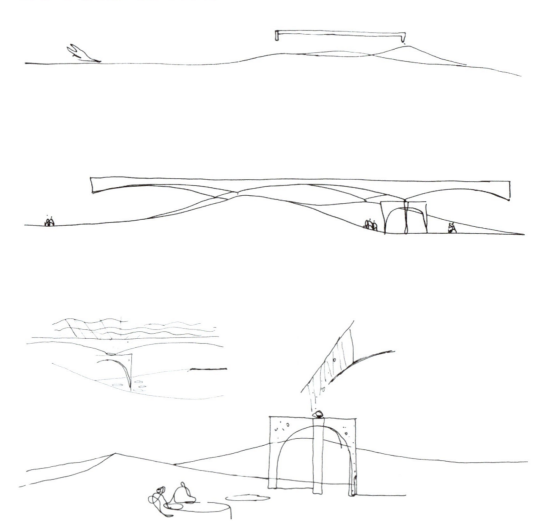

1.2 Various sketches of the Brazilian Pavilion by Paulo Mendes da Rocha. The sketches convey a dune-like landscape framed in its horizontal extent by the canopy and light touched by structural elements. Copyright: Paulo Mendes da Rocha.

Abstract land form, a continuous yet sectionally particularized space, a continuous (landscape) surface and a transition from a sheltered to a burrowed space appear in a particular line of projects in da Rocha's work, such as the unbuilt Caetano de Campos Education Institute (1976) or the Brazilian Museum of Sculpture (MuBE) (see p. 87). Such projects clearly de-emphasize the architectural object and integrate the architecture within an extensive landscape design.

What is interesting to note is a condition brought to light when colour images of the scheme were made available: the ground is painted flamboyantly in the colours of the Brazilian flag but the canopy is left in its exposed raw state. This feature is not evident in the typical black and white photographs of the project under construction that are best known today and that are preferred by Mendes da Rocha, thus indicating that he may not have approved of the colour scheme. In consideration of this feature it is of interest to speculate further and to pay some attention to the specific way in which the constructed landscape meets the extended surface of the surrounding context. One may consider three different versions: (1) clear demarcation of the extent of the constructed landscape by changing materiality and coloration of the ground surface at the border of the plot; (2) continuation of the surface material and coloration of the surrounding context throughout the project; (3) gradual change in the materiality and coloration of the ground surface from the border towards the centre of the plot. The first and actually built version emphasizes the discreteness and objectness of the scheme in spite of the existence of a continuous space, based on the perception of a demarcation line between project and context. The second version would operate on the perception of some kind of contraction of the context into an unfamiliar configuration. The third version would operate on the perception of a gradual movement

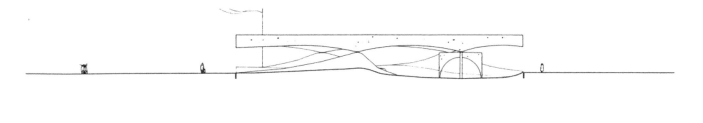
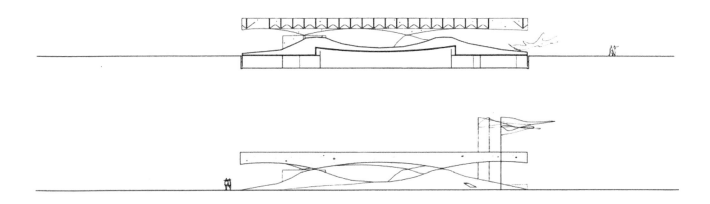
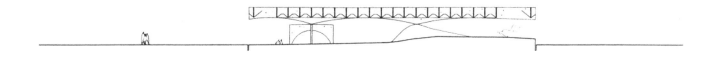
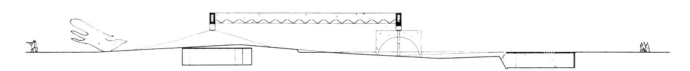

1.3   Five sections of the Brazilian Pavilion. The sections reveal both the continuity of the ground surface and the fact that the ground is constructed. The subterranean spaces seem to float in the mass of the ground. No complete architectural object can be discerned. Copyright: Paulo Mendes da Rocha.

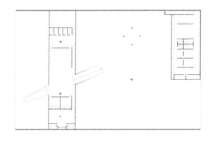
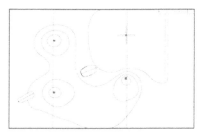
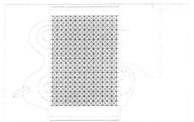

1.4   *Left to right*: Below ground level, ground plan and roof plan of the Brazilian Pavilion. Copyright: Paulo Mendes da Rocha.

1.5 Photo of the Brazilian Pavilion under construction. The photo shows one of the meeting points between canopy and undulating ground, and on the right-hand side a ramp descending to the below-ground spaces of the project. Copyright: Paulo Mendes da Rocha.

from the familiar to the unfamiliar. Clearly each of these perceptions is fundamentally different. The first adheres to the logic of discreteness while giving no primacy to the architectural object as sharply separated from the ground, while the second and the third erode this perception and offer two distinct emphases on non-discreteness.

1.6 Photo of the canopy and architecturally expressed column of the Brazilian Pavilion. Copyright: Paulo Mendes da Rocha.

PROJECT 2
MuBE – BRAZILIAN MUSEUM OF SCULPTURE
Sao Paulo, Brazil, 1988
Paulo Mendes da Rocha

Museums are typically designed as entirely discrete and prominent buildings of heightened cultural value and institutional importance. As such they would seem to constitute a specifically pronounced typological antithesis to non-discrete architecture. And yet, there exist a number of projects that challenge this assumption. One particularly notable example is the Brazilian Museum of Sculpture (MuBE), designed by Paulo Mendes da Rocha, which is located in a predominantly residential area in Sao Paulo, Brazil. The initial brief asked for a combined sculpture and ecology museum. While the ecology part was later abandoned it had nevertheless a strong impact on the design of the building. Paulo Mendes da Rocha said of this project that it was 'conceived as a garden' (da Rocha 2007: 86).

MuBE's architecture comprises: (1) a constructed landscaped terrain with a continuous surface, (2) a series of integrated gardens and water features, (3) a portico of considerable span and width, and (4) interior spaces 'burrowed' within the thickened constructed ground of the project. The terrain is formed by a constructed ground, which comprises the specific programmes of the museum that require enclosure, such as the exhibition spaces, auditoriums, archives and offices. The gardens and water features reinforce the reading of the project as a landscaped terrain. Designed by the distinguished Brazilian landscape

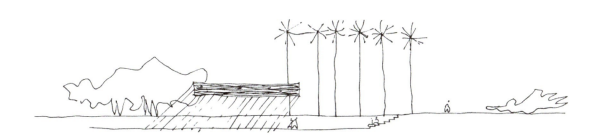

2.1 Sketch of MuBE by Paulo Mendes da Rocha, highlighting the intended landscape approach by showing the principal elements of terrain as spatial organizer, and portico as shading canopy and plantation. This sketch strongly resonates with those of the Brazilian Pavilion by Mendes da Rocha. Copyright: Paulo Mendes da Rocha.

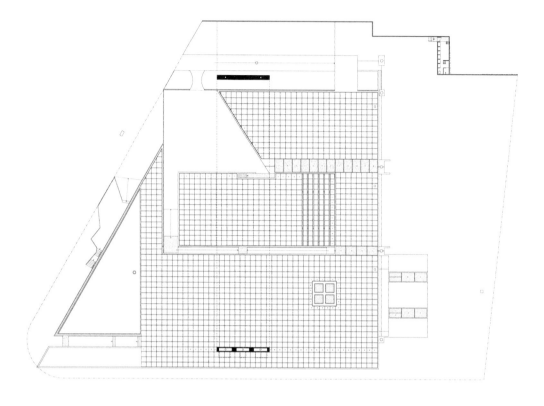

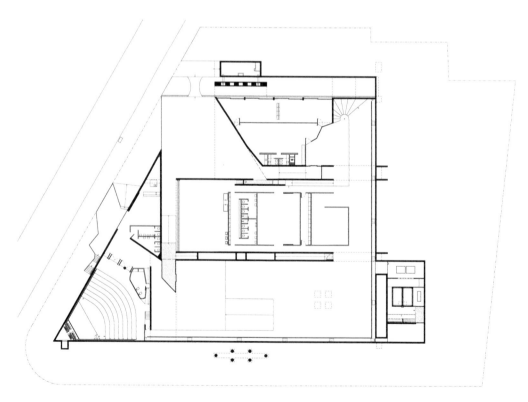

Plans of MuBE. *Top*: Tectonic landscape of the 'above-ground' level showing the square and sunken theatre. *Bottom*: 'below-ground' level showing the museum, auditorium and associated functions. Redrawn by Ricardo Rodrigues Ferreira.

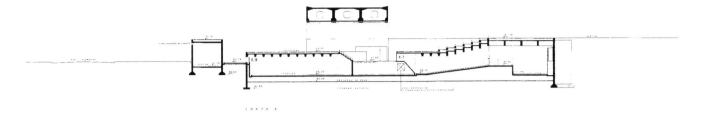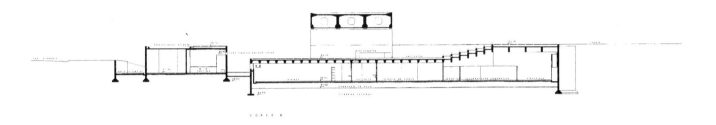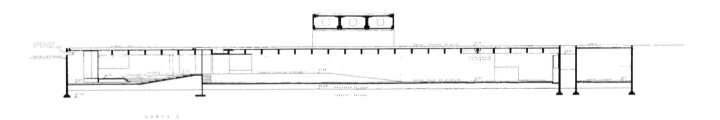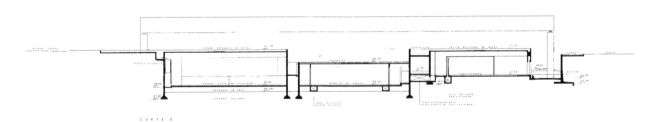

Various sections of MuBE showing how the project benefits from the level change of the site and how the lower level appears to sit within the ground. Copyright: Paulo Mendes da Rocha.

2.4 View of the level changes in the tectonic landscape of MuBE. Photography: Nelson Kon.

architect Roberto Burle Marx, the gardens include water features, tree groves and indigenous fauna.

The building itself is not visibly readable from the surrounding street level except for the portico. This immense 12m-wide and 60m-spanning structure unifies the varied levels of the terrain, defines a landscape-related scale reference for the visitor, and marks, partly shelters and provides for the programmable spaces embedded in the tectonic terrain, such as the sunken outdoor theatre. MuBE was conceived by Mendes da Rocha as a tectonic landscape that is not about the production of a discrete architectural object but, instead, an architecture that aims at providing an extensive landscape experience, and a smooth spatial transition from outside to inside through the articulation of a continuous terrain that defines exterior and interior spaces and

2.5 View of the main entrance area to the plot and interior spaces of MuBE paved in white cobbles used for the pedestrian pavements and walkways that surround the site. Photography: Nelson Kon.

provisions. This is further emphasized by how the project sits within the site, how it negotiates the sloping terrain and how it meets the neighbouring plots. The site is confined along its south-western edge by a residential road and along its south-eastern edge by a larger avenue. The edge along the residential road acts as the formal entrance to the site and museum, and the plot edge along the avenue side would have offered an uninterrupted datum of access, leading from the walkway on to the public plaza and gardens, were it not for a subsequently mounted perimeter fence. The north-western and north-eastern edges border neighbouring plots. These edges initiate the blurring of the limit of the site through the plantation of the gardens

2.6 and 2.7 Views of the exterior plaza and sunken theatre of MuBE partially sheltered by the concrete portico. Photography: 2.6 Nelson Kon. 2.7 Lito Mendes.

designed by Burle Marx that conceal the borders with the neighbouring plots. The portico establishes a notional arrival point to the tectonic landscape, the plaza and sunken theatre. On the residential side it sits back from the plot edge in the same way as the local villas and reflects a similar reading of the vertical proportions of that residential streetscape. Besides the more obvious spatial and proportional relations it is also the material articulation of the horizontal surfaces that is noteworthy. There are two exterior horizontal surface treatments, both of which are found in abundance in the surrounding fabric of the city: square

2.8 View of one of the water pools integrated into the tectonic landscape of MuBE. These were some of the key features of what was initially also intended as a museum of Brazilian ecologies. Photography: Lito Mendes.

concrete tiles and white cobbles used for the pedestrian pavements and walkways that surround the site. The plot of MUBE's edge along the south-western and eastern edges features white cobbles. This surface material is brought into the site along the south-western edge as the formal entrance to the scheme and is used throughout the exterior ground condition at this entrance datum. At the sunken theatre and the level that meets the south-eastern edges concrete square tiles are employed. The vertical surfaces and the large spanning canopy, similar to the canopy of the Osaka Pavilion, are left raw and exposed. By way of avoiding lavish materials and finishes, the project is subtly embedded into the context as terrain. As the selected materials are associated with the public domain they begin to bring this cultural institution into different and more continuous social and cultural affiliations through extraordinarily modest and subtle material means.

The material thresholds and changes that separate the horizontal datum into construction and gardens remain, however, clearly delineated. Here an opportunity presented itself to consider different options for a more detailed blending of the tectonic landscape with the gardens. There are not many projects that have attempted to thoroughly tackle this design problem, as it may have been considered too minute, perhaps even irrelevant, as design criteria, and solutions are not readily at hand. Yet, once microclimatic and ecological considerations such as designing for biodiversity and related habitat and niche-provision considerations come into play, this may change the picture.

PROJECT 3
SPREEBOGEN – INTERNATIONAL URBAN PLANNING COMPETITION
Berlin, Germany, 1992
Andrew Zago

The 1992 International Urban Planning Competition for the Spreebogen area in the centre of the German capital Berlin asked for an urban scheme for a new federal capital complex that comprises the German Parliament, Federal Council, the Federal Chancellery and the Federal Press Conference Centre on a 62-hectare site. The required area for governmental programmes amounted to about 250,000 square metres. Additional programming of the site was left open to the architects who participated in the competition. The green areas adjacent to the River Spree and the adjacent Tiergarten Park offered the possibility to pursue this large urban design competition from a landscape perspective. In parallel, the disruption of the city fabric due to the former division of Berlin brought with it the question of how new connections were to be articulated.

The American architect Andrew Zago described his competition entry as 'a viscous and differentiated plenum [that makes]

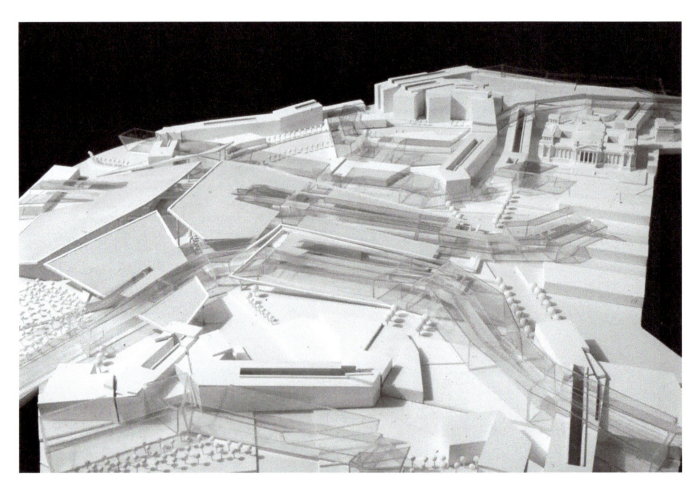

3.1 Model of the entire competition site and scheme showing existing and proposed government buildings (the Reichstag building at the top right-hand corner), and the proposed exhibition halls, 'urban tubes' – connective public spaces and infrastructure – and the World Garden and Festival structure with its large 'floating' canopies. Copyright: Zago Architecture.

3.2 Partial view of the model showing the relation and directionality of the ground articulation, built volume, 'urban tubes' and canopies of the Festival structure. Copyright: Zago Architecture.

the void of space thematic [and that] appears in many forms simultaneously, variously connecting and then separating from its context. It is a permeable and convoluted entity, eluding clear outline' (Zago 1993: 11). The relinquishment of clearly delineated figures or objects in favour of a continuous and continually varied

3.3 Views of the northern section (*top*: view northwards, *bottom*: view southwards) of the site showing the large festival structure with its canopies. Copyright: Zago Architecture.

urban fabric and landscape served as an alternative to a traditional ensemble of discrete architectures based on the canonic figure/ground arrangement.

The proposed scheme comprised four main systems: (1) exhibition halls, (2) so-called 'urban tubes' (connective public spaces and infrastructure), (3) long and slender corridor-like government buildings, and (4) the World Garden and Festival structure. The proposed 24 exhibition halls, which were to serve a broad range of purposes and activities, were organized on a

3.4 Colour-coded model. *White*: Reichstag building; *turquoise*: government buildings; *orange*: exhibition halls; *transparent*: 'urban tubes'; *green*: World Garden. This model does not show the large canopies of the Festival structure. Copyright: Zago Architecture.

3.5 Colour-coded axonometric showing the area around the Reichstag building. Copyright: Zago Architecture.

3.6 Colour-coded axonometric showing the area around the Festival structure. Copyright: Zago Architecture.

3.7 Axonometric showing the volumetric scheme and its relation to the River Spree. Copyright: Zago Architecture.

grid that was distorted in relation to existing landscape features and public transport routes. The 'urban tubes' established the primary means for articulating the plenum and for connecting adjacent districts across the site. They were proposed to comprise elongated arcade and winter garden-type spaces that originate as sectional extrusions from the characteristic spaces of the adjacent districts and serve recreational and retail functions,

pedestrian connections and reduced vehicular traffic. The governmental functions were organized in programmatic bands of 'continuous relationships rather than as a collection of separate destinations' (Zago 1993: 11). The World Garden features plantation typical of the different continents and serves as the primary ground articulating system of the scheme. Across the site the ground datum was to vary continually in height. This was meant to subvert the dominance of a singular continuous ground surface in favour of providing an experience of a spatial, differentiated and provisional ground condition. Together, the World Garden and the Festival structure provide the open public and ceremonial spaces of the site as a national and international centre. The extensive canopies of the Festival structure – perhaps reminiscent of Festival plazas with large canopies, such as in the World Expo in Osaka in 1970 – together with the numerous close adjacencies and intersections of different types of enclosures and the varied ground datum provide a large amount of sheltered transitional interstitial and residual spaces. The combination of an abundant amount of interstitial space resulting from multiple extensive envelopes and varied ground datum entirely diminish the perception of the urban scheme as an ensemble of discrete architectural objects and ground as passively occupied.

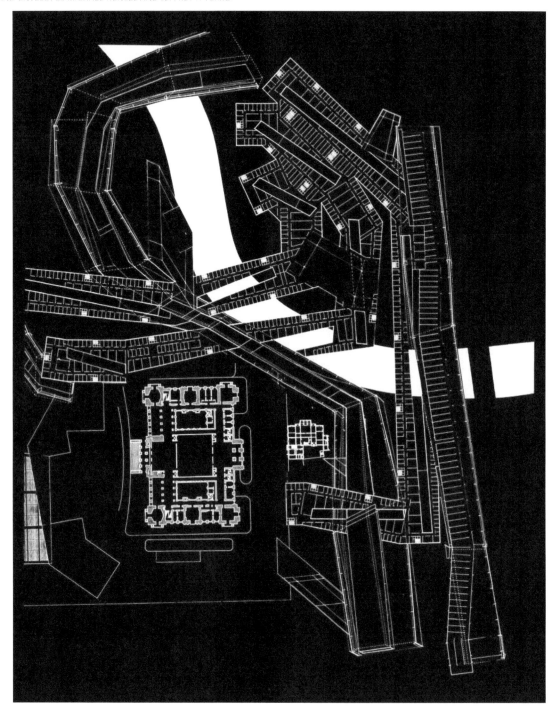

3.8 Plan view of the area around the Reichstag building with the proposed linear governmental buildings that bridge the River Spree. Copyright: Zago Architecture.

While the urban and organizational levels of the scheme are intriguing, the way in which the architecture would be articulated remains regrettably, yet understandably, elusive due to the size and scale of the project. There are however a number of projects that may indicate a way forward, such as Mendes da Rocha's MuBE project (see p. 87) that articulates a tectonic landscape, RCR's Marquee Les Cols (see p. 99) in the way it defines the tectonics of a canopy condition lightly set within a constructed terrain, and Helen & Hard's Geopark playground (see p. 172) in the way it materializes provisional ground conditions.

PROJECT 4
MARQUEE AT LES COLS RESTAURANT
Olot, Girona, Spain, 2007 to 2011
RCR Arquitectes – Ramón Vilalta, Carme Pigem and Rafael Aranda

The Marquee at Les Cols is located in the town of Olot, in the foothills of the Pyrenees. Like the Les Cols restaurant and pavilions that are located on the same site adjacent to the Garrinada volcano, the Marquee was designed by RCR Arquitectes. And, like some of RCR's other works, such as the Les Cols pavilions (2003–2006) or the unbuilt House for an Architect (2005) and Mas

4.1   Rendered views of the Marquee at Les Cols showing the approach from the south. Copyright: RCR Arquitectes.

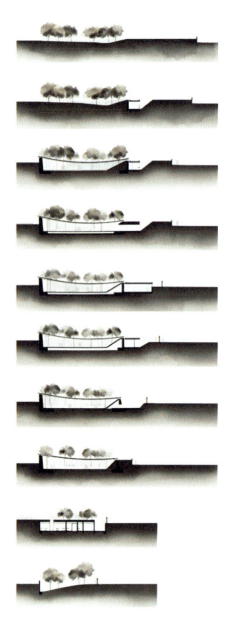

4.2 Serial cross-sections of the Marquee at Les Cols showing how the project sits within the landscape and how its canopy and the roof of the kitchen area enter into different affiliations with the surrounding ground datum. Copyright: RCR Arquitectes.

Salvá Stables (2007), the Marquee offers an interesting approach to rearticulating the relation between architecture and landscape and outside and inside.

Traditional marquee tents, most commonly associated with English countryside summer weddings, provide shelter for outdoor events. Likewise, the Marquee at Les Cols is conceived of as a venue for wedding banquets and social events. Its architecture merges with the surrounding landscape and offers a setting for a variety of different events. Rafael Aranda of RCR Arquitectes described the design intention as focusing on 'a space, which could not exist inside a building: a place where people would sense the changing time of the day and the weather, how rain or light vary from minute to minute' (Curtis 2011: 19).

The Marquee is located to the east of the Les Cols restaurant and pavilions on the eastern and lower part of the site. On its shorter southern and northern sides the Marquee opens to the landscape and gardens respectively. The main approach to the Marquee is from the south down a gently sloping landscape surface that continues into and through the project.

Along its length the Marquee is flanked by a masonry wall to the west and by an artificial rise of volcanic rock to the east. Its enclosure and canopy, made from ETFE, are transparent and enable maximum visual access to the surrounding landscape. In addition, the climatic enclosure and exposure is varied from exterior entrance area to interior 'filtered' space, to exterior covered and exterior air-conditioned space. The primary space is organized in parallel bands defined by transparent sheets, paving and rows of trees. The layers of transparent and reflective materials visually collapse landscape and architecture into one another. The trees pierce through the canopy, which is aligned with the top of the masonry wall and the volcanic rock rise, suggesting a new provisional ground datum. The kitchen area and additional secondary spaces are burrowed beneath the ground datum. The combination of the strategies of burrowing and seemingly dematerialized sheltering makes it possible to avoid the appearance of an architectural object.

The design of the Marquee at Les Cols clearly resonates with and rearticulates the design strategies of the Brazilian Pavilion by

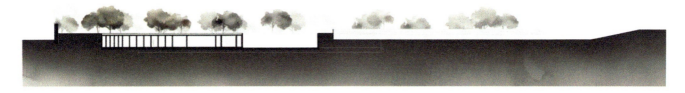

4.3   Three longitudinal sections of the Marquee at Les Cols showing how the project sits within the landscape. By being partly burrowed and partly light and seemingly dematerialized, the project sidesteps settling into a discrete architectural object. Copyright: RCR Arquitectes.

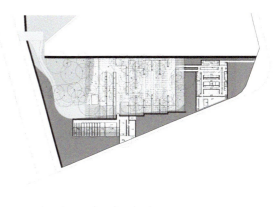
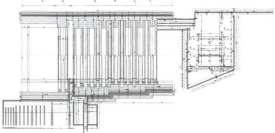

4.4   Site plan of the Les Cols complex showing the restaurant to the south-west, the pavilions to the northwest, and the Marquee to the east. Copyright: RCR Arquitectes.

4.5   Plan of the Marquee at the Les Cols complex showing the burrowed kitchen and restroom area and the organization of the primary space under the canopy that is flanked by parallel rows of trees, paving and furnishings. Copyright: RCR Arquitectes.

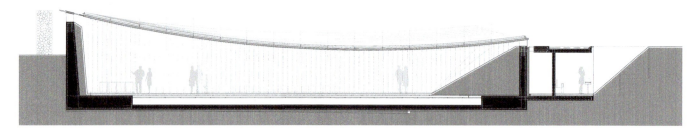

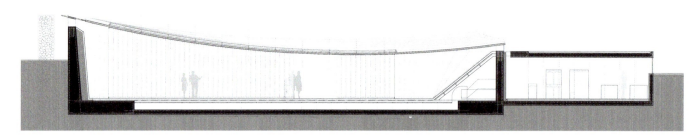

4.6 Cross-sections of the Marquee at the Les Cols complex showing the articulation of the primary space by the catenary canopy and the secondary spaces burrowed in the artificial volcanic rock rise. Copyright: RCR Arquitectes.

4.7 Various views of the Marquee at Les Cols. *Top*: View of the Marquee at Les Cols from the south. *Centre*: Transitional area. *Bottom*: Layering of spaces below the canopy. Photography: Hisao Suzuki.

4.8 View of the Marquee at Les Cols showing the entrance area in the south, the canopy and the way it is pierced by rows of trees. The canopy suggests a provisional new ground datum suspended above the actual inhabited one. Photography: Hisao Suzuki.

4.9 View of the primary space of the Marquee at Les Cols, showing the layering of space by way of suspended transparent sheets and the rows of tree trunks. Photography: Hisao Suzuki.

Paulo Mendes da Rocha (see p. 83). Yet, the question arises as to how a larger ensemble of such schemes might be organized and how such schemes might respond to directly adjacent existing architectures. While the Marquee can suggest how parts of much larger schemes, such as Andrew Zago's entry to the Spreebogen competition, might be articulated in a detailed manner (see p. 94), such larger projects may in turn begin to suggest how schemes like the Marquee might be organized into an urban fabric.

PROJECT 5
SEATTLE ART MUSEUM: OLYMPIC SCULPTURE PARK
Seattle, Washington, USA, 2001 to 2007
Weiss/Manfredi

The Olympic Sculpture Park designed by Weiss/Manfredi is located on a brown-field industrial site that was formerly used as an oil transfer facility and is one of the last sites to be developed along the Seattle waterfront. A primary road and railway lines divide the site into three separate parcels that descend 40 feet from the city level to the water's edge.

Frequently architects respond to this type of design problem with schemes that cover the entire site with a landscape surface or a concrete deck, resulting in an undercroft that hides the existing infrastructure and produces an abundance of unusable residual spaces.

In contrast, Weiss/Manfredi's scheme steers clear of this tendency and proposes instead a design that maintains the infrastructure as a visible and vital part of the city. Their competition-winning scheme reconnects the three parcels and various levels via a Z-shaped inclined platform. Besides a primary

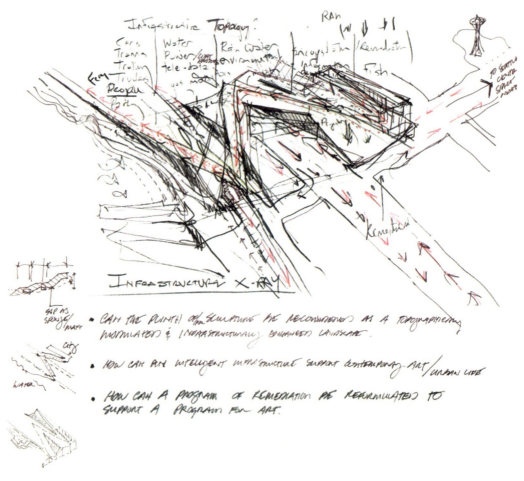

5.1 Initial sketch of the Olympic Sculpture Park, as an X-ray view of the layers of infrastructure including road, rail, waterfront, and the cultural infrastructure of the sculpture park. Copyright: Weiss/Manfredi.

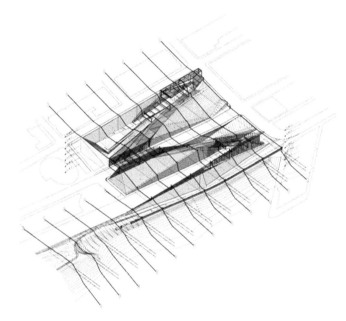

5.2 Axonometric X-ray view of the Olympic Sculpture Park, illustrating the sectional articulation of the new infrastructural and cultural grounds that connect the city fabric to the waterfront. Copyright: Weiss/Manfredi.

pedestrian route the scheme offers a number of additional routes that take advantage of the sectional shift across the site.

An exhibition pavilion is situated on the city level in the eastern corner of the site where the primary pedestrian route starts. From this point of entry the path descends to the waterfront and offers views of the Olympic Mountains, the city and port. It terminates at the waterfront with views to the beaches. Along the path the landscaping changes from temperate evergreen forest, to deciduous forest and to shoreline gardens made up of tidal terraces for salmon habitat and saltwater vegetation.

These enhanced landscape zones also become secondary territories that allow access on to this new ground and begin to define discrete pockets of space within it. Optional points of entry are created along the primary road and from other bordering roads that would otherwise cut off areas of surrounding city fabric if it were not for the sectional articulation of the scheme. The vegetation in relation to the articulation of the ground defines areas of the enhanced ground as an interior. This is most clearly seen in the area that comprises the evergreen forest. The ground in this area is sunken to create a theatre-like condition that is further enhanced as an interior on this landscape by the surrounding evergreen forest that acts as a natural enveloping condition. The combination of the sunken ground and the enveloping forest produces a somewhat consistent condition that offers shelter from the otherwise present conditions of urban life such as traffic noise and from some climate conditions such as wind.

Contaminated over years of use as an industrial site the new ground constructed for the Olympic Sculpture Park acts as an environmental cap over the affected land to limit the recurrence of further contamination.

Consequently the scheme includes strategies for groundwater preservation, including (1) a strategy of remediation of the existing ground and (2) a drainage strategy to limit any further expansion of the contaminated zones.

Monitoring of this condition is made possible by wells that are embedded in this new environmental cap over the affected zones. The drainage strategy works in conjunction with the capping and includes a surface drainage strategy that runs along the tarmac surface of the primary circulation path and a subsurface drainage system that is embedded at varied heights within the thickness of the new ground. A part of this system is used to irrigate the groves of trees and new landscape, with excessive run-off flowing into Puget Sound.

The way in which the ground is articulated and traversed by its Z-shaped platform also divides the site into specific surface conditions that provide for the implementation of specific programmatic uses, as well as the accommodation of local ecologies. These surfaces are categorized into four types: (1) turf – which accommodates structured art events; (2) meadow – which accommodates flexible-use art events; (3) groundcover – which also accommodates flexible-use art events; and (4) beaches – where environmental art events take place. Among these are two groves of trees, one made up of evergreen trees that remain constant throughout the year, and the other made

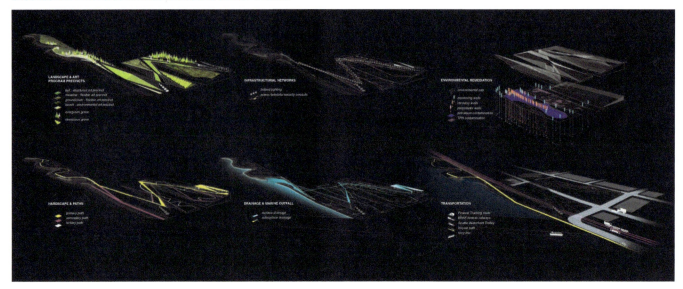

5.3 Olympic Sculpture Park's key diagram elaborating the layers of systems that make this new ground of the city: (i) programmatic conditions of the park and art precincts; (ii) environmental considerations of the remediation of the ground, (iii) the water drainage towards the waterfront; (iv) the localized infrastructures of the park itself, (v) the varied pedestrian circulation paths, and (vi) the citywide infrastructure that passes through and around this new ground. Copyright: Weiss/Manfredi.

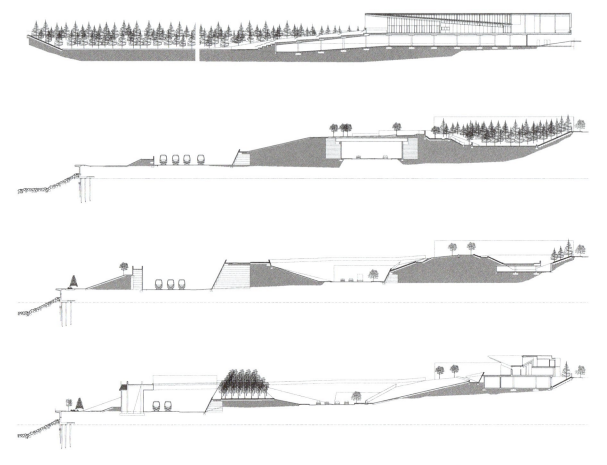

5.4 Cross-sections of the Olympic Sculpture Park showing the variation and articulation of the constructed ground, the placement of the pavilion as part of the new ground, the placement of evergreen and deciduous vegetation, and the relation of these features to the existing infrastructures of the railway, waterfront and motorway. Copyright: Weiss/Manfredi.

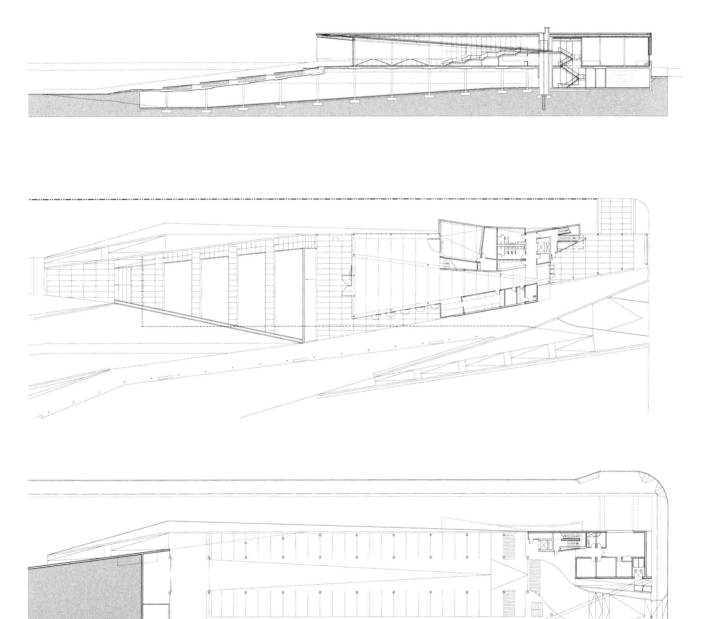

5.5 Section and plans of the Olympic Sculpture Park pavilion, showing the car park and the primary interior space, and how it is embedded into the ground, as well as how it links to the primary path of circulation of the scheme. Copyright: Weiss/Manfredi.

5.6 View of the Olympic Sculpture Park following the axis of the waterfront's edge, showing the layers of the scheme and how it integrates the park with the dominating local infrastructures of the waterfront, railway and road network. Photography: Benjamin Benschneider.

5.7 View of the Olympic Sculpture Park showing how the new ground connects the sectional divide of 40 feet (12 metres) from the city fabric to the waterfront. Photography: Benjamin Benschneider.

5.8 View of the Olympic Sculpture Park showing its inhabitation and use as a ground for events, as well as an infrastructure that links the city back to the waterfront for the public. Photography: Benjamin Benschneider.

up of deciduous trees that register the seasonal changes. The combination between systems of paths, surfaces, vegetation, irrigation and groundwater management, and allocated provisions for indoor and outdoor use, as well as semi-sheltered landscaped spaces, render this scheme an extended threshold condition that is operative because of its serial, sequenced and synthesized sectional articulation and variation in various scales, ranging from the macro-section of the Z-shaped platform to the micro-sections of the paths, surfaces and water systems.

PROJECT 6
MEYDAN – UMRANIYE RETAIL COMPLEX & MULTIPLEX
Istanbul, Turkey, 2007
Foreign Office Architects

Foreign Office Architects' Meydan – Umraniye Retail Complex & Multiplex project is located on the Asian side of Istanbul. The project features an interesting approach to both ground and envelopes. The project is set within a larger context of urban development that currently favours a car-based urbanism and large climatized shopping malls, often combined with a set of apartment towers located atop the volume of the mall. The perimeter of such projects is frequently hostile and almost impenetrable on a pedestrian scale. Here, like in other parts of Istanbul that are rapidly changing at a staggering scale and pace, the city has turned into a car-based metropolis. FOA's scheme does not deny this development, but places the required parking underground with access to a central open plaza, while at the same time opening the perimeter of the site to pedestrian movement from the surrounding neighbourhood. The emphasis on the open public plaza with its generous pedestrian connections to the adjacent areas implies that the project is not one large climatized interior, but is instead a publicly usable connective tissue that articulates the different retail and leisure functions as separate and more humanly scaled units. In so doing the project does not settle into the 'Junkspace' condition that characterizes other such complexes, whether in Istanbul or elsewhere. What comes to the fore instead is the typology of an urban square. Overall, the project is defined by a landscape-inspired approach: a continuous landscaped surface organizes the perimeter of the site, pedestrian circulation, distribution of (enfolded) built volume, hard surfaces, green surfaces and so on. This public landscape is either entered from the access points along the perimeter of the site or from below by way of ramps from the underground parking that surface in the open central square of the site. Surface materials are kept to a few that aim for unifying the scheme into a coherent whole: grass for landscapes surfaces, brick and colour-coordinated cladding for the building volume that is not enfolded in the surface, and glass as interior/exterior threshold and climate envelope in the building volume which features a box-within-box section. On the whole the project stands out positively against the vast amount of hard-nosed and superficially branded profit-driven development in Istanbul that often seems to entirely disregard what the accumulation of such projects amounts to.

Projects like the Meydan – Umraniye Retail Complex & Multiplex invite speculation as to what an extensive urban scheme based on its underlying design principles might look like and how it would negotiate other extensive systems such as road

6.1 The Meydan project may be discerned in mid-distance. What appears on first sight as extensive urban green landscape is mostly leftover space of an enormous amount of inner urban freeway and road system that severely separates neighbourhoods. In addition, an increasing number of mega-malls combined with apartment towers (eerily resembling a medieval castle typology) is only accessible by car. The Meydan project is a noteworthy exception in that it is accessible on foot and offers ample social public space. Photography: Courtesy Metro Management.

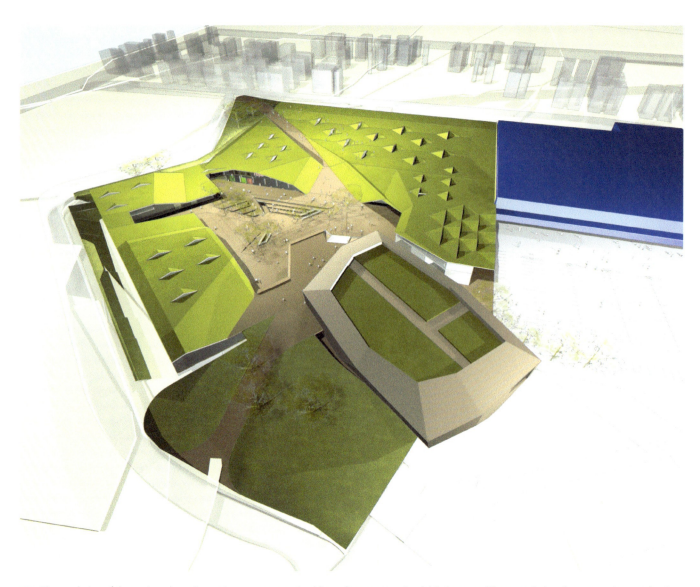

6.2 The rendering of the project shows its continuous green and public surface areas and enfolded spaces. The central plaza features various pedestrian connections to the surrounding areas. Copyright: Foreign Office Architects.

6.3 *Bottom to top*: Parking level, retail and multiplex levels, roof plan. The plans of the project show the connective role of the central plaza as a connection and distribution point. All access, whether on foot or by car, is directed in plan and section to this open social public space. Copyright: Foreign Office Architects.

6.4 The section through the whole site reveals the role of the central plaza as the main connection and distribution point for all publicly accessible surfaces, whether programmed or landscaped. Copyright: Foreign Office Architects.

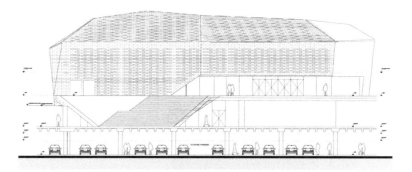

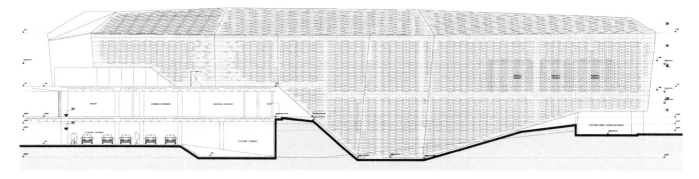

6.5 The two sectional elevations show the articulated and perforated outer envelope of the building volumes that is not enfolded in the landscaped surface. The format and coloration of the cladding of these outer envelopes is aligned with the brick paving of the plaza and pedestrian circulation surfaces. In this way the volumes blend into the surface scheme instead of standing out as separate objects. Copyright: Foreign Office Architects.

6.6 Various views of the Meydan project showing the joined landscape and pedestrian circulation surface, enfolded spaces, open courtyards and central plaza. Photography: Michael Hensel.

6.7 This photo shows the correlation between the articulated landscape surface of the project and the hilly landscape in the mid- and far distance, as well as the way in which the landscape surface frames the central plaza that is simultaneously connected to and visually shielded from the surrounding neighbourhood. Photography: Cristobal Palma.

infrastructure or housing. Some landscape projects, such as the renowned Flamego Park in Rio de Janeiro, designed by Lota de Macedo Soares, with its undulating landscape and many pedestrian bridges across roads, is set within the troughs of the rolling landscape. The project also resonates with the urban design of the Turf City project by Nekton Design (see p. 145). The partners of the now dissolved FOA practice experimented extensively with their students on urban-scale projects. One would wish for them to deliver a masterplan for a larger area in Istanbul or elsewhere based on the traits of the Meydan project. It would also be of interest to allow local fauna to encroach upon the landscaped surface of the project instead of limiting it to the generic grass surface, particularly since the green surfaces are not accessible to the public.

PROJECT 7
CITY OF CULTURE OF GALICIA
Santiago de Compostela, Spain, 1999 to 2012
Peter Eisenman

The City of Culture of Galicia is a cultural complex situated at the top of Monte Gaiás in Santiago de Compostela in the La Coruña municipality of Spain.

The project was presented in the media as resembling a scallop shell in plan, thus referencing the local tradition of bringing a shell to the shrine of St James in Santiago de Compostela. However, it was not a discrete symbolic form that Eisenman pursued, but instead a new geography of contours, a design approach that embeds architecture and landscape within one another. In so doing, the prevailing figure/ground-type urbanism was relinquished in favour of a different vision of urbanism that treats both landscape and architecture as a continuous tectonic condition.

In Eisenman's work this approach began to take shape from the early 1990s onward, commencing with projects like the Rebstockpark masterplan in Frankfurt and the Nördliches Derendorf masterplan in Düsseldorf. In the Rebstockpark project Eisenman confronted the notions of the static discrete objects of post-war-era urbanism by way of a masterplan that predicated the notion of event and the formal operation of folding. The latter subjects both the ground plane and the architectural objects to the same continuous transformation that articulates the geometry of both. Yet, the relation between ground and object remains otherwise discontinuous and the treatment of the ground surface and that of the envelopes are distinctly different, as shown in a series of perspectival and elevational views. In the masterplan scheme for Nördliches Derendorf this approach was taken a step further by deploying a different formal operation that resulted in a more smooth transition between building mass and landscape, rendering them as different intensities of ground contraction and a cohesive field. This approach resonates with the City of Culture scheme in which the architecture constitutes at the same time and in a non-decomposable manner a constructed tectonic landscape.

The initial scheme for the City of Culture comprised six buildings organized in three pairs, each of which were treated as a geological tectonic plate that would affect and be affected by the others: (1) the Galician Library and Periodicals Archive, (2) the

7.1 View of the City of Culture of Galicia looking west towards Santiago de Compostela and the towers by John Hejduk. *Foreground*: The Periodicals Archive. *Middle-ground*: The Galician Library. *Background*: The Museum of Galician History. Copyright: Eisenman Architects.

7.2 View of the City of Culture of Galicia showing the articulation of the overall building forms and how they may collectively be read as a new ground condition rather than as discrete cultural buildings. Copyright: Eisenman Architects.

7.3 Close-up view of the City of Culture of Galicia with an emphasis on the stone surface material of this new ground. Copyright: Eisenman Architects.

7.4 View of the City of Culture of Galicia looking at the articulated courtyard space attached to the Galician Library. Copyright: Eisenman Architects.

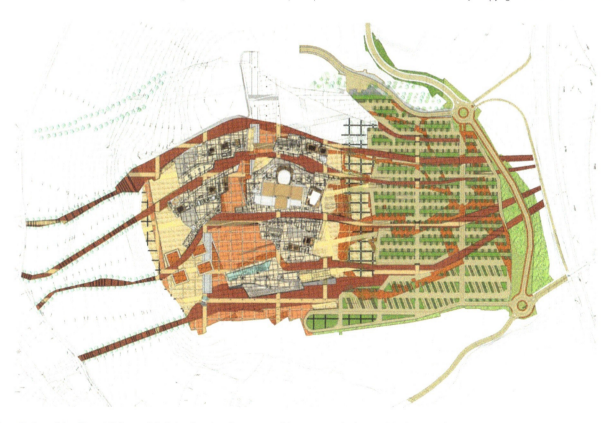

7.5 Overall plan of the City of Culture of Galicia, showing the extent of the proposed scheme. *North to south*: The Museum of Galician History, Technology Centre and Music Theatre, Galician Library and Periodicals Archive. Located to the east are the parking landscape and local motorway infrastructure. Copyright: Eisenman Architects.

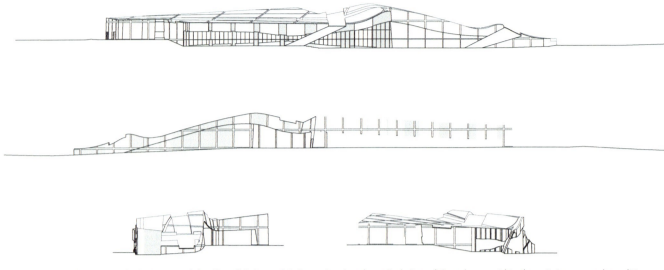

7.6 Elevations of the Periodicals Archive of the City of Culture of Galicia, showing the articulation of the scheme within the existing ground condition and the towers by John Hejduk. Copyright: Eisenman Architects.

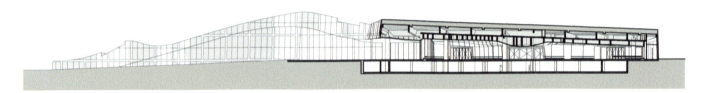

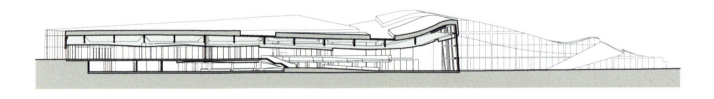

7.7 Sections of the Periodicals Archive of the City of Culture of Galicia, showing the internal articulation of space through the deep poché of the soffit. Copyright: Eisenman Architects.

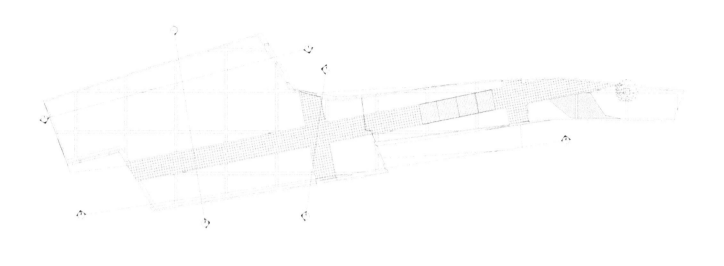

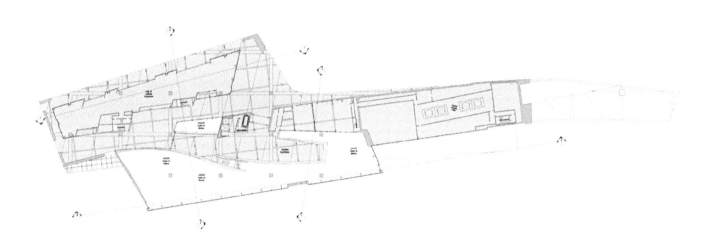

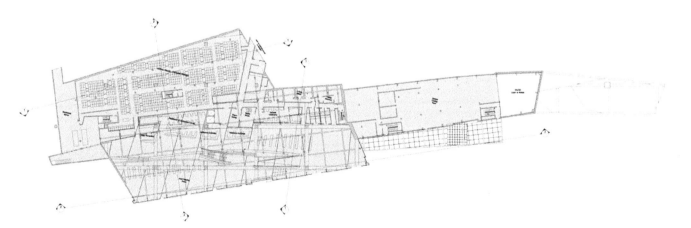

Plans of the Periodicals Archive of the City of Culture of Galicia, showing Level 1 which houses the stacks and reading rooms, Level 0 which houses an exhibition space, and the roof plan. Copyright: Eisenman Architects.

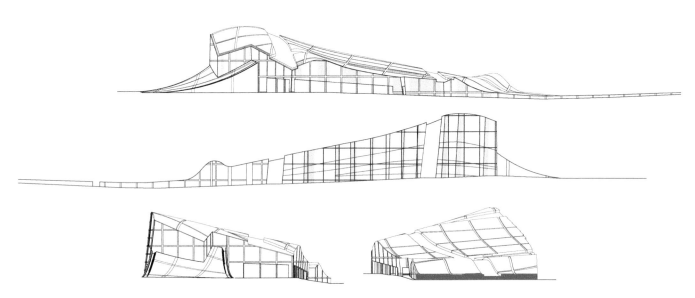

7.9   Elevations of the Galician Library of the City of Culture of Galicia, giving the impression that the building is an extension of the existing ground. Copyright: Eisenman Architects.

Museum of Galician History and the New Technology Centre, and (3) the Music Theatre and Central Services and Administration. Yet, the New Technology Centre and Music Theatre's construction were eventually cancelled. Although this leaves out two of the largest buildings of the scheme it does not take away from the spatial organization and the tectonic landscape theme of the project.

As a way of circumventing traditional urbanism that relies on the figure/ground methods of collage, Eisenman embeds the planar figure of the medieval city of Santiago into the ground. Ground is thus no longer treated as a plane to which figures are applied. Instead, ground, with its topographical and geological features, is treated as a spatial medium. The thick mass of the ground with the figure of the medieval city embedded within is subjected to a design process that deforms this mass into a fusion of landscape and architecture that in its sectional articulation accommodates the programmatic and spatial demands of the scheme. The question which arises is similar to that of Paulo Mendes da Rocha's Museum of Sculpture (see p. 87): namely how such a large scheme is treated along its perimeter. Is this perimeter sharply separating the scheme from its larger setting, thus rendering the project a large figure, or does the perimeter feather out and enable a more nuanced transition between local setting and the scheme? Likewise, and above and beyond the external perimeter of the scheme, are there internal perimeters that enable the scheme to be infiltrated by the setting, resulting in an extended interface? Such questions arise increasingly with such large 'landform buildings' as Stan Allen terms this approach and the answers will determine whether such schemes will remain primarily formal gestures or whether they are strategically opened to landscape-related contingencies and imbued with the capacity to sustain landscape-related processes.

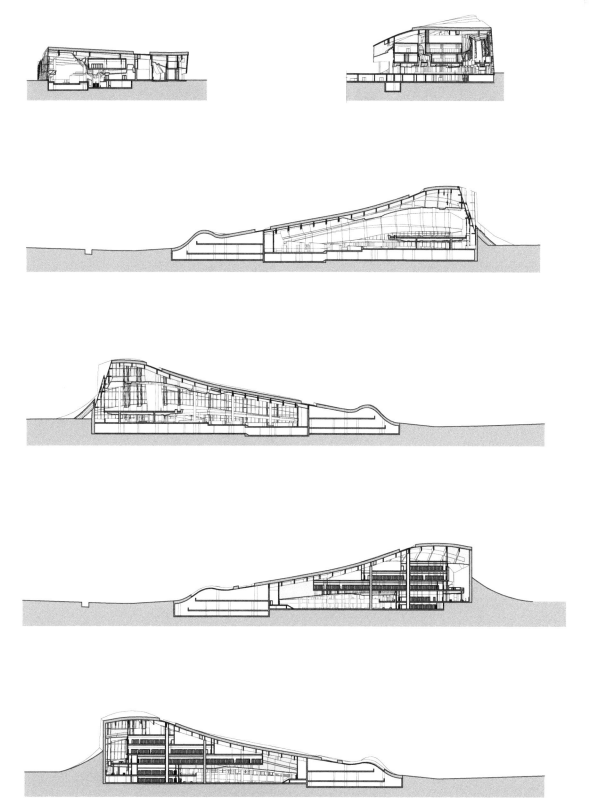

7.10 Sections of the Galician Library of the City of Culture of Galicia, showing the internal articulation of space through the deep poché of the soffit and the depth of the soffit becoming a ground to inhabit in the interior as space gets embedded into it and as it begins to wrap other spaces. Copyright: Eisenman Architects.

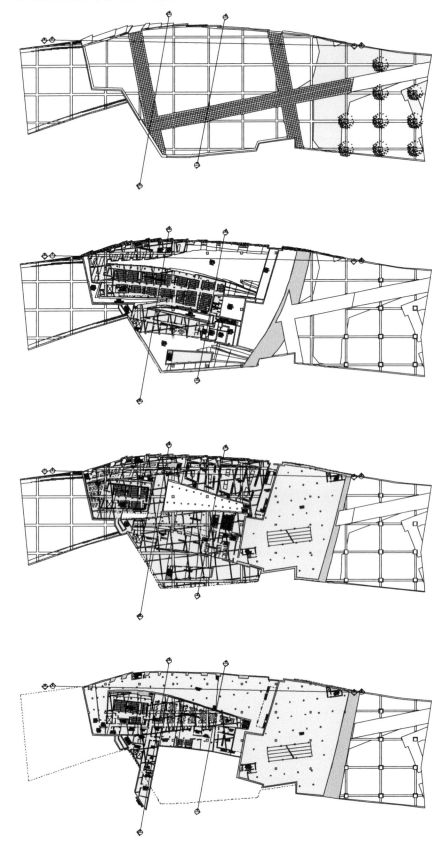

7.11 Plans of the Galician Library of the City of Culture of Galicia, showing levels 1, 0, +1 and the roof plan. Copyright: Eisenman Architects.

PROJECT 8
XI'AN HORTICULTURAL EXPO
Longgang, China, 2011
Plasma Studio and GroundLab

Situated between the local airport and the ancient city centre of Xi'an, the Xi'an Horticultural Expo, completed in 2011 by Plasma Studio and GroundLab, comprises a 37-hectare landscape that houses the International Horticultural Expo and Legacy Park for the City of Xi'an, the 5,000sqm Creativity Centre building and the 4,000sqm Greenhouse, and lastly the 3,500sqm Guangyun Entrance Bridge. Conceived of as flowing gardens, the scheme aimed to integrate the functionality of the landscape into a future vision of sustainability that carefully integrates programmed elements, water, planting, circulation and architecture.

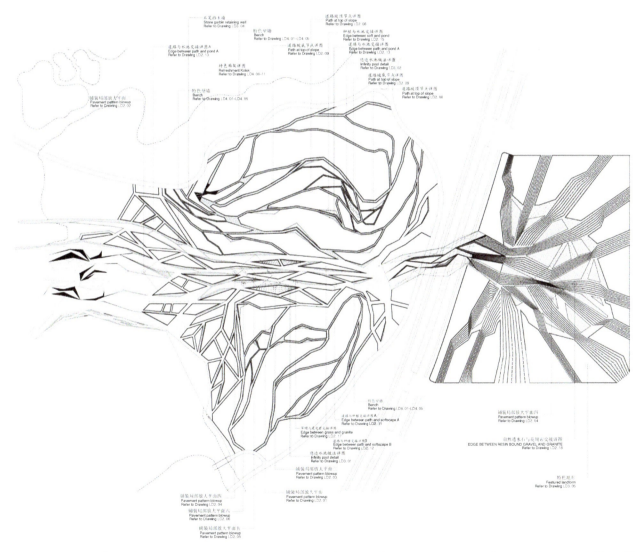

8.1 Site plan of the Xi'an Horticultural Expo, showing the system of footpaths that cross the Guangyun entrance bridge through the varied fields of floral species of the Legacy Park to the Creativity Pavilion situated on the lakeside. Copyright: Plasma Studio and GroundLab.

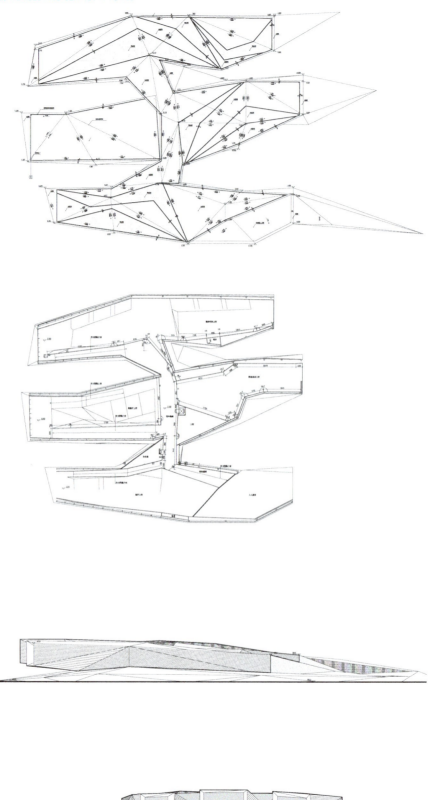

8.2 Roof plan, first-floor plan, front elevation and side elevation of the Xi'an Horticultural Expo Creativity Pavilion, showing the treatment of the envelope of the building as an extension of the surrounding articulated ground of the Legacy Park. Copyright: Plasma Studio and GroundLab.

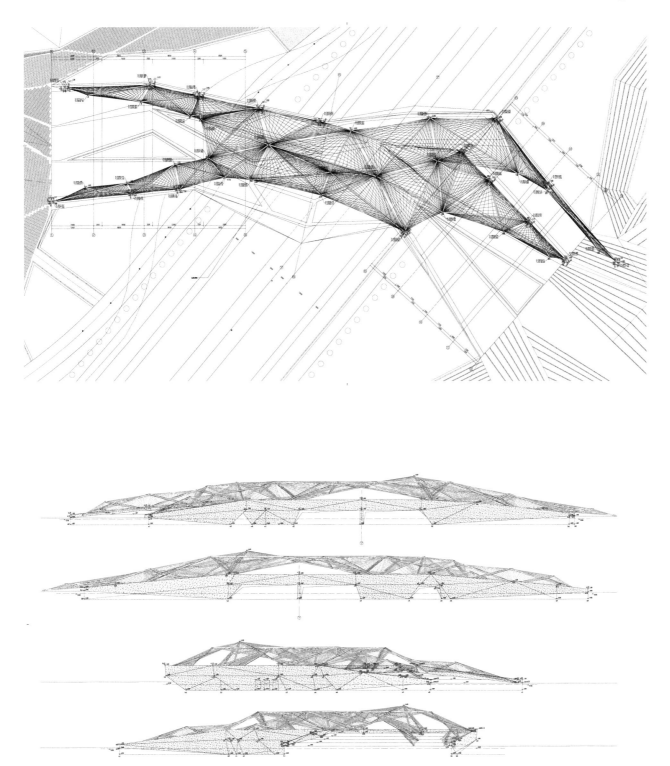

8.3 Plan and various elevations of the Xi'an Horticultural Expo Guangyun entrance bridge. There are two elements at work that both act as extensions of the ground: (1) the bridge itself that, in addition to having pedestrian pathways, also has pools and extended areas of planting that make the bridge a 'place' to view from and rest, and (2) the trellised canopy structure that will be naturally overgrown with climbing vegetation, thus forming a green canopy. Copyright: Plasma Studio and GroundLab.

8.4 Night-time view of the Xi'an Horticultural Expo, showing the integrated lighting scheme that highlights the floral patchwork planting of the Legacy Park which runs from the Guangyun entrance bridge to the Creativity Pavilion. Copyright: Plasma Studio and GroundLab. Photography: Cristobal Palma.

Plasma Studio and GroundLab used the given topography as a source for a new set of formal strategies that incorporates sinuous pathways, landscape planting and water features which together generate a networked terrain condition that parcels the vast landscape. With 12 million visitors over a six-month period (10,000 per day on average), circulation and crowd management constituted a primary consideration and design parameter. The pathways with their varying widths and gradients of slopes naturally mediated the velocity and pace of movement of visitors to the Expo. This averted crowding and long queues, and access to the Creativity Centre and the Greenhouse. The landscape in which the network of pathways is embedded constitutes a hybridized landscape of natural and artificial systems that culminate in a series of waterscapes. With the need for large amounts of irrigation for this proposal, Plasma Studio and GroundLab saw this as an opportunity to use the Expo as an initial investment in the transformation of the site for the future, a future of natural and artificial conditions combined into a synergistic sustainable system that becomes maintenance-free over time. This was set out by using terrain and pathways for collecting and channelling rainwater, allowing run-off to flow into the wetland areas where it is cleaned through passive methods of filtration, and subsequently dispersed for irrigation. By having these water bodies in close proximity with the pathways they begin to act as a passive cooling element and, where the waters aggregate into larger pools, these areas become moments to pause in oasis-like conditions.

The three built structures for the Expo, the Creativity Pavilion, the Greenhouse and the Guangyun entrance bridge, are placed strategically within the plan of the scheme.

The Creativity Pavilion and the Guangyun entrance bridge are located on the north side of the Horticultural Expo and at the intersections of the major pathways within the pedestrian network. The bridge connects the two parts of the site that are divided by a major road and acts as the primary orientation point for the visitors that arrive at the Expo, channelling them from the entry plaza into the main Expo area and back along three bands of circulation. Moreover, the bridge stands out as a physical

8.5 View of the Xi'an Horticultural Expo, looking from the Creativity Pavilion along the primary bundled pedestrian pathways to the Guangyun entrance bridge, highlighting the variation of occupation of the vast landscape. Copyright: Plasma Studio and GroundLab. Photography: Cristobal Palma.

8.6 View of the Xi'an Horticultural Expo Creativity Pavilion, showing the cantilevered projection of the scheme's conceptual ground. Copyright: Plasma Studio and GroundLab. Photography: Cristobal Palma.

8.7 Night-time view of the Xi'an Horticultural Expo Guangyun entrance bridge, showing the integrated lighting scheme in the tensegrity canopy, transforming what would be read as pure infrastructure into a place to be experienced. Copyright: Plasma Studio and GroundLab. Photography: Cristobal Palma.

8.8 The Xi'an Horticultural Expo Greenhouse, which is situated across the lake from the Creativity Pavilion, is embedded in the terrain and deploys folded transparent surfaces as a tectonic landscape infill. Copyright: Plasma Studio and GroundLab. Photography: Cristobal Palma.

indicator of the Expo's theme 'Flowing Gardens' as it weaves and braids together the circulation paths, planting, water features, along with a tensegrity shading canopy which itself acts as a hovering ground for climbing vegetation. The Creativity Pavilion is located at the lake's edge on an axis with the Guangyun entrance bridge. This is also the starting point for the ferryboats that cross the lake to the Greenhouse. The volume of the Creativity Pavilion derives from extending the terrain into a landscaped interior event space, which is organized as three cantilevering volumes that project out over the lake. The Greenhouse is located on the island and embedded within the landscape, by way of a cut in the ground that takes visitors through three different zones of varied climates and environments. The envelope is made up of a tessellated transparent mesh. The formal move of tessellation stitches smoothly across the cuts into the ground so as to suggest affiliation between enclosure and ground. The transparency of the envelope allows the visitor to register the interior and exterior terrain conditions that change and modify as one traverses through it.

The scheme for the Xi'an Horticultural Expo offers a number of formal and organizational strategies for integrating landscape and architectures within an ecological scheme. This involves the use and articulation of landscape, infrastructural or architectural surfaces in a coherent and often synthesized mode, one that often transcends the exterior–interior threshold.

PROJECT 9
A THOUSAND GROUNDS: SPREEBOGEN
Berlin, Germany, 1992
Michael Hensel, Chul Kong, Nopadol Limwatanakul and Johan Bettum

This project was undertaken in the context of the Graduate Design Program at the Architectural Association in London in 1992/1993 (Directors: Jeffrey Kipnis and Donald Bates) and was therefore largely experimental in character. The search for and development of instrumental design methods was an integral part of the project and the research theme of tectonic landscapes.

This entry to the competition for a new governmental centre for Berlin in 1992 aimed at synthesizing architecture and landscape into a notionally non-decomposable tectonic landscape. Massing and interior spaces of the Federal Parliament, Chancellery and Council, the related offices, as well as the press conference, media, educational and foreign culture centres and exhibition areas, emerge from the sectional arrangement and intensification of folded and layered grounds. A large amount of interstitial and residual spaces resulting from intersecting volumes, multiple envelopes and extended thresholds were intended to provide sheltered yet non-climatized transition areas between exterior and interior for season- and weather-specific use. In order to provide flexible circulation and security arrangements 110 weirs were projected for the River Spree that were intended to enable selective drying or flooding of portions of the landscaped areas of the scheme. In addition to the changing waterscape, seasonally specific fields of native plant species were proposed as a rotational planting scheme. Changing water levels and density and continually changing datums established by the plant canopies were intended to shield, reveal or shelter public assembly areas. The latter are conceived of as spaces for both planned and unplanned events. Along the perimeter of the large competition site the landscape scheme was designed to blend seamlessly with the existing context of the surrounding neighbourhoods by way of continuous public landscape areas as well as gradual modification of the built fabric bordering or within the site.

The scheme was clearly emphasized in the main organizational aspects of the site, including landscape-related processes. Yet, the architectural scheme was only very generally defined as a series of guidelines for massing and landscape relations, and the project therefore remained quite elusive. Today, however, there exist a number of projects which begin to indicate how

9.1 A conceptual model indicates the fusion of landscape and built mass into one another, using colour-coding for the various surface systems that make up the *tectonic landscape*. Yellow and red denote the areas of massing enfolded within the landscape utilizing a box-within-box arrangement and multiple envelopes. Copyright: Hensel, Limwatanakul, Kong and Bettum. Photography: Limwatanakul and Hensel.

the architecture of the scheme could have been articulated. These include, for instance, Foreign Office Architects' Meydan – Umraniye Retail Complex & Multiplex (see p. 111), which demonstrates clearly how a tectonic landscape can be effectively

9.2 This programme and event map conveys information about activities, circulation, landscape items and surfaces for programme and public appropriation, assembly fields, time-specific plantation schemes and lighting systems, river regulation and flooding areas, in short all systems that organize the site and its specific provisions. *Top*: Overall programme and event map. *Bottom*: Detail of the map. Copyright: Hensel, Limwatanakul, Kong and Bettum.

9.3 This axonometric of landscape systems and massing elaborates spatial transitions and degrees of interiority in conjunction with landscape surfaces that make up the *tectonic landscape* together with other spatial elements such as season-specific plantation instructions, 110 weirs for regulating the river, etc. *Top*: Overall axonometric. *Bottom*: Detail of the axonometric. Copyright: Hensel, Limwatanakul, Kong and Bettum.

9.4 This colour axonometric consists of ten layers serving as an instrumental tool to organize the detailed landscape and massing interaction. Copyright: Hensel, Limwatanakul, Kong and Bettum.

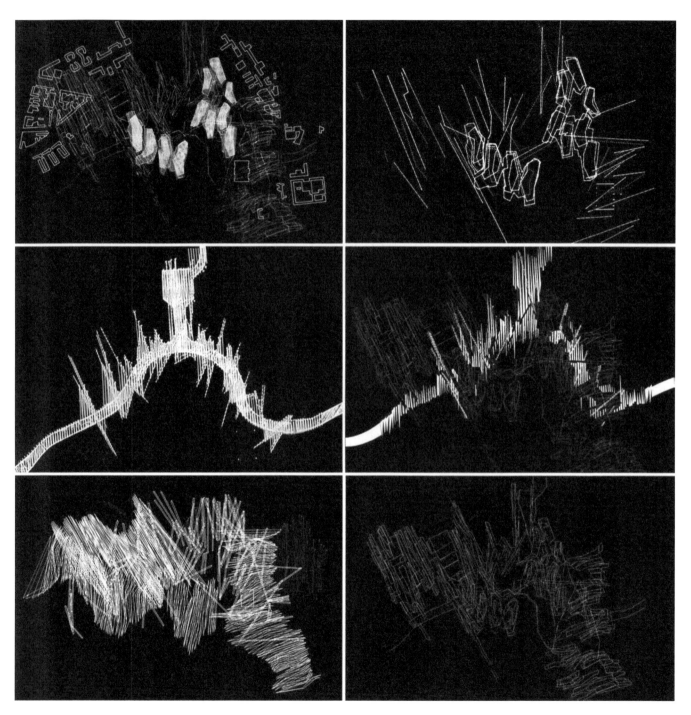

9.5 These diagrams describe various landscape systems and their interaction, such as (1) existing and proposed massing and proposed tectonic landscape (*top left*); (2) proposed massing and ground lighting system (*top right*); (3) the River Spree and the proposed 110 weirs (*centre left*); (4) minimum water level in the site and accordingly available assembly fields (*centre right*); (5) all landscaped areas and systems (*bottom left*), and (6) all available assembly and event areas (*bottom right*). Copyright: Hensel, Limwatanakul, Kong and Bettum.

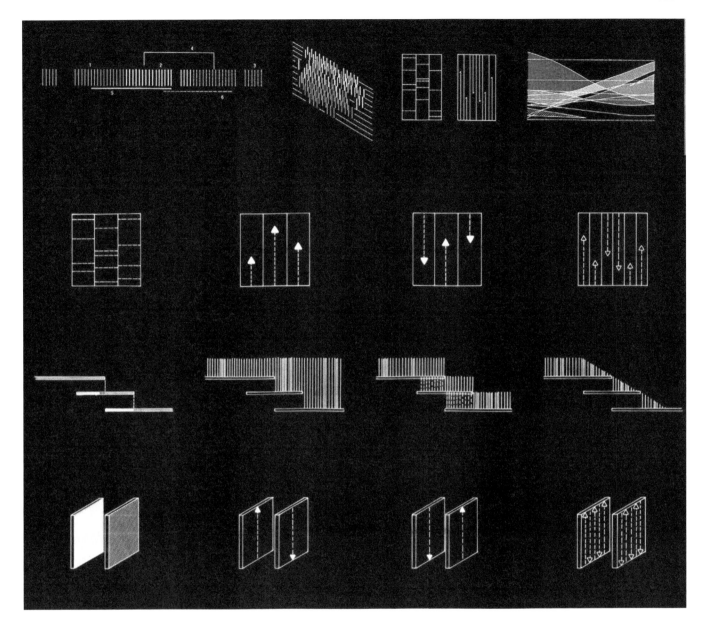

9.6 These diagrams describe a number of strategies relating to the planting scheme for the tectonic landscape, including: (1) the interaction between fauna and massing and its seasonal variations (*top row*); (2) plant distribution and rotation (*second row from the top*), and (3) sectional strategy for planting and the provisional datum resulting from the plant canopies, as well as their variation over time (bottom rows). Copyright: Hensel, Limwatanakul, Kong and Bettum.

articulated. At the same time the Spreebogen – The 'A Thousand Grounds' project – can contribute some insights into how an urban fabric may be thought of which comprises projects such as Foreign Office Architects' Meydan – Umraniye Retail Complex & Multiplex.

Moreover, hints may be taken from other projects such as Mendes da Rocha's MuBE project (see p. 87) and Miralles and Pinós' Olympic Archery Range (see p. 230) that both articulate tectonic landscapes, RCR's Marquee Les Cols (see p. 99) in the way it defines an architecture lightly set within a constructed terrain, and Helen & Hard's Geopark playground (see p. 172) in the way it materializes provisional ground conditions. The first two projects can contribute an approach to the stereotomic landscape elements of the A Thousand Grounds scheme, while the latter two can help articulate a relation between the tectonic elements and the constructed ground and landscape of the scheme, as well as its micro-sectional articulation respectively.

PROJECT 10
YOKOHAMA INTERNATIONAL PORT TERMINAL
Yokohama, Japan, 1995 to 2002
Foreign Office Architects

The Yokohama International Port Terminal by Foreign Office Architects (FOA) strikes with surprise, as it is on the one hand thoroughly modernist in character while on the other hand it just as thoroughly transcends its modernist characteristics. The project clearly features Le Corbusier's five points of architecture, namely pilotis, free façade, free plan, ribbon windows and roof garden, and his notion of the architectural promenade as perhaps most clearly embodied in his seminal Villa Savoye (1929–1931).

Yet, one needs to imagine Villa Savoy, stretched to 400 metres in length and 70 metres in width, with one short end compressed into a single layer from which all levels of the building bifurcate and the organization of which evolves from a looped circulation pattern.

FOA won the international design competition for the new terminal in 1995.

10.1   Aerial view of the Yokohama International Port Terminal showing the terminal as an extension of the city infrastructure and green spaces, as well as a distinctly landscaped surface. From this viewpoint the presence of the building as a separate entity diminishes and what comes to the fore is a non-discrete architecture at the city scale. Copyright: Foreign Office Architects. Photography: Satoru Mishima.

10.2 View of the end of the pier. Copyright: Foreign Office Architects. Photography: Satoru Mishima.

10.3 View of the entrance to the terminal and the landscape roof. Here all surfaces of the building meet in a circulation plaza. Copyright: Foreign Office Architects. Photography: Satoru Mishima.

10.4 View of the ramped spaces that constitute extended thresholds between the parking level, terminal hall and the landscape roof. The appearance is partly one of burrowed spaces within a thick ground and partly suggests the continuation of the timber decking of the landscaped roof level. Copyright: Foreign Office Architects. Photography: Satoru Mishima.

Based on the starting concept 'ni-wa-minato' proposed by the client, which addresses a mediation between harbour and garden, as well as the local citizens and the world, the scheme integrates public spaces and the controlled spaces of the terminal. In so doing the scheme constitutes a 'hybridisation between a shed like canopy – a non-discrete container – and a ground' (Moussavi and Zaera Polo 1995: 14).

FOA took explicit interest in how circulation could shape space with circulation organized as loops and choices between multiple paths through the building. This was articulated and intensified by the articulation of the building surface which coordinates and correlates circulation, activities and events.

The scheme was developed through a sectional approach that deployed serial sections and that treated the entire built volume as a thick ground. Inspired by the principles of origami, the traditional Japanese art of paper folding, the folding of the surfaces of the project produces creases along the length of the building volume that provide both paths as well as structural capacity.

In deploying this approach across scales, the initial scheme featured an interesting approach towards articulating the surfaces that the architects termed 'mille-feuille' and that make up the building as a series of self-similar folded steel sheets in various sizes nested within one another. In articulating the scheme in this way the project transcends the traditional modernist paradigm of separating building elements in functional terms.

The final scheme adapts the structure to the continual changing in its cross-sectional requirements. Each section is particularized to create varying spatial conditions and provisions ranging from circulation paths to large halls to inclined areas that integrate stairs with seating for spectators, semi-sheltered conditions and so on.

This new ground defined by the scheme employs two primary and two secondary surface materials that define and provide for

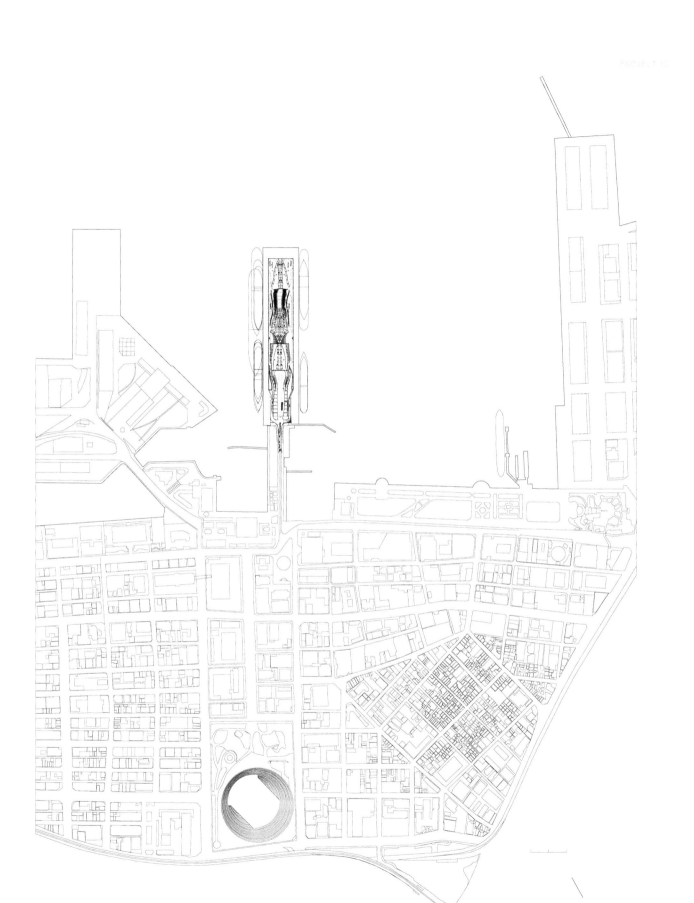

10.5 Site plan of the Yokohama International Port Terminal. Copyright: Foreign Office Architects.

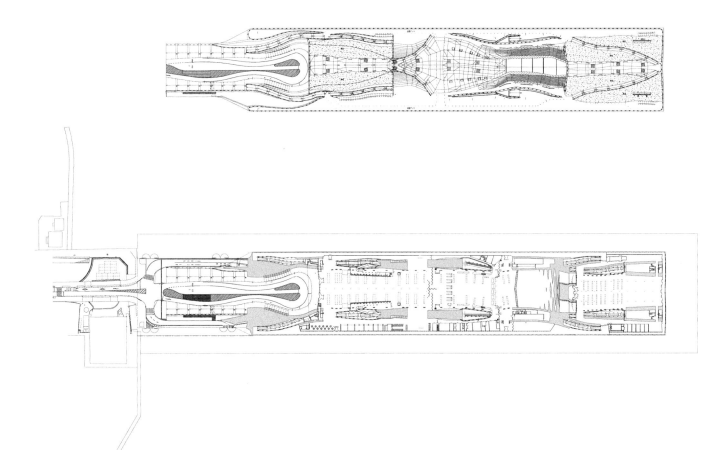

10.6 The plans of the Yokohama International Port Terminal show the two key levels of the scheme: (1) the landscape roof/park level and (2) the arrival/departure hall and exhibition hall level. Copyright: Foreign Office Architects.

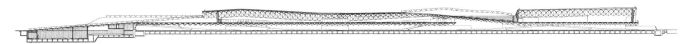

10.7 The long section through the terminal building shows how the cross-sectional folded structural elements aggregate into a thick multi-layered ground, which incorporates a smooth, undulating landscape roof that connects to the city fabric, and provides varied interior spaces for the arrival/departure hall, exhibition spaces and related infrastructures. Copyright: Foreign Office Architects.

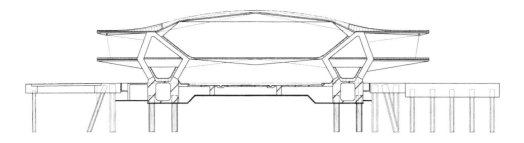
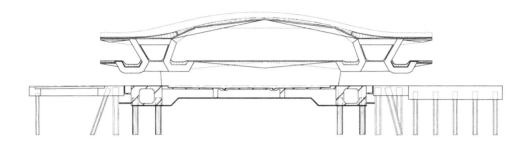
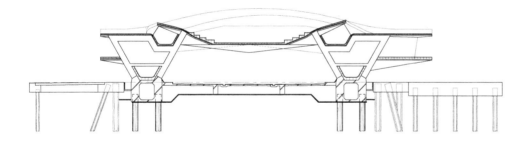
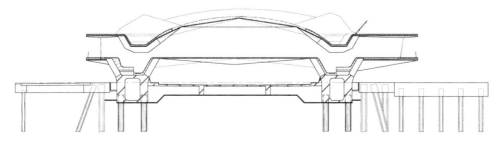

10.8 These four cross-sections show the sectional variation that runs through the scheme, as well as the spatial transition from interior, to semi-interior exterior, to full exterior and back again. Copyright: Foreign Office Architects.

the use of these surfaces. These include the painted steel plate structure that defines the underside of the new ground condition and which also becomes the ceiling surface of the interior spaces and the timber surface which defines the walkable areas and that becomes the roof landscape and the floor of the programmed interior spaces. Both of these surface materials have a grain and directionality to them. The folded steel plate's directionality and grain are linked with the structural demands of span and to the cross-sectional spatial requirements that it needs to achieve. Where it defines the ceiling plane of the interior it acts additionally as a lighting reflector to illuminate the deep spaces, and some areas of the surface are perforated to accommodate air-conditioning systems located between that surface and the timber surface of the roof. The timber surface has a grain operating within a more intimate human scale of tactility. This is the surface with which visitors come more readily into contact. This surface has a directionality that is oriented opposite to the direction of the steel surfaces. Running along the length of the building this surface grain leads visitors into and on to it, and provides for transitional spaces such as ramps and steps, as well as informal areas for seating and events. The timber used for this project is a Brazilian hardwood called Ipe that is commonly used in the construction of piers, which is resistant to weathering and acquires a grey coloration. In so doing this subtle change begins to define the transition between interior and exterior based on the tonal shift of the same material: as one walks across the roof landscape one notices the gradient shifts in tones from a lighter grey to a darker richer coloration.

The secondary materials are the grass patches on the roof surfaces and the vertical surfaces of glazing that complete the climatic enclosure of the scheme. The former is used on the exterior roof landscape; it provides areas for informal use and implies the extension of the surrounding public gardens. In so doing the combination of timber decking and grass surfaces articulates the concept of 'ni-wa-minato', the mediation between harbour and garden, on a material scale. The broad range of public activities that take place on the roof landscape confirms the validity of FOA's intentions and approach to the design of a public landscape. Given the programmatic needs of the passenger terminal and its location on a pier, the perimeter of the scheme needed to be clearly demarcated and, when seen from a distance at pedestrian level, the object remains necessarily accentuated. Yet, when approaching the project and entering it, the object no longer takes primacy and recedes, giving way to the perception of various ways of inhabiting ground. In a series of unbuilt projects with different, more gradual perimeter conditions FOA experimented with a similar design approach, thus blending the respective schemes in such ways that give no primacy to the architectural object, while at the same time maintaining distinct architectural traits. In this respect it is of interest to compare the Yokohama scheme with their later project for the Meydan Retail Complex & Multiplex in Istanbul, Turkey (see p. 111).

PROJECT 11
TURF CITY
Reykjavik, Iceland, 2008
Nekton Design
Jeffrey Paul Turko & Gudjon Thor Erledsson

Designed in 2008 by Nekton Design, the Turf City masterplan was a finalist entry in the Vatnsmyri 102 Reykjavik masterplan competition. The competition rules stipulated the redevelopment of the existing domestic airport that borders the city of Reykjavik to its south.

The Turf City project constitutes a synthesis between a further development of the mat-building typology and a multiple ground and continuous surface approaches. In so doing, the project explored the spatial and organizational relationships produced between building mass and envelopes, the existing and projected landscape and ground conditions, and how these conditions may be fused into a coherent scheme that displays a strong relation to the local setting and spatial and formal ambience that conveyed Icelandic traits and sensibilities. A driving conceptual theme was that of the traditional Icelandic turf house which combines building envelope and landscape as a thick constructed ground. Thus, the site was conceptually treated as a city-sized turf house. Although the proposal covered a range of criteria and strategic aims, the two elements that were key in its formation were the strategies for the production of an integrated urban fabric and landscape.

The Turf City scheme constitutes a series of multiple ground conditions, each with its own continuous surfaces as a new urban terrain and roofscape: sport and leisure scapes as landscaped surfaces for human use, landscape surfaces reserved for other species, etc. This new terrain is articulated according to the programme and occupation of the plan and registers sectionally as a change in height and in the degree of articulation of the

11.1 Rendered view of Turf City showing the massing organized in a mat-building-type manner and its relation to the surround context (i.e. the existing city fabric of Reykjavik in terms of building heights), and to the wider landscape in terms of surface continuity. Copyright: Nekton Design.

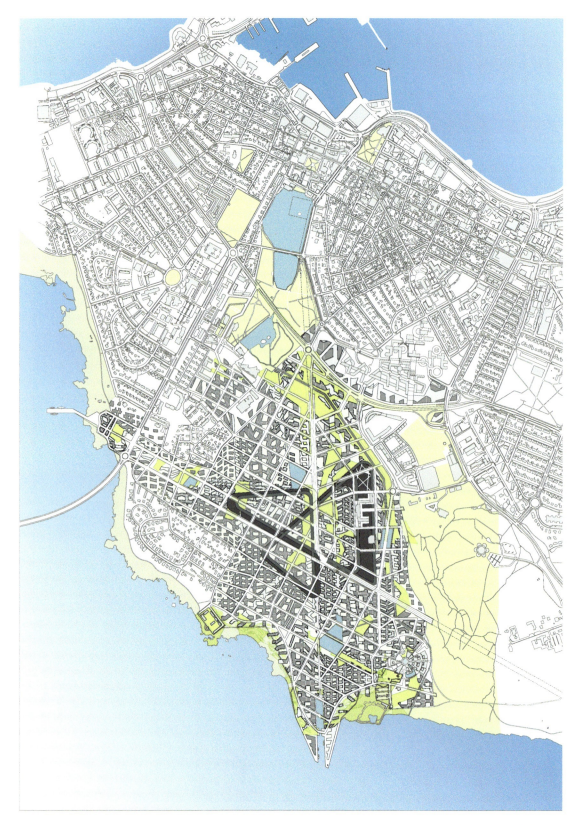

11.2 Masterplan of Turf City, showing the use of the existing Reykjavik city grid as a device to proportion the new urban fabric, with the new city block type being articulated by the surrounding grain of built fabrics and the projection of the local landscape features and parklands. Copyright: Nekton Design.

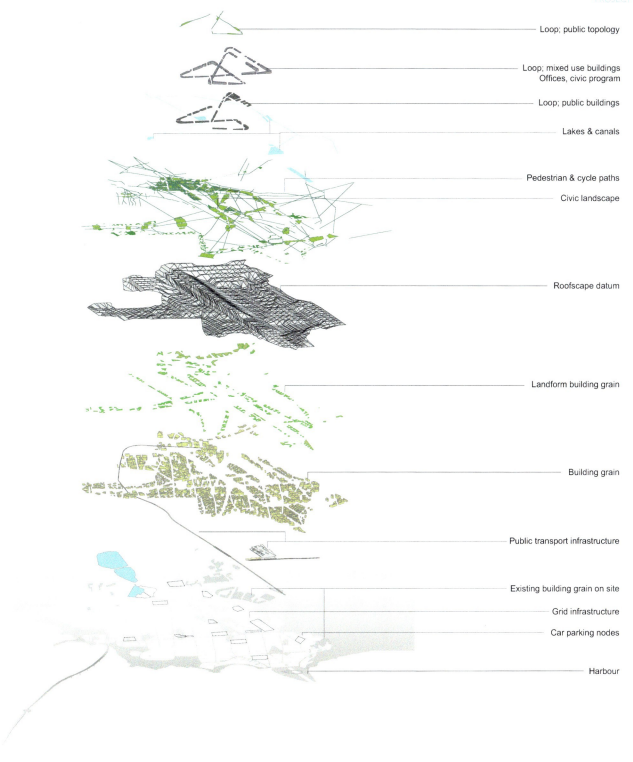

11.3 Exploded axonometric of the Turf City masterplan, showing (1) the civic buildings placed in the footprint of the old runways; (2) the civic landscape which acts as the primary infrastructure that connects the old city to the new through boulevards, cycle paths and a network of parklands and canals; (3) the land-form buildings conceptually informed by the Turf House vernacular that are positioned along some of the main paths of the civic landscape, and the various continuous surfaces that articulate the roofscape datum; and (4) the city grid that acts as the framework for infrastructures and services. Copyright: Nekton Design.

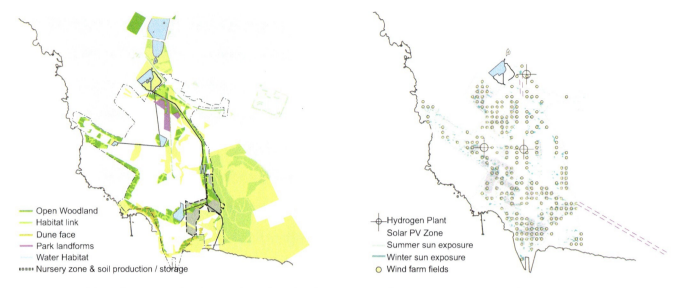

11.4 Diagrams of the Turf City masterplan, showing the ecological and energy strategy for the scheme. The ecological strategy offers varied landscapes and habitats for local species and wildlife to evolve and incorporates a strategy for replenishing the parklands and ground soil with zones dedicated to its production and storage via nurseries. The energy strategies include both mechanical and passive options, from solar PV zones to capture energy, to offering zones for sun exposure during the summer and winter months. Copyright: Nekton Design.

terrain. This fabric of 150 hectares was then organized by grid equivalent with that of Reykjavik city, which divides the massive ground into manageable territories for finer articulation, as well as proportionally relating the new fabric to the existing urban grain. The plan was developed through the strategic use of positioning and expanding the current landscape conditions that were present and used as the key infrastructural elements that connect existing conditions into the new scheme. This included the existing parks and nature reserves; the site bordered one of the few areas in Reykjavik with dense tree foliage, as well as the coastline that borders the site to the south. To the north of the site the existing open park extends southward into the new fabric acting as a passive infrastructure that includes cycle paths and walkways. In addition to this, a new network of canals also extends southward, creating an intricate water system and new ponds that act as new habitats and focal points for new residential districts and which support present ecologies. This expansion from the north also includes the Nordic House designed by Alvar Aalto whose original scheme included a nature reserve water feature that was integrated into the Turf City scheme. From the east of the site where the current woodland area is located there was proposed an expansion westward which would see the implementation of a tree nursery as a vital part of an expanded woodland condition across the site. To the south of the site the shoreline was intended to be reinforced with the new woodland, as well as the implementation of new dune land forms to support a range of microclimates and ecological niches. The landscape and urban fabric strategies are merged in the formation of the building mass. Acting as building, landscape and infrastructure, this element is stitched into the network of foot and cycle paths, as well as canals and lakes and woodland. These elements were intended to culminate in a city fabric with human comfort and multi-species provisions as a priority. Comfort in the urban fabric of Reykjavik is determined mainly by high winds rather than by low temperatures. The roof stratum encourages the wind to skim over the planned development and the building articulation is planned to shelter key public areas from strong winds. The expansion of the landscape features such as the woodland and the strategic placement of the building mass as hard landscape also act as windbreaks for open spaces.

Located at the centre of the masterplan are the looped public buildings that take their planar formation from the runway corridors from the old airport. These buildings act as the primary hub for public transport and establish a core that connects to the various areas of the masterplan. The loop houses a new bus terminal for Reykjavik as well as a proposed high-speed rail link to Keflavik international airport.

The formation of the scheme on the scale of the city block was akin to the mat-building typology. This low and horizontal building type became the underpinning architectural departure point for the proposed ground-related urbanism. Most of the urban fabric was proposed within a single- to double-storey

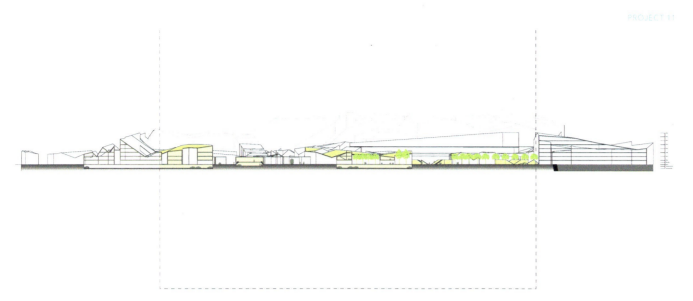

11.5 One general section across the Turf City masterplan, looking to the north, showing the variation of the scale and density of the new city fabric with the maximum height of the fabric sitting on the most northern position of the scheme (background). In the foreground one gets a sense of the sectional grain of the standard building fabric as well as the single-storey land-form buildings. Copyright: Nekton Design.

11.6 Detail plan of the Turf City masterplan fabric, showing the mix of conditions on the scale of the city block: the figuration of the looping public buildings is integrated with the mat-building-type fabric of the city blocks and the Turf House-type land-form buildings. Parkland, gardens and unprogrammed public spaces begin to filter across and through these fabrics in section. Copyright: Nekton Design.

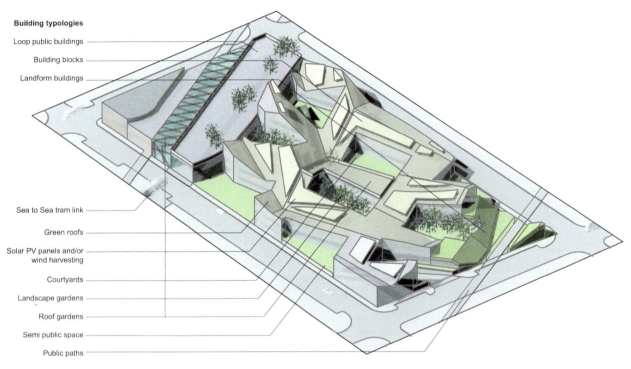

11.7 Detail of axonometric, showing a city block of the Turf City masterplan scheme, which includes the loop public building, the mat-building blocks and the land-form buildings. Also shown is the integration of the varied landscapes and infrastructures. Copyright: Nekton Design.

height range and, with the prevailing environmental constraints of high winds and limited sunlight in winter months, the use of a conventional figure–ground approach to the block parcelled plan was avoided. The production of a mat urbanism that focused mainly on the articulation of its section was paramount. This led to the plans being articulated with courtyard insertions that were deployed on varied levels and with varied uses, with some being connected to the adjacent interiors and others being part of a larger parkland strategy.

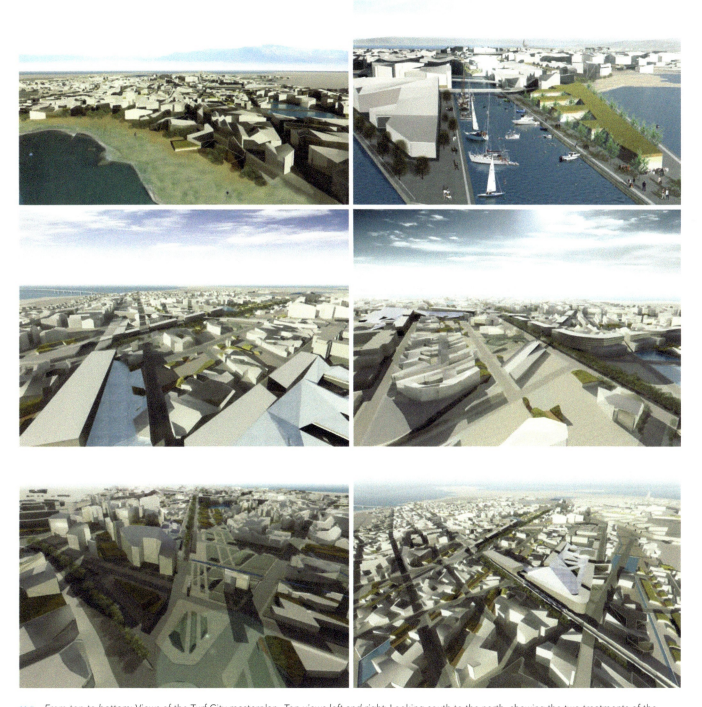

11.8 *From top to bottom*: Views of the Turf City masterplan. *Top views left and right*: Looking south to the north, showing the two treatments of the water's edge that includes the implementation of new grasslands, dunes and beaches and a new harbour. *Middle view left*: Looking across the scheme to the west showing an overview of the loop public building and how this is integrated into the surrounding fabric. *Middle view right*: Looking across the scheme to the south also showing an overview of the loop public building and how this is integrated into the surrounding fabric. *Bottom left*: Giving a view north to south looking down the main boulevard condition of parkland and infrastructure. *Bottom right*: Looking to the west with the new bus station and railway link to the international airport highlighted in the centre of the image. Copyright: Nekton Design.

PROJECT 12
BRAGA MUNICIPAL STADIUM
Braga, Portugal, 2003
Eduardo Souto de Moura

The 30,000-seat Braga Municipal Stadium was designed by the Portuguese architect Eduardo Souto de Moura and completed in 2003. Due to its location in the former Monte Castro quarry it features the nickname 'The Quarry' – a sobriquet funnily shared with Antoni Gaudí's Casa Milà. The project takes advantage of its setting in a remarkable way, with seating stands flanking only the sides of the pitch. The back of the pitch is open towards the rock face of the quarry, while its front opens on to the wider landscape and overlooks the lower lying city of Braga and the landscape beyond. The L-shaped quarry site entails that one stand is set against the rock face, while the other is free-standing and monumental, and provides the main entry area. Beneath the pitch the stands are connected by way of a 5,000-square-metre plaza.

The design of Braga Municipal Stadium resonates with that of the Leça da Palmeira Swimming Pool by Alvaro Siza (see p. 159) in the way it utilizes adjacent landscape features and opens to

12.1 The model photos of the Braga Municipal Stadium show the relation between the project and the quarry. The quarry delimits the stadium on two sides, on one side as the back of seating ranks and on the other as exposed to the rock face. The opposing seating ranks are free-standing and monumental. On the north side the stadium opens to the landscape. Copyright: Eduoardo Souto de Moura.

1- TICKET OFFICE
2- PARKING
3- ENTRANCE SQUARE
4- ENTRANCE GATES
5- UEFA TEMPORARY PARKING
6- ALLEY
7- WATER LINE
8- EAST SQUARE (LOWER LEVEL)
9- EAST STAND
10- TRAIL
11- FIELD
12- WEST STAND
13- WEST SQUARE (UPPER LEVEL)
14- GRASS STORAGE BUILDING
15- VIP PARKING
16- TV COMPOUND

SITE PLAN

The site plan reveals how terrain form and building elements are correlated in the design in order to articulate a unique stadium that bears a close relation to its context. Copyright: Eduardo Souto de Moura.

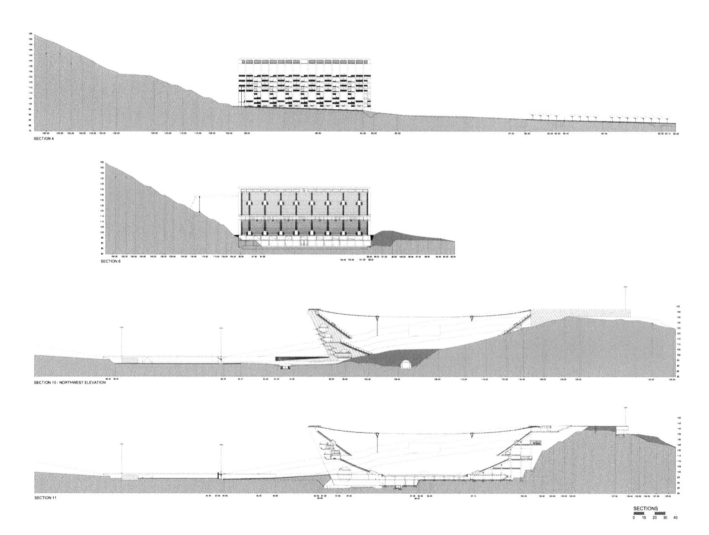

12.3 Various sections of the stadium, showing its relation to the terrain form. Copyright: Eduardo Souto de Moura.

the wider landscape, thus embedding the project comfortably into its setting. In the case of the stadium this is done without relinquishing the possibility to emphasize parts of the building as monumental, while de-emphasizing the architectural object as a whole. The project also resonates with RCR Arquitectes' Marquee at Les Cols (see p. 99) in the way in which the roof is articulated and how it is aligned on one side of the stadium with the higher terrain level of the quarry and, in so doing, suggests a second yet provisional datum. In this way the stadium seems halfway part of the ground, while on the other hand contrasting it as both a constructed landscape and clearly defined architecture on the opposing side. Open space continues through the stadium from the higher altitude of the quarry through its exposed slope and into the wider landscape. There is never any uncertainty

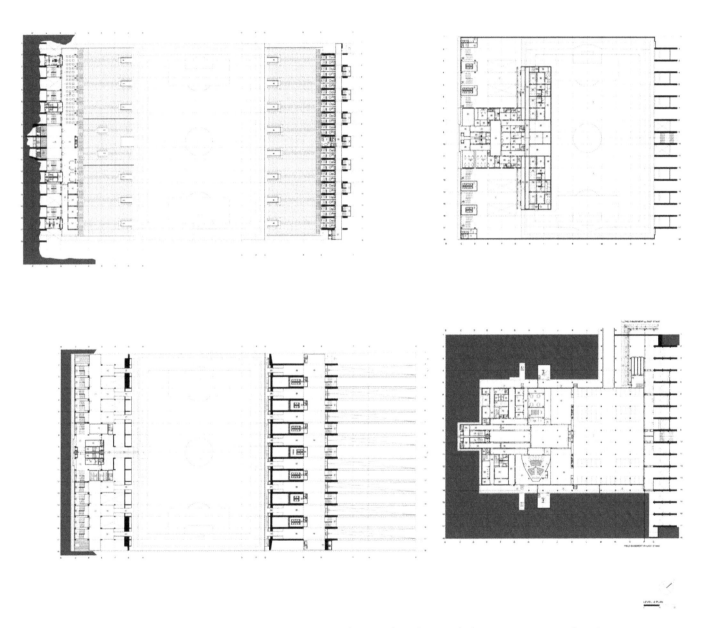

12.4 Various plans of the Braga Municipal Stadium, showing the seating ranks, vertical circulation and subterranean connection from the entrance area to the seating ranks that are placed against the rock face of the quarry. Copyright: Eduardo Souto de Moura.

12.5 This photo, which was taken at a higher vantage point, shows how the stadium sits within the quarry with the roof on one side aligning with the higher level of the quarry, and the seating ranks on the other side constituting the free-standing monumental part of the stadium. Also evident is the open continuous space through the stadium that connects it with the wider landscape. Photography: Bjarte Stav.

12.6 This photo shows the monumental free-standing part of the stadium, which serves as the main entry area to the stadium. Photography: Bjarte Stav.

12.7 In this photo the open space to the back of the stadium and the rock face of the quarry may be seen. Photography: Bjarte Stav.

12.8 This photo was taken from a higher vantage point at the exposed rock face of the quarry at the back of the stadium. At the back of the pitch both terrain and vegetation was left as it was. In the far distance the city lights of Braga may be discerned. Photography: Bjarte Stav.

as to where one is located, nor does the stadium become an entirely inaccessible space when there is no match being played. At any time its space remains part of the visual continuity of the wider landscape. With this, the question arises how this design approach may be rearticulated to meet dense urban settings or, to turn the question around, how urban settings may be thought of in which such an approach would be momentous. It would not be too challenging to imagine a project like this in the context of landscape urbanism-type settings such as the Turf City scheme (see p. 145) in which the wider landscape is largely constructed and enmeshed with layers of natural systems. In an urban context it would also be conceivable that the large subterranean plaza of the Braga Municipal Stadium is part of a more extensive public space, whether above or below ground, with an alternating sectional location across the urban fabric.

PROJECT 13
SWIMMING POOL
Leça da Palmeira, Portugal, 1966
Álvaro Siza

The Swimming Pool in Leça da Palmeira is one of the earliest and most striking projects by the eminent Portuguese architect Álvaro Siza. The project is located between the main boulevard and boardwalk along the coast of the Atlantic Ocean and the natural seashore, which consists of sandy beach strewn with rocky outcrops. Between the boulevard and the beach the terrain drops a few metres, a change that is accommodated by a retaining wall.

The swimming pool's facilities are placed against this wall and, due to the sectional change, they are not immediately visible from the boardwalk. Ramps lead down to the facilities, which are austere in material expression using only cast concrete for exterior walls and roofs and concrete tiles on the floor. This choice of material enables the perception of a smooth transition from the boardwalk into the swimming pool's facilities. However, the

13.1 This aerial photo of the Swimming Pool in Leça da Palmeira shows the entrance area and facilities located along the sectional drop between the promenade and the beach. The pools are integrated into the natural landscape of the beach. The pools seem to glow from within due to the white-painted surface of the pools. This element is perhaps the most strongly visible design feature of the project. Copyright: Fernando Guerra/VIEW/Corbis.

13.2 This aerial photo shows the way in which the large pool is integrated into the natural landscape of the beach. Existing landscape features such as the terrain form and the rocks are used to define the location, extent and parts of the perimeter of the pool. The added architectural elements complete the perimeter, pool floor and access platform and stairs. Other than that, all natural features remain exactly as found. Copyright: Fernando Guerra/VIEW/Corbis.

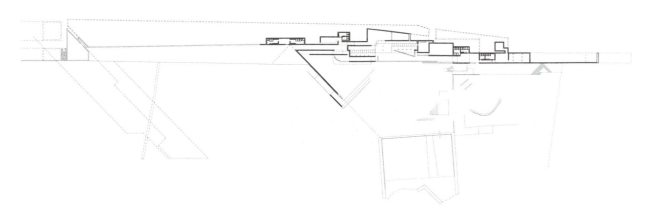

13.3 Elevation and plan of the Swimming Pool in Leça da Palmeira. Redrawn by Ricardo Rodrigues Ferreira.

13.4 When approached from the boardwalk, the Swimming Pool in Leça da Palmeira is almost entirely unnoticeable. Its facilities barely project above the low wall along the boardwalk. Only a modest sign announces its presence. Photography: David Leatherbarrow.

13.5 The materials used for the facilities are entirely unassuming: concrete, stone and wood with a plain finish. *Top*: Entrance area. *Bottom*: Changing rooms. Photography: David Leatherbarrow.

13.6 Both the small and the large pool are carefully integrated and in parts formed by natural landscape features. Photography: David Leatherbarrow.

13.7 Constructed elements and chosen materials complement the existing landscape features. Both are sensitively integrated into a scheme that remains non-discrete, although all its newly introduced elements are clearly noticeable. Photography: David Leatherbarrow.

13.8 From a lower vantage point the new introduced elements step back due to their coloration and texture, which correspond with those of the natural features of the site. Only the turquoise colour of the water of the pool indicates that something special is located in this setting. Photography: David Leatherbarrow.

perception changes dramatically when entering the changing rooms. Here the use of wood treated with oil together with sparse opening for natural light from above and the wet shimmer of the concrete surfaces create the feel of a cavernous space carved into the ground, even though this is clearly not the case. The main volumes of the project are articulated by horizontal and vertical concrete surfaces that often do not meet in corners or that are not within the same plane, thus recalling the approach to a more continuous space pursued by Frank Lloyd Wright. This results in the perception that the volume is provisional in spite of the heavy material used. The gaps between vertical surfaces result often in the absence of corners and allow glimpses of spaces beyond. In so doing this relatively small project appears upon approach not only open to the sky as one descends the ramped space, but also suggests in a subtle way a horizontal spatial continuity that is not dependent on literal transparency of materials. This experience of a subtly dissolved enclosure alone is remarkable; however, another equally stunning experience is given by the way the pools are set into the natural sandy and rocky shore.

Here natural features of the landscape such as rocky outcrops are used to define the perimeter of the large pool by adding only the length of concrete wall necessary to enclose and hold the water body of the pool. A similar strategy is used for the smaller pool as well. The horizontal concrete surfaces of the sundeck, of ramps and of stairs are interspersed with rocks cutting into the surface and with sand burying corners. When examining aerial photos of the project, uncertainty arises as to what preceded what: was the landscape here first and did the architecture encroach upon it to enter into a symbiotic relation? Or was it the other way around? This remarkable project really sets the tone for how to negotiate a relation between architecture and terrain that transcends the typical tabula rasa attitude of commonplace architecture. One feels reminded of sensibilities that are abundant in particular vernacular traditions that link architecture and terrain in subtle and differentiated ways. Hence, where such land form exists it would thus seem futile to construct one in its stead.

PROJECT 14
ASPHALT SPOT
Tokamashi, Japan, 2003
R&Sie(n)

R&Sie(n) is a transformative practice in many respects. François Roche described the general approach of R&Sie(n) to architectural design as follows:

> Our tools for the codification and transformation of territories work not through an ideal projection, but a local inventory ... this ... gives rise to our unstable and unique scenarios.
>
> (Roche 2004: 5)

The Asphalt Spot project, designed for the Echigo-Tsumari Art Triennial 2003 in Tokamashi, Niigata Prefecture, Japan, is a perfect demonstration of a scheme that is based on this approach, one that delivers to the beholder a destabilizing experience.

Asphalt Spot integrates a 300-square-metre outdoor exhibition space and parking lot into an undulating surface scheme, which reflects the surrounding close, mid- and far-distance terrain articulation, while extending it into the tectonic landscape of the project. The undulating asphalt surface, or 'elastic surface' as R&Sie(n) describe it, with its marked parking spaces and the leaning columns that support it in locations where it peels of the ground, appears as if deformed by abrupt geomorphic processes or seismic force. In this the perimeter of Asphalt Spot plays a critical role in the way it connects, peels away and disconnects from the surrounding ground datum of the site, locally resulting in undulant edges. This edge treatment evokes the images of the unnerving documentation of 'Galloping Gertie' – the Tacoma Narrows Bridge – that collapsed on 7 November 1940, apparently

14.1   This view of the Asphalt Spot project in its immediate context makes apparent its relation to the undulating adjacent and mid-distance terrain. In this way the project seems to seamlessly integrate with its setting in spite of plot boundaries and changes in the surface material. Copyright: R&Sie(n).

14.2 View of Asphalt Spot in relation to the near-, mid- and far-distance terrain. Copyright: R&Sie(n).

due to aeroelastic flutter, and other images of roads and asphalt surfaces that are split and rolled up due to the impact of strong earthquakes. The variation between smooth continuation of the terrain form adjacent to the plot and the asphalt surface and its splitting in various locations, with the asphalted surface continuing in the undercuts, diminishes the objectness of the scheme in spite of its strongly delineated footprint and abrupt material change from grass to asphalt.

This scheme resonates with Greg Lynn's description of burrowed space in that 'labyrinthine organisations such as the burrow … are essentially ungrounded, or rather they are not grounded by the single gravitational force of the earth's horizon' (Lynn 1998 [1994]: 95). While in some ways Asphalt Spot is clearly of the ground it is also off the ground, or rather it is part of the ground becoming ungrounded, momentarily suspended in mid-rupture that eliminates in conjunction with the surrounding landscape horizon as a fixed reference. In addition, all vertical references are eliminated. The columns that support the asphalt surface wherever it peels off the ground are poised at varied angles, as are the fence poles on the asphalt surface.

This generates a sense of disequilibrium and compels the visitor to remain in motion in search of spatial orientation and certainty. This effect is enhanced when parked cars are present, as they seem precariously suspended at odd angles and poised to momentarily roll off the asphalt surface. Fences cut across the parking spaces at an odd angle and appear randomly deposited

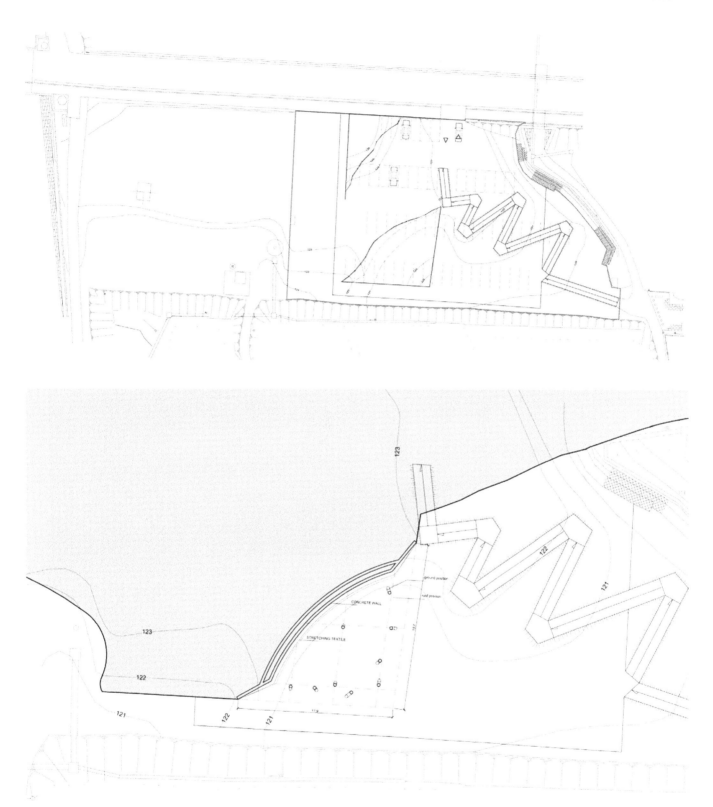

14.3 *Top*: Site plan. *Bottom*: Plan showing the relation of the project to the adjacent terrain and the space under the asphalt surface with its inclined columns. Copyright: R&Sie(n).

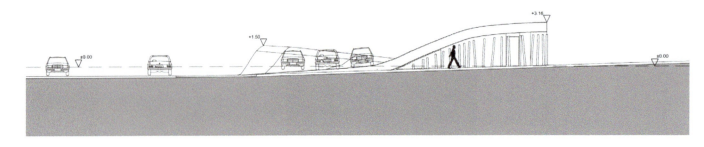

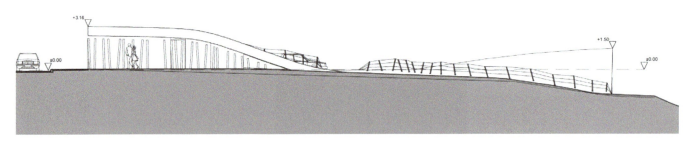

14.4 The elevations show both the continuity between the terrain and the asphalt surface and the discontinuities resulting from the peeling off of the asphalt surface from the ground. Copyright: R&Sie(n).

14.5 Various views of the project, showing terrain and surface continuity and local discontinuities. Copyright: R&Sie(n).

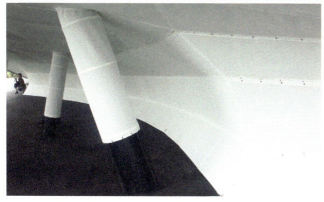

14.6 *Top to bottom*: Progression from moving atop to below the asphalt surface. Copyright: R&Sie(n).

14.7 Parked cars seem poised to start rolling down the inclined surface. Smaller undulations are placed in the asphalt surface to prevent this from happening. Copyright: R&Sie(n).

by the same force that seems to have deformed the entire project. Their purpose is to secure the raised edges of the asphalt surface without resorting to a perimeter balustrade that would diminish the experience of the sharp edge of the raised surface.

It is the particular combination between the spatial and material articulation of this tectonic landscape in conjunction with the surrounding setting that instils a sense of dynamic in the visitor and that renders the ground constituted by this project provisional. One question that arises concerns therefore how such an approach would have to be articulated when the surrounding context is more contrasting and densely built. Clearly the project would be perceived in a different way. It would also be of interest to enable a wide range of different planned and unplanned uses and activities of the project in order to examine how such an undulating surface affects use. Here the link to Paul Virilio's and Claude Parent's notion of the *oblique* and the way in which inclined surfaces foster dynamic activities seems obvious and worth further consideration.

PROJECT 15
GEOPARK PLAYGROUND
Stavanger, Norway, 2008
Helen & Hard

The Geopark Playground, designed by Helen & Hard for the Stavanger European Capital event in 2008, is located in the centre of Stavanger in direct adjacency to its lively waterfront and Petroleum Museum. As the project was originally intended to be on site for only one year it was possible to explore some quite radical ideas in its design. Placed instead of a formal representative square as an arrival point to the museum, the project discards the commonly expected characteristics of formal public space. It does so by giving full priority to a provocative design experiment based on the informal and itinerant theme of playground. The scheme negotiates the use of this urban surface and waterfront with harbour activities, displays of industrial objects related to the museum (to which the objects of the playground contribute), and other public activities. The coexistence and blending of this broad range of activities together with the material and micro-sectional articulation of the ground provides the experience of constant change and an intensely provisional public landscape.

The playground was designed in the shape of the Norwegian Troll natural gas and oilfield, which is located 2,000 to 3,000 metres below the seabed of the Norwegian sector of the North Sea. The design evolved around the theme of suggested geological strata and their geomorphic transformation. Beyond the design narrative the reference to the Troll field is less discernible, and perhaps less important, as another and much more momentous condition comes to the fore: the appearance of a random aggregation of stuff only momentarily deposited in its current place. Overlapping patches of sand, gravel, asphalt and industrial-grade plastics are strewn with industrial equipment acquired from abandoned oilfields, offshore bases and scrap-yards. Materials and artefacts seem as if washed ashore by the sea or spilled from within the museum on to the urban surface. The evoked image of petro-industrial jetsam, stranded tarpaulin, asphalt carpets, piles of sand and stone, and long-defunct gear accumulates to a peculiarly jolly signal-coloured industrial wasteland apparently deposited by force of nature and only marginally affected by human intervention. Weathering, decay and accumulative graffiti add to this perception. In so doing the project constitutes a playground of contingencies that are effortlessly

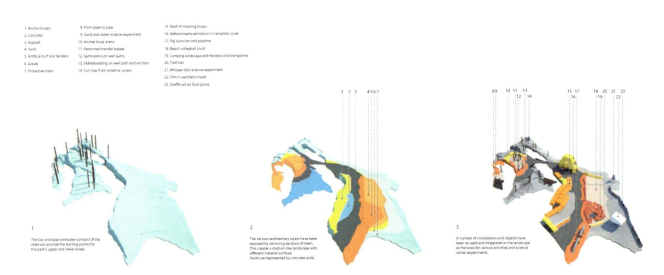

15.1 Three stages of the Geopark design development. *Left*: Terrain articulation. *Centre*: Material layering. *Right*: Objects and installations. Copyright: Helen & Hard.

15.2 Siteplan of the Geopark Playground. Copyright: Helen & Hard.

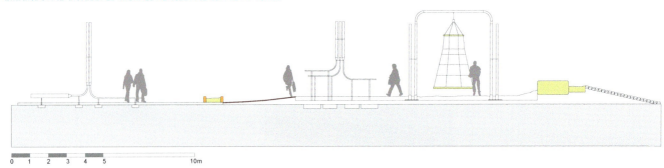

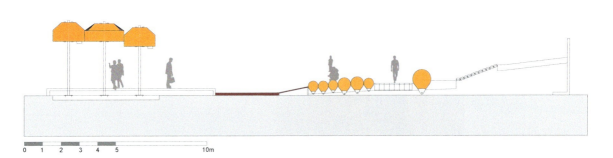

15.3 Sections showing the subtle terrain changes and object and installation placement. Copyright: Helen & Hard.

15.4 Overview of the Geopark Playground at the time of its completion in 2008. Photography: Emile Ashley.

15.5 Shipyard, industrial fair, playground? Along the waterfront harbour, exhibition and playground activities are directly adjacent. No sharp border separates them into distinct territories. Their related objects blend visually into a coherent (post-) industrial landscape. Photography: Michael Hensel.

absorbed by the scheme and that promote rather than diminish its specific characteristics.

The project was developed in two stages. Siv Stangeland and Reinhard Kropf of Helen & Hard explained that:

> The first stage … created a park sloping towards both the sun and the centre of the square. The second phase consisted of workshops with youth groups. Here the functions [of the landscaped square] were programmed for activities such as biking, climbing, exhibitions, concerts, jumping, ball games, and chilling out.
>
> (Braathen et al. 2012: 201)

Although, as mentioned above, the project was intended to have a lifespan of only one year, the chosen emphasis on temporality was by no means self-evident, as a much more formal and

15.6 Weathering, decay, graffiti. The impact of contingencies adds temporary layers to the strata and objects of the assemblage, and heightens its provisional character without necessarily suffering any perceivable loss of quality. Such markings have not reduced this popular playground to an abandoned junk yard. Photography: Michael Hensel.

conventional scheme could have been pursued. Instead the Geopark Playground constitutes an explicit design experiment and choice that projects noteworthy potentials for architectural and urban design:

1. Promoting close affiliations between activities, objects and ground-surface materials with those bordering the site emphasizes seamless transitions instead of strict separation.
2. The intensification of a scheme's specific features from its perimeter zones to its focal points yields its own individual character without necessitating separation from its setting.
3. Careful micro-sectional articulation and material assemblage of the ground surface promote subtle thresh-

15.7 Jetsam? Debris? Wandering dunes? The ground articulation of the Geopark Playground appears markedly provisional and suspended in ceaseless transformation. Minute sectional changes in height or surface inclination, and material changes and overlaps, subtly indicate miniscule thresholds or transitions between overlapping zones. Photography: Michael Hensel.

old conditions instead of strict separations (a move that requires the presence of common sense in cohabiting space).

It will be interesting to see the effect of these design choices implemented in schemes that may initially seem to offer fewer opportunities to do so than a playground. As for the playground site in Stavanger, there are currently efforts underway to replenish the project every three years with a new design for a playground by varying practices. If this takes place, some of the inherent qualities of the current scheme will hopefully be further explored and developed by the projects that may follow.

ENVELOPES

PROJECT 16
VILLA VPRO
Hilversum, The Netherlands, 1993 to 1997
MVRDV

The multi-storey broadcasting centre Villa VPRO, the first realized project by the Dutch practice MVRDV, is located in Hilversum in The Netherlands. It is the new headquarters of the VPRO broadcasting corporation, which was previously housed in a group of 13 villas. Maintaining a feel of the latter constituted a driving design intention of the project on the side of the client and the architects in order to preserve the informality of VPRO's previous work environment. In so doing the scheme is based on a three-part spatial strategy by (1) intersecting the rectangular enclosure of the project with exterior spaces, (2) spatial and surface continuity between the exterior spaces that intersect the rectangular volume and

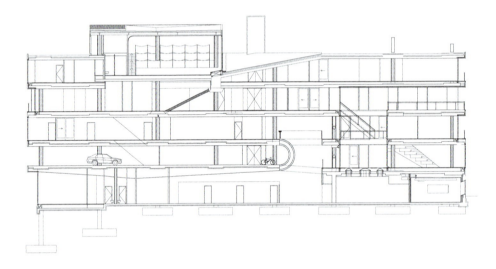

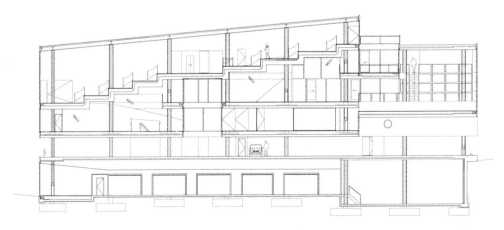

16.1 Cross-sections of Villa VPRO, showing the sectional variation of the scheme. *Top*: East–west section. *Bottom*: North–south section. Copyright: MVRDV.

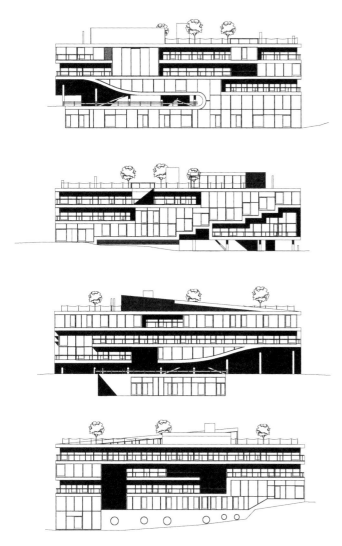

16.2 Elevations of Villa VPRO, showing the modifications of the building's envelope articulation that vary the relation between interior and exterior conditions. *Top to bottom*: North elevation, south elevation, east elevation and west elevation. Copyright: MVRDV.

interior spaces, and (3) an internal spatial organization based on a promenade between spatially distinct entities set within the overall enclosure. Using elements that reference the space of the villas, such as antique furniture, carpets and chandeliers, further enhances this.

The site in which the Villa VPRO sits is subjected to a zoning regulation that limits the height of the building to be no taller than the surrounding tree heights. This resulted in a constrained footprint and therefore a very compact volume, resulting at the time in the deepest plan building in Holland. This restriction resulted in a scheme that is reminiscent of contemporary versions of the mat-building typology, such as OMA's unbuilt Agadir Convention Centre (1990) or their realized Nexus World Housing project in Fukuoka, Japan (1991). These all constitute finite mat typologies with a fixed and non-expandable perimeter, which due to this constraint depend on a sectional strategy for organizing expansive and often habitable circulation and compact arrangements of varied spatial requirements and qualities.

Consequently the sectional approach of Villa VPRO reflects the spatial intentions. Yet, in so doing it has to straddle the difficult relation between the need for a standard column-and-slab arrangement à la Le Corbusier's Maison Domino in order to address the needs of a contemporary office building and, on the other hand, instances of a tectonic terrain form, whether smoothly inclined surfaces or steeply stepped and terraced zones. The element of ground is in this way addressed in various ways, involving the sectional articulation of the project, the exterior spaces that intersect the main rectangular volume, and the rearticulation of the ground on the roof garden of the project.

The slabs become the primary space-making device and element that define the building's envelope condition. Accordingly, the slabs were articulated by spatial extensions that extend vertically into the deepest parts of the plan and horizontally out to the façade edge. As discussed above, this strategy enables an extended interface of threshold between exterior and interior, and links with the surrounding landscape, allowing for daylight and airflow to reach into the deep plan and space of the project, and resulting in the impression of the offices being embedded into a tectonic extension of the landscape. This is enhanced by the varied landscaped connections between the slabs, thus articulating them to some extent as continuous surfaces using ramps, slopes, grand staircases and so on. This is

16.3　Floor plans, slab diagram and interior sketch of Villa VPRO. *Plans top to bottom*: Top row Level 4 and Level 5; middle row Level 2 and Level 3; bottom row Level 0 and Level 1. The slab diagram, which is the primary element of the building's envelope, shows how surfaces are punctuated and articulated in plan and section, allowing for visual and spatial connectivity between the varied landscapes of the interior, as well as having a connection to the landscape in which it is situated. Copyright: MVRDV.

best illustrated on Level 1 of the scheme, where the parking deck is given a canopy and a key entrance extends up into the plan.

The treatment of the slabs is coordinated with the placement spatial types that reference the previous arrangement of the 13 villas, such as terrace, attic, patio, corridor and salon. This collision of office and domesticated space in the interior is registered in the materials used and their deployment in the space.

Instead of materials associated with contemporary office buildings, a range of materials associated with the previous villas is used.

A key aim of MVRDV on this project was to not have a façade, but to only have a minimal environmental barrier of air. The original intention was to use heaters that would project an air barrier which would separate the interior and exterior, thus resonating with conceptual projects such as Yves Klein's Air Architectures of the early 1960s. Yet, this radical proposition was legally not possible at the time and glass was used instead. Thirty-five different types of glazing were used in order to accommodate the varying heights, cooling capacities, colour, reflectivity and transparencies needed for the interior requirements.

This intention to not have a façade, which would traditionally be the element to define the building's envelope, highlights the slab as the key generator of the primary envelope condition of the Villa VPRO project. This sectional approach resonates

16.4 View of the east elevation of the Villa VPRO, showing how the articulated slabs begin to form the building's envelope on Level 1 that is an extension of the exterior ground surface and projects deep into the building's footprint. Copyright: Robert Hart. Image courtesy of MVRDV.

16.5 Views of Villa VPRO. *Clockwise starting top left*: (1) interior view showing the articulation of the slab to connect to levels above, folding of the surface, and below, punching through; (2) exterior view showing the effects of the articulated slab on the elevation, and how this also mixes the interior and exterior of the envelope; (3) interior view form Level 1 looking through the slab down into Level 0; and (4) view on Level 1, capturing how the envelope's articulation allows a mixing through the section of interior and exterior conditions. Copyright: Robert Hart. Image courtesy of MVRDV.

16.6 Views of Villa VPRO. *Clockwise starting top left*: (1) overview of the Level 3 and Level 4 courtyards looking to the west; (2) view to the south of the Level 5 roof landscape; (3) detail view of the west elevation showing the connection to the surrounding ground and the deep punches of the exterior space that enters the building; and (4) view of the exterior courtyards to the surrounding landscape. Copyright: Robert Hart. Image courtesy of MVRDV.

16.7 View of the western elevation of Villa VPRO, highlighting how the building envelope is articulated through the slab, thus generating a variety of exterior conditions across and deep into the building. Copyright: Robert Hart. Image courtesy of MVRDV.

16.8   Night view of the north elevation of Villa VPRO, highlighting how the building envelope is articulated through the slab. Here it shows how Level 1 establishes a new artificial ground datum for the scheme that smoothly stitches the building into the surrounding context. Copyright: Robert Hart. Image courtesy of MVRDV.

with projects such as OMA's unbuilt Jussieu Library scheme for Paris (1992) in which two of the three founders of MVRDV participated in the design development. Recently, schemes like Snøhetta's Oslo Opera House (see p. 10) have exteriorized the approach by way of overlaying a continuous public surface over the enclosed space of buildings. However, there is further potential in the spatial and sectional strategies embodied in the Villa VPRO scheme. Hence, in spite of the currently prevailing obsession with the making of discrete objects and superficial exterior façades, alternatives readily exist that demonstrate a radically different take on the envelope as a sectional and spatial extension.

PROJECT 17
PALAZZO DEL CINEMA
Venice, Italy, 1990
Steven Holl

Located on the Lido Island of Venice, Steven Holl's unbuilt competition entry for the Palazzo del Cinema is a key example of a multiple envelope or box-within-box scheme with an open perimeter threshold. The scheme consists of a horseshoe-shaped perimeter building with the cinema theatres suspended above an extension of a canal. Holl's integration of the scheme into the context of Venice began with the proposed extension of the canal entry from the lagoon deep into the site. This resulted in a harbour condition that acts as the primary entry point for those arriving by water from the other islands in the lagoon. The cinemas were to be suspended over the canal as a large urban

17.1 The model of the Palazzo del Cinema scheme shows the permeable perimeter volume and the suspended cinema volumes. The elevations feature different-sized openings in the perimeter volume that afford glimpses of the monolithic cinema volumes. Copyright: Steven Holl Architects.

17.2 The watercolour paintings of exterior views of the Palazzo del Cinema scheme show the massing and envelope strategies of the permeable perimeter and the monolithic cinema volumes, as well as some of the intended material conditions and effects. Copyright: Steven Holl Architects.

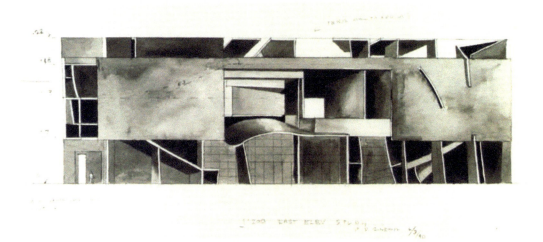

17.3 The watercolour paintings of sectional views of the Palazzo del Cinema scheme show the spatial permeability of the scheme, as well as the cinema and grotto space. Copyright: Steven Holl Architects.

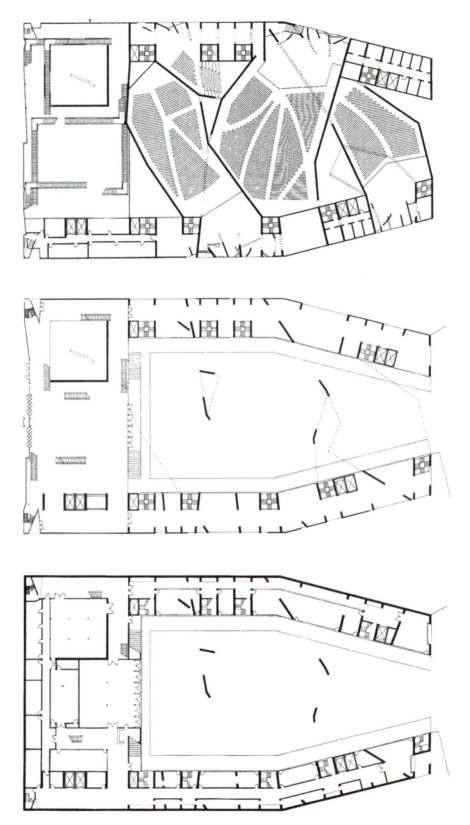

17.4 The plans of the Palazzo del Cinema exhibit the spatial interrelation between the perimeter volume and the structure and volumes of the suspended cinemas. Copyright: Steven Holl Architects.

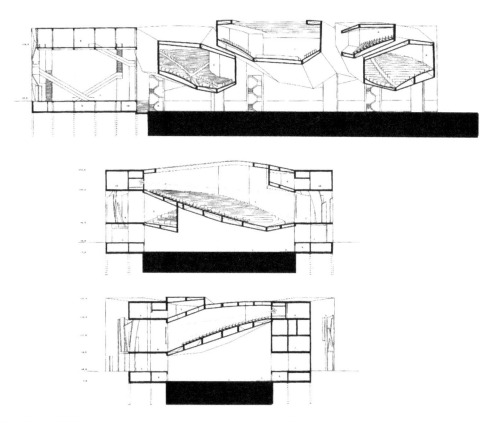

17.5 The sections of the Palazzo del Cinema show the suspended cinema volumes and their spatial separation or continuity with the perimeter volume. Copyright: Steven Holl Architects.

canopy, thus producing the 'grand public grotto' that could be used for marina functions and with arcades along its perimeter that could house shops. Thus the extended threshold of the scheme with its permeable perimeter could serve as an extended interface between different activities of the urban life of Venice and the programme of the Cinema Palace.

The scheme correlates the building's massing and envelope strategy in a manner that renders the scheme permeable along its perimeter and monolithic in its suspended mass. There are two distinct envelope conditions in the scheme. First, the horseshoe-shaped perimeter volume enables the exchange of the site with the surroundings and houses the lobby (situated along the south-eastern edge of the site), offices (in the basement level), circulation to the cinemas, and also becomes the public threshold to access the new marina condition. This envelope follows a more rational geometry and is read as one element. The second enveloping condition houses the cinemas, which constitute a thick canopy and envelope for the public marina beneath. The envelopes of the cinemas are folded, resulting in a crystalline appearance.

The proposed material for the structure of the scheme is concrete. The concrete is also expressed as the material finish in the thick cinema canopy. The horseshoe-shaped perimeter volume was proposed to be clad in a sand-blasted acrylic along the main façade and brass alloy, which would have been used as the formwork for the concrete work, around the remaining perimeter. This would have resulted in a red patina that resonates with the colour palette of Venice's historical fabric.

Opening in the massing occurs for two reasons: (1) to enable access and exchange with the surroundings along the ground level – these openings manifest as rectilinear punches that occur on the vertical planes, providing openings into the interior of the cinema lobby and into the interior of the site in order to access the grotto and marina – and (2) at elevated levels the openings expose the suspended monolithic volumes and crystalline geometry of the cinemas. The ends of the cinemas that meet the exterior of the perimeter volume are the ends of the spaces where the projection screen is placed and, whenever possible, the screens were meant to be withdrawn in order for the projections to extend out on to the cinema volumes and animate the envelope in that area with light and colour. The cinema canopy acts as shading and rain protection, and also produces a rich palette of light conditions and effects. The thick folded cinema volumes interlock with the perimeter volume, producing fissures and crevices which accentuate the permeability of the volume in spite of its monolithic aspects. Through the fissures light enters the public grotto. Steven Holl (1993: 136) described the related intentions as follows:

> Time in its various abstractions links architecture and cinema. The project involves three interpretations of time and light in space:
> [1] *Collapsed and extended time* within cinema is expressed in the warp and extended weave of the building. ...
> [2] *Diaphanous time* is reflected in sunlight dropping through fissure space between the cinemas into the lagoon basin below. Ripples of water and reflected sunlight animate the grand public grotto.
> [3] *Absolute time* is measured in a projected beam of sunlight, which moves across the cubic pantheon in the lobby.

A series of watercolour paintings by Holl describe the effect of the interplay between space, mass, light and reflectivity. These give evidence to the intention to arrive at both a vast space and an intimate series of conditions produced within and the phenomenological inclination of the scheme. Even though this project remained unbuilt, it constitutes a prime example of how envelopes may be thought of so as to enable rich interaction and experience across its deep threshold and to be permeated with the activities and events of urban life.

PROJECT 18
LE FRESNOY ART CENTRE
Tourcoing, France, 1991 to 1997
Bernard Tschumi

Bernard Tschumi's competition-winning scheme for Le Fresnoy Art Centre in Tourcoing, France was completed in 1992. This project has a special status among the selected range in that it constitutes an adaptation and transformation of an existing set of buildings instead of an entirely new scheme, even though the competition brief allowed for the latter.

The competition brief asked for an art and audio-visual research centre, including a school, film studios, media centre, performance and exhibition halls, cinemas, laboratories for research in sound and production, electronic imagery, video and film, administrative offices, housing, as well as a bar and restaurant. The site for the project featured an old leisure complex from the 1920s that included an array of facilities for ballroom dancing, horse riding and skating, as well as film theatres. Tschumi chose to maintain the existing buildings and to unify them with a new envelope/roof that is largely open to the surroundings. It is in this

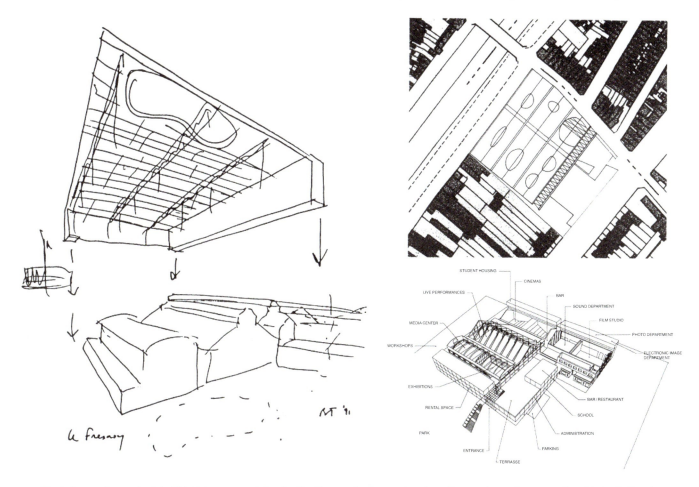

18.1 *Clockwise starting on the left*: (1) Initial conceptual sketch of Le Fresnoy Art Centre electric roof inserted over the existing box fabric. (2) Site plan of Le Fresnoy Art Centre, showing the grafting of the new electric roof on to the existing urban fabric. (3) Axonometric diagram of Le Fresnoy Art Centre's programmatic deployment showing the mix of interior and exterior occupation. Copyright: Bernard Tschumi Architects.

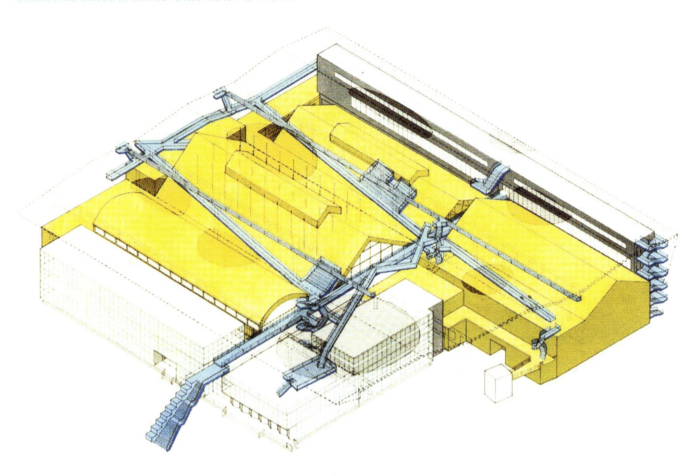

18.2 The axonometric diagram of Le Fresnoy Art Centre displays the relationship between the existing built fabric (yellow), the new gangways that animate the 'in-between' space (blue), the new building fabric (white) and the 'electric roof'. Copyright: Bernard Tschumi Architects.

project in particular that Tschumi demonstrated his 'box-within-a-box' approach that articulates a large amount of interstitial space between the outer and inner envelopes, while at the same time protecting the already existing buildings from further direct weather impact.

The concept of the box-within-a-box section was deployed and developed along the three main considerations. (1) The electric roof is the contemporary and technological element of the scheme. Although closed along the northern edge, this element is open along the other sides, providing visual connections to the old and new buildings and the surrounding context. This horizontal rectangular surface that measures approximately 8,000 square metres is punctuated with large openings so as to enable natural light and ventilation into the vast interstitial space between the new and existing roof surfaces. The structure of the new roof also includes the technical services for the heating, cooling and ventilation of the fully climatized interior spaces. (2) The existing leisure complex buildings house the interior fully climatized spaces of the project. Some demolition was required on the northern edge and the south-eastern corner due to the degree of dereliction of these parts. These were replaced with boxes of corrugated steel along the northern perimeter and a curtain wall system on the south. (3) The 'in-between', as Tschumi termed it, is the space between the electric roof and the roofs of the boxes of the building complex below. Although the restaurant and bar and the grand staircase that connects to the adjacent gardens would be located in this space, the primary intention was to provide a non-programme-specific event space.

The application of the 'box-within-a-box' concept that Tschumi deployed in this project is of interest in the way it articulates the new elements of the scheme as a powerful auxiliary architecture that showcases how it is possible to enable a vast transitional space for planned and unplanned events.

The 'electric roof' and the 'boxes under the roof' stage a transition between degrees of exposure, shelter and interiority. The volumes under the large roof display varied envelope conditions

18.3 The view of the north-eastern edge of Le Fresnoy Art Centre clearly shows the relationship between the 'electric roof' and the suspended stairway and gangways to the existing buildings, as well as the scale relation of the project to the existing built fabric of the neighbourhood. Copyright: Bernard Tschumi Architects.

18.4 The view of the south-eastern face of Le Fresnoy Art Centre shows the primary entry up into the in-between space and the openness and transparency of the 'electric roof'. Copyright: Bernard Tschumi Architects.

18.5 The interior view of Le Fresnoy Art Centre reveals the vast 'in-between' space of the scheme produced by the 'electric roof' surface. Copyright: Bernard Tschumi Architects.

18.6 Interior view of Le Fresnoy Art Centre, showing sectional variations of the scheme. Copyright: Bernard Tschumi Architects.

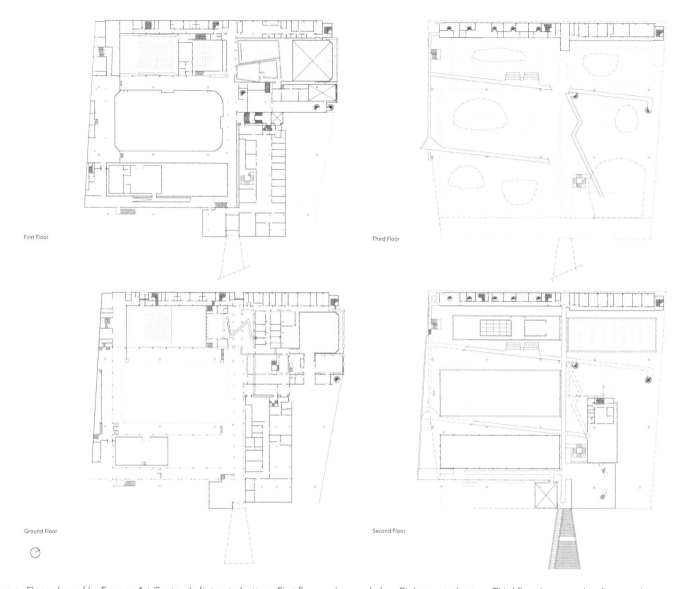

Floor plans of Le Fresnoy Art Centre. *Left, top to bottom*: First floor and ground plan. *Right, top to bottom*: Third floor (gangway level), second floor.

and are articulated as two different types. The existing buildings of the leisure complex became the spaces that house the specific programmes of the media centre, performance spaces, sound department, cinemas and film studio. The second newly constructed buildings that replaced the existing derelict ones contain housing, administration and rentable space. The difference is evident in the materiality of the two. The existing buildings, which were constructed for a similar purpose such as a cinema and ballroom, contain large halls made either of masonry, glass, steel or in some instances timber. Their exterior finishes are a standard yellow render with pitched or vaulted red-tiled roofs. The new buildings with their generic use are constructed in a basic concrete and glass curtain wall system. Together with the large roof these new volumes resemble industrial buildings.

The roofs of the new volumes are flat and used as terraces inhabited by the bar and restaurant. The roofs of the existing volumes act as a kind of tectonic landscape element within the vast interstitial space and articulate smaller spaces particularized by the sectional relation between the upper and lower roof surfaces. Within this interstitial space circulation is provided by an extensive system of suspended stairways, catwalks and platforms. Mounted on to the roof surfaces of the existing buildings is bleacher seating for spectators enjoying a variety of different

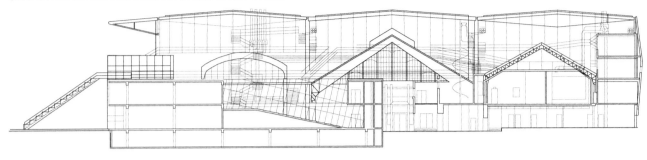

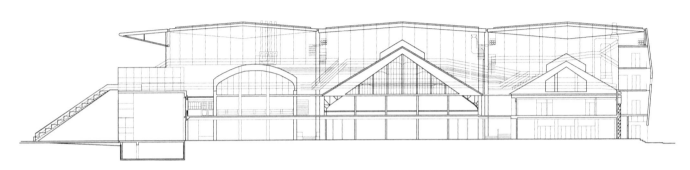

18.8 Sections of Le Fresnoy Art Centre, showing the sectional variations of interior and semi-interior/exterior spaces.

performances and events. Other existing roof surfaces are used as projection screens.

The 'electric roof' with its three-sides open perimeter constitutes a permeable threshold that allows for spatial and visual connections to the surrounding city fabric. By way of deploying a largely accessible perimeter that stages a vast interstitial space for a wide range of uses, Le Fresnoy Art Centre resonates with projects like Steven Holl's Palazzo del Cinema in Venice (see p. 184), while demonstrating the potential of supplementary or auxiliary architectures to transform existing object-emphasizing architectures without transitional spaces into extended threshold arrangements that can provide for a broad spectrum of use. That such sectional approaches need not be limited to larger projects is demonstrated by schemes such as FAR's Wall House (see p. 200) or Joakim Hoen's Seaside Second Homes (see p. 207).

PROJECT 19
WORLD CENTRE FOR HUMAN CONCERNS
New York City, USA, 2001 to 2004
OCEAN

Shortly after 9/11, Max Protetch, gallerist in New York City, invited 50 architectural practices from around the world to propose schemes for Ground Zero, the site of the destroyed World Trade Center. OCEAN took this invitation as an opportunity to address the question of limited forms of political representation as a cause of conflict. Today when Nation State status appears to be the one singular form of legitimate political representation and the United Nations constitutes the assembly of Nation States, the question arises as to how peoples are represented who do not constitute a Nation State or who are involuntarily represented by one not of their choosing. As a result, conflict is bound to unfold. This raises the genuine question as to whether there could exist concurrent forms of political representation that are not in contradiction with one another. One such example is the Sami people

19.1 View of the proposed World Centre for Human Concerns in the context of Lower Manhattan, showing the building volume and the large urban canopy. Copyright: OCEAN Design Research Association.

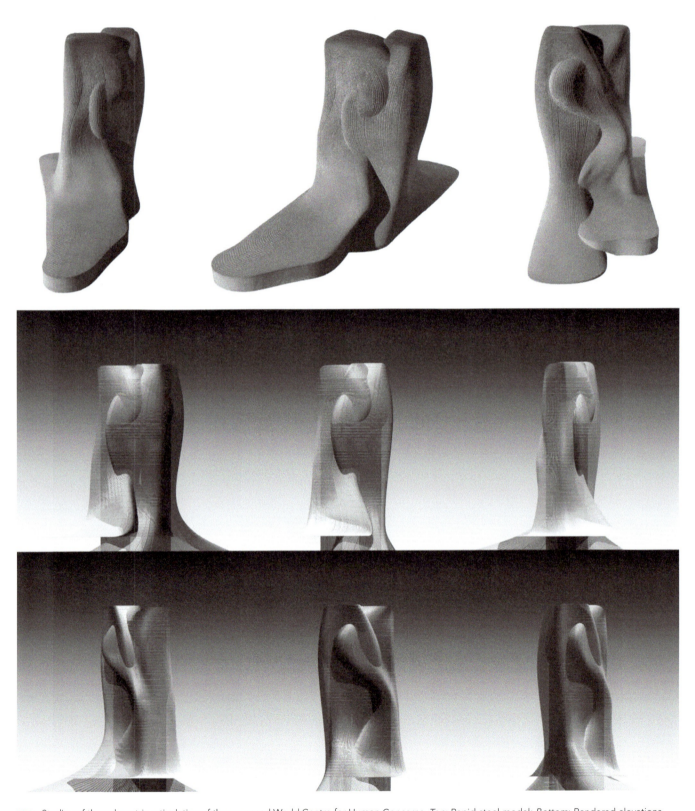

19.2 Studies of the volumetric articulation of the proposed World Centre for Human Concerns. *Top*: Rapid-steel model; *Bottom*: Rendered elevations. Copyright: OCEAN Design Research Association.

 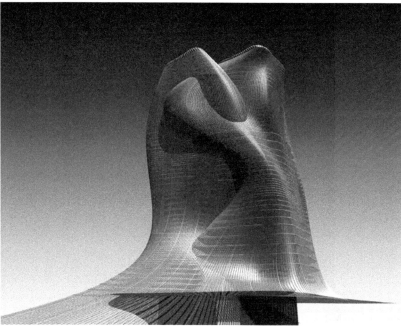

19.3 Studies of the volumetric articulation of the proposed World Centre for Human Concerns with and without adjacent buildings. Copyright: OCEAN Design Research Association.

with their semi-autonomous status and their own parliaments in Norway, Sweden and Finland. In pursuit of projecting an architecture and a notion of inclusive forms of political representation, OCEAN proposed a World Centre for Human Concerns as a space for all peoples and cultures, whether existing or emergent.

This task required careful consideration of the question of the spatial and formal articulation of the architecture as a very large building. In search of an architecture that is free from associations with other forms of political representation, while not resorting to the entirely arbitrary, OCEAN chose to articulate the project in reference to one of the counter-proposals to Minoru Yamasaki's Twin Towers by the German architect and spatial net pioneer Conrad Roland. In 1963/1964 the latter had proposed a radically novel 120-storey twisting double-curved volume with a central core and a structural net on its perimeter.

The 430-metre-tall volume of the World Centre adopts this formal language but redefines it spatially and structurally. Its twisted double-curved volumes inscribe the voids of the former Twin Towers, which may be gleaned as vague figures through the textured and folded skin of the new building. Every viewpoint grants a unique view of the scheme, which thus escapes full comprehension as an object. The World Centre's spaces result from the draping and folding of the building mass around the volume of the twin towers, and articulates the new building volume as a set of intersecting interstitial spaces that circumvent a singular or established spatial hierarchy. Different architects can design the spatial pockets that result from the intersecting volumes. The scheme is unified by its envelope treatment and the correlated programme and interior environment strategies.

The main envelope of the building does not connect to the ground, as is commonly the case. Instead it forms a very large urban canopy that provides shelter over several adjacent plots and connects to adjacent buildings. In this way the transition from outside to inside is significantly extended. Moreover, when approaching the building the perception of the ungrounded volume as an architectural object disintegrates.

The scheme relinquishes the common high-rise organization of central structural, service and circulation cores and uses instead the building envelope as a space for circulation and social encounter, with 120 vertical circulation channels nested within it. This results in a countless number of ways of moving around the building. The basket-like circulation channel system is developed into a structural principle, resulting in a system with plenty of redundancy and capacity to withstand local disruption. The striated articulation of the envelope in tandem with its double curvature enables a modulated transparency of both the envelope and the spaces within and beyond it, according to day- and night-light conditions.

The very deep plan of the building necessitates a rethinking of interior climate modulation and daylight. By questioning an equal need for daylight, differentiated interior habitats may be articulated instead. Rainforests and the oceans serve as organizational models, where even in the lowest and darkest regions microecologies flourish. This suggests a redefinition of what

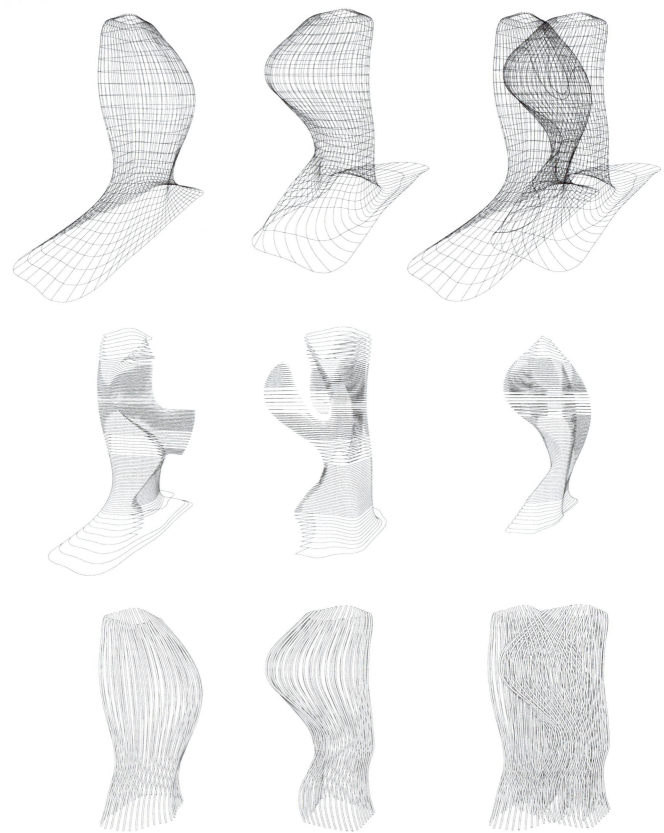

19.4 *Top*: Intersecting envelopes result in different spatial pockets. *Middle*: Three primary spatial pockets and floor plan arrangements. *Bottom*: System of vertical structural and circulatory elements. Copyright: OCEAN Design Research Association.

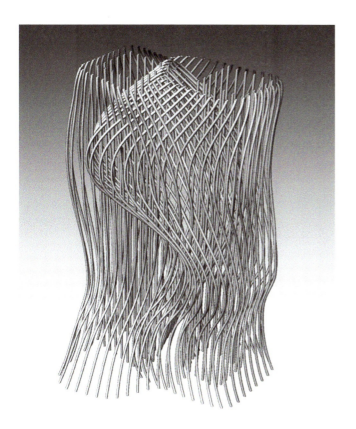

19.5 One hundred and twenty vertical channels on the internal and external perimeters of the scheme serve as both structural and circulation elements. Copyright: OCEAN Design Research Association.

constitutes a 24-hour city. So far this notion implied available programmes around the clock. The alternative entails diverse

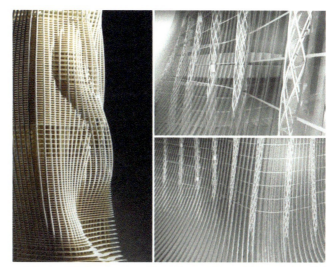

19.6 *Left*: Rapid-prototype model showing the vertical channel and floor plate arrangement. *Right*: Studies of the relation between the vertical channels and the primary envelope of the building of which they are a part. Copyright: OCEAN Design Research Association.

daylight conditions at all times. The darker core constitutes a 24-hour night programme zone, while the outer and peripheral areas enable a flexible negotiation of programmes relative to less constant ambient conditions. The correlated environmental modulation strategy and 24-hour programme strategy was only developed to concept stage. However, projects like OCEAN's Czech National Library (see p. 224) with its interior climate and programme relation, Sean Lally's Estonian Art Academy (see p. 253) with its pockets of heterogeneous interior climate modulation, and Cloud 9's MediaTic (see p. 258) with its deep plan begin to show how this approach can be developed and implemented.

PROJECT 20
WALL HOUSE
Santiago de Chile, Chile, 2007
FAR – Frohn and Rojas

Located in the suburbs of Santiago de Chile, the Wall House, designed by Frohn and Rojas, was completed in 2007. The project consists of (1) a concrete and timber core that defines the primary structure, floors and parts of the furnishings such as walls that double up as shelves, (2) a primary polycarbonate glassed climate envelope, and (3) a textile covering of the volume of the house. Wherever the timber core does not reach all the way to the glassed envelope it results in an interstitial space between these two layers, effectively organizing the house concentrically into a protected core and a surrounding interstitial yet interior space. Likewise the textile and glassed envelopes result in an exterior sheltered interstitial space. This spatial organization raises an interesting question regarding the relation between so-called primary and secondary spaces, in particular since cantilevering areas of the upper floor render the transition between peripheral and central space a spatial zone rather than a linear division. What emerges from this spatial strategy may be perceived on the ground floor as a continuous flow of space

20.1 Exterior view of the eastern face of the Wall House, showing how the textile envelope begins to define the overall geometric volume of the house and how the landscape begins to slip through it into the semi-interior space between it and the climate envelope. Copyright: FAR – Frohn and Rojas.

20.2 Exterior night view of the south-eastern face of the Wall House, showing the range of transparency and opacity resulting from the interplay between material layers and light sources. Copyright: FAR – Frohn and Rojas.

that is particularized in section. The articulation of space on the upper floor is primarily accomplished by the walls, which do not terminate in an opaque ceiling. Instead, the walls stop short of the slanted glazed roof with the exterior textile cover regulating light and thermal impact. This varied spatial strategy renders the spatial experience provided by the scheme surprisingly rich.

In this project three enveloping conditions exist. The timber walls are either open or clad on one side with timber panels. These partitions double up as shelves and cupboards that are either occupied or not occupied with objects, and thus offer a variety of closure and porosity. What one might expect to be a purely solid condition is often transparent and ever changing by the use of the inhabitants. This enveloping condition facilitates the internal social and spatial relationships. The climate envelope is made of polycarbonate and glass. Wherever the timber core reaches to the climate envelope's surface it becomes opaque due to the timber panelling. Otherwise the climate envelope is either translucent (polycarbonate) or transparent (glass).

The textile exterior envelope performs on a number of levels. First, it is used to prevent or diffuse the impact of direct sunlight on the interior and exterior transitional spaces and thus provide a manageable interior climate for the house. Due to the presence of the textile cover it was possible for the climate envelope to feature large translucent and transparent surface areas. Moreover, the exterior textile cover engenders a variation of opacity, translucence and transparency that changes with light direction and time of day. While appearing relatively opaque from the outside and translucent from the inside during daytime, the change during night-time is dramatic. Interior light sources render the textile semi-transparent. Moreover, on closer inspection the textile envelope is not uniform in material across its entire surface; instead the material varies in density and porosity, and thus in visual effect. For instance, the textile patches adjacent to the openings that provide entry points are more transparent.

The interplay between spatial strategy, materiality and material effects renders the scheme provisional and temporal, which is not merely a result of the suggestion of a tent typology. In so doing it resonates in some way with the ground articulation of Helen and Hard's Geopark (see p. 172), yet without the element of casual accidentiality. Another interesting consideration is the

20.3 View from the spatial transition from the exterior interstitial space between textile and climate envelope to the interior space on the ground floor that ranges from double-storey height to space under a cantilever. The latter shows how space can be particularized in section without having to revert to the primary use of vertical elements to accomplish this goal. Moreover, it is possible to grasp the flexible use of space in response to different times of the day and seasonal climate change. Copyright: FAR – Frohn and Rojas.

20.4 Interior view of the Wall House, looking from the primary living space through the partly closed and partly open timber envelope into the kitchen space. Copyright: FAR – Frohn and Rojas.

20.5 Interior view of the Wall House on the first floor, showing the most private spaces of the project. Clearly the walls do not terminate in a ceiling. Instead space remains continuous above the height of a person, resulting in the perception of an unbound space. Copyright: FAR – Frohn and Rojas.

20.6 Interior view of the Wall House, on the first floor showing the interstitial space between the climate envelope and the timber wall and shelving. One can also catch a glimpse of the wet room in the concrete core through the unfilled shelving. Copyright: FAR – Frohn and Rojas.

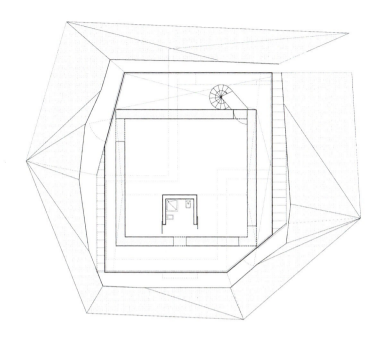

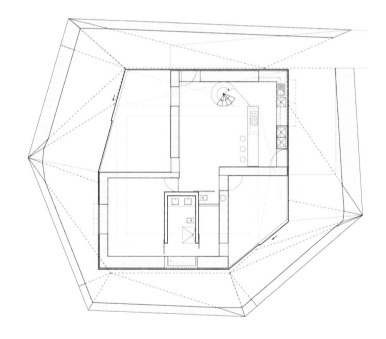

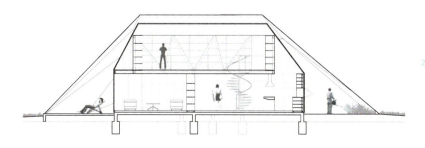

20.7 *Top*: First-floor plan. *Centre*: Ground-floor plan. *Bottom*: Section cutting on an east–west axis; all show the relationships between the envelope types and the resulting spatial organization and layered transitional spaces. Copyright: FAR – Frohn and Rojas.

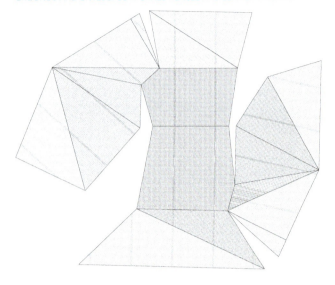
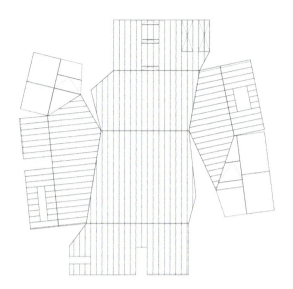

20.8 Unfolded surface diagrams of the different envelopes. *Top left*: Textile envelope. *Top right*: Climate envelope. *Bottom*: Unfolded elevations of the ground- and first-floor timber walls and shelving. Copyright: FAR – Frohn and Rojas.

way in which R&Sie(n)'s Spidernethewood house (see p. 212) and FAR's Wall House might inform one another. The former inverts the relation between textile membrane and solid enclosure and extends the exterior threshold with netting and plantation. Hybrid variations on the combined approaches of these two projects have the potential to yield a range of different kinds and degrees of embeddedness of a scheme that can vary in accordance with the conditions it meets along the perimeter.

PROJECT 21
THREE SEASIDE SECOND HOMES
Norway, 2012
Joakim Hoen

The unbuilt Seaside Second Home project by Joakim Hoen constitutes a reflection on the potentials of what may be termed informed non-standard architecture. This project combines a series of spatial strategies, with a non-standard approach to the articulation of three individual buildings, each made particular to one of three sites by way of a computational data-driven design process. Programmatically, the second homes are a version of the ubiquitous Norwegian seaside holiday cottages that are only used during the summer season, except that the projected second homes cater for habitation during all seasons.

The three sites along the Norwegian west and south-west coast were selected as principally similar coastal landscapes, but with different local terrain form and weather conditions and exposure. Instead of levelling the sites, as is typically the case, the intention was to preserve the terrain in detail and to use it to inform the design. The specific terrain form of each location was derived from detailed terrain scans provided by the Norwegian authorities.

Local weather stations delivered data pertaining to the site-specific wind conditions as input into the generative design process. Solar impact was evaluated by means of computer-aided analysis.

The design system for all three variants consists of two envelopes: an outer permeable screen that shelters a transitional zone, and an inner climate envelope of variable thickness. The outer envelope surrounds the inner envelope except for the

21.1 Rendered exterior view of one of the variants of the Seaside Second Homes project, showing the large glassed elevation facing the sea and the landscaped interior, which corresponds with the exterior terrain. Copyright: Joakim Hoen.

21.2 Rendered interior view of one of the variants of the Seaside Second Homes project, showing the landscaped interior and, on the far side of the interior, the alcoves for sleeping that are set into the climate envelope. Copyright: Joakim Hoen.

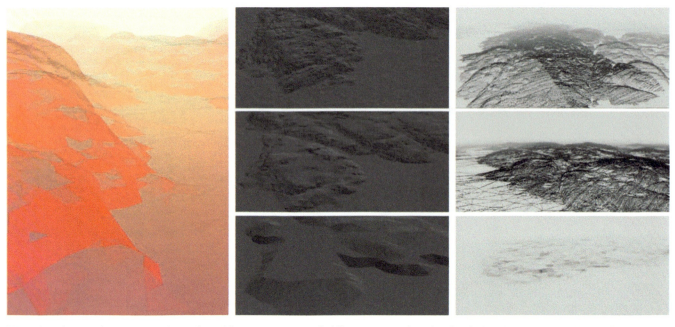

21.3 Chart showing the terrain articulation derived from terrain scans with different accuracy based on height-line density. *Bottom*: Lowest density. *Centre*: Medium density. *Top*: High density. For the purpose of taking the specific terrain form and its impact on local climate conditions into account it is necessary to obtain highly accurate data. Copyright: Joakim Hoen.

entrance area, the large glazed elevation facing the sea and the concrete core enclosing the bathroom.

The articulation of the outer screen-like envelope concerns primarily the dissipation of horizontal wind loads and modulation of solar impact on the inner envelope. In addition, it is articulated in such a manner as to shade the transitional space while providing sufficient daylight, and to decelerate airflow velocity from the exterior to the transitional space, so as to make it usable during

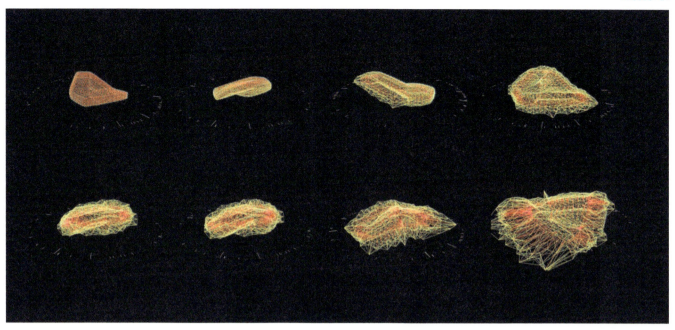

21.4 Various frames of an animation that simulates and visualizes the generation of the form of the outer envelope in response to airflow conditions and velocity. Copyright: Joakim Hoen.

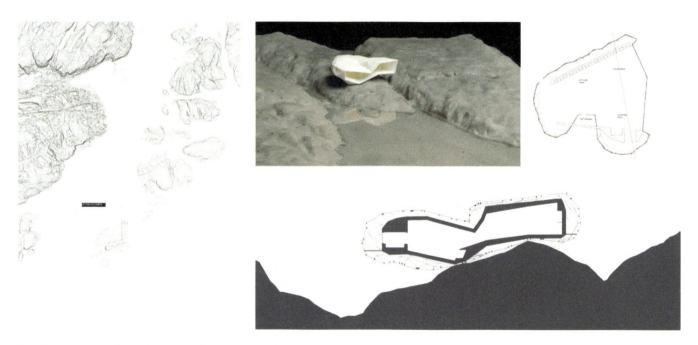

21.5 Terrain map, sections, plan and rapid prototype model of site one variant. Copyright: Joakim Hoen.

more severe weather conditions. The outer screen-like envelope and the outer surface of the inner envelope articulate the transitional space based on combined spatial requirements, needs for different activities and environmental performance.

The interior is an open space that is articulated as an extension of the landscape and motivated by the notions of the *oblique* and *habitable circulation* (Parent and Virilio 1996). The sectional articulation of the landscaped interior is defined and constrained by considerations pertaining to providing or obstructing sightlines by way of the relation between the floor and ceiling surfaces. The variable thickness of the inner envelope evolves on the one hand from the algorithmic procedures

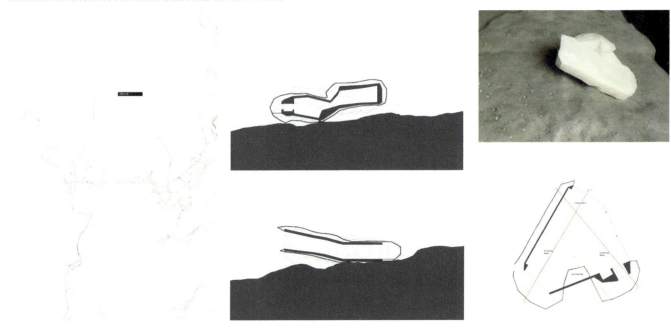

21.6 Terrain map, sections, plan and rapid prototype model of site two variant. Copyright: Joakim Hoen.

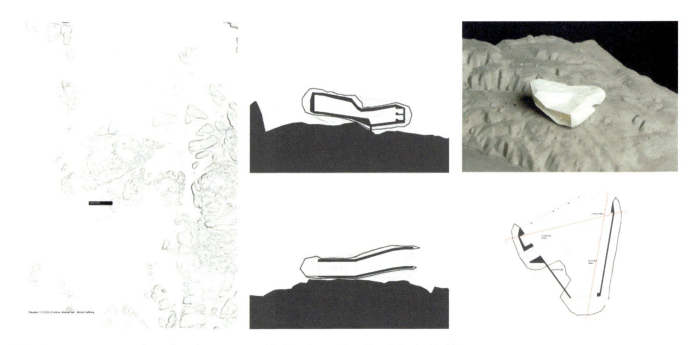

21.7 Terrain map, sections, plan and rapid prototype model of site three variant. Copyright: Joakim Hoen.

pertaining to the outer and inner surface of the inner envelope, and, on the other hand, from the desire to nest smaller spaces for use within the thickness of the envelope, such as alcoves for sleeping reminiscent of traditional Norwegian designs, shelving and so on.

The multiple envelope approach that underlies the Seaside Second Home project clearly resonates with that of FAR's Wall House (see p. 200), Bernard Tschumi's Le Fresnoy Art Centre (see p. 189) and Steven Holl's Palazzo del Cinema (see p. 184). However, it is the comparison with FOA's Meydan – Umraniye Retail Complex & Multiplex in Istanbul (see p. 111) that is of interest. FOA's project is located in an urban context in which terrain articulation is all but erased and therefore, if desired, needs to be constructed, while the Seaside Second Home project operates

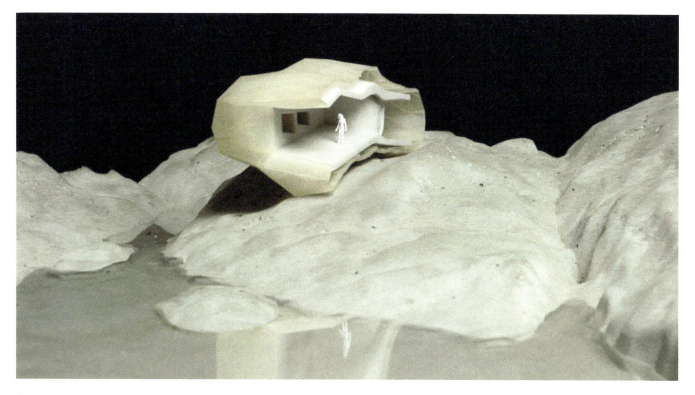

21.8　Sectional rapid-prototype model of site one variant showing the relation between massing and terrain, as well as the relation between the envelopes and the resulting transitional interstitial space and the interior space, including the nested alcove pockets in the climate envelope. Copyright: Joakim Hoen.

on untouched sites as found. This raises the question as to what kinds of criteria might be employed to construct a landscape, and how one might define and account for an interrelated extended surrounding context and its articulation and transformation over time. A systematic comparative analysis of such projects may yield rather useful insights into this problematic.

PROJECT 22
SPIDERNETHEWOOD
Nîmes, France, 2007
R&Sie(n)
François Roche, Stéphanie Lavaux, Jean Navarro with Nicolas Green

The Spidernethewood project designed by R&Sie(n) is a two-storey single family house of 450 square metres located in Nîmes, France. The project combines a series of interesting spatial and material strategies in its design:

1. From the perimeter of the site and from the exterior spaces adjacent to the building no discrete architectural object can be perceived, as the dense vegetation conceals the building. In this way the project constitutes a promising inroad towards non-discrete architecture.

2. Nets are used to constrain the growing vegetation, which is trimmed in the plane of the nets. From the resulting exterior spaces of the scheme the perimeter of the site cannot be perceived, due to the dense vegetation. As a result the spatial depth and extent of the site is rendered indeterminable. This strategy delivers a spatial buffer zone to the project that provides a heightened sense of privacy to the exterior spaces, which as a result cohere with the interior space.

3. While the exterior-to-interior threshold is marked by a clear change in material articulation, the space is rendered

22.1   The site plan of the Spidernethewood project shows the volume of the house and the exterior spaces that are articulated by the design vegetation, which is constrained by nets. Copyright: R&Sie(n).

22.2 *Top*: Ground-floor plan. *Bottom*: First-floor plan. The ground-floor arrangement shows how interior and exterior spaces are correlated and form a continuum across the exterior–interior threshold. Copyright: R&Sie(n).

continuous by way of the continual sectional articulation of the space across this threshold. In other words, the 'surfaces' that define the space and section are geometrically continuous, even though net that delimits this space changes into textile. For the articulation of the ground surface across the threshold two different strategies are employed. The interior floor surface is made from concrete, which is also used around the outdoor swimming pool, thus rendering this spatial zone more strongly related to the interior. In all other interior–exterior threshold conditions the floor surface changes from concrete in the interior to gravel for the exterior surfaces. This approach negotiates on the one hand a clear delineation by way of material change with one that is continuous in terms

22.3 Four axonometric views of the Spidernethewood project, showing the volume of the building with the interior spaces as an X-ray, and the exterior extension of these spaces by way of the nets. Copyright: R&Sie(n).

22.4 *Top*: View of the Spidernethewood project from the perimeter of the site, showing how dense vegetation on site masks the building volume. *Centre*: Two views showing (1) the transition from the wild vegetation to the spaces constrained by the nets, and (2) the transition from the exterior space defined by nets and vegetation to the interior space of the project. *Bottom*: Interior views of the project, showing the use of textile surfaces that articulate the interior spaces and which are a denser version of the exterior netting. Copyright: R&Sie(n).

of the shared material characteristics that continue across the threshold.

The strategy of employing vegetation in the production of a space of indeterminable depth may in some way be likened to employing a deep structure for the same purpose. However, projects may also employ these strategies for the exact opposite purpose of rendering an idiosyncratic object that stands out due to its fuzzy envelope, as evidenced, for example, by the GC Prostho Museum Research Centre designed by Kengo Kuma (see p. 238) or the British Pavilion at the Shanghai Expo 2010 designed by Thomas Heatherwick. What yields the difference is the way in

22.5 These four views show the exterior spaces of the project that are defined by the nets just after completion of the project and before the vegetation has grown to co-articulate the exterior spaces. Copyright: R&Sie(n).

22.6 Two views of the threshold between exterior and interior. While changes in the material articulation of surfaces clearly render the threshold as an abrupt delineation, the sectional articulation of the space is continuous across the threshold. Copyright: R&Sie(n).

which vegetation or structure is extensive to such an extent that the seam between architecture and setting is rendered imperceptible to quite some degree. This does not necessitate the masking of all seams and thresholds, as the Spidernethewood project demonstrates. It would be interesting to see how such schemes might be aggregated into denser settlement patterns. As the interstitial spaces between such projects can be left to local species to populate, the potential of this project in terms of providing for the local biological environment seems entirely obvious. However, the artificial introduction of non-native species would render such an effort a superficial greening gesture with potentially disruptive effects on the local biological environment. Hence, the relation between gardening and freely evolving wilderness comes to the fore. The Spidernethewood project relinquishes the former for the sake of the latter. The sole intervention with the existing vegetation is that of trimming, which results in a firmly delineating threshold activated by the most permeable element of the scheme: the nets. At this threshold the perceived continuity of space undergoes a sudden change in gradation and constrained/unconstrained depth as the space available for physical inhabitation changes into the tangled space of dense wild growth of the local fauna. It is these unexpected combinations and changes in gradation and depth between delineation and continuity that may be found everywhere in the scheme that suspends the perception of its space in a state of oscillation.

An interesting consideration concerns the aggregation of this project into an urban fabric. What comes to the fore is a

22.7 *Top*: Transition from the wild vegetation to the spaces constrained by the nets. *Bottom*: Transition from the exterior space defined by the nets and vegetation to the interior space defined by textile surfaces. Copyright: R&Sie(n).

22.8 Two interior views of the Spidernethewood project showing the 'blank' uniform articulation of the interior. The view on the right resonates with the interior space of Toyo Ito's seminal white U project in that it renders the space continuous beyond the view of the beholder. Copyright: R&Sie(n).

possible shift from landscape urbanism as a vast expansion of the front yard as a designed tectonic landscape towards what might be considered wilderness urbanism, in which the direct interfacing between freely evolving local ecosystems and architectures becomes the centre of design attention. This may also be applied to schemes that multiply grounds which are at the same time continuous.

PROJECT 23
SERPENTINE PAVILION 2002
London, England, 2002
Toyo Ito

In 2002 Toyo Ito designed the Serpentine Pavilion for the Serpentine Gallery's temporary summer pavilion programme. This annual event has become a hallmark for architectural experimentation and was set up as a platform for internationally renowned architects who had never built in the UK to have an opportunity to showcase their architectural visions. Toyo Ito's pavilion made its appearance in the third year of the programme following designs by Zaha Hadid in 2000 and by Daniel Libeskind in 2001. The temporary pavilion was used as a café during the day and a space for events such as lectures and talks during the evenings.

Ito and Arup's Advanced Geometry Unit under the leadership of Cecil Balmond evolved the design of the pavilion from the application of an algorithmic procedure based on a square

23.1 View of the Serpentine Pavilion 2002 in its initial location in Hyde Park, London. The pavilion is a clearly discrete architectural object that is distinct from its context. In a countermove, its envelope appears fragmented, transparent and open to the surroundings. Copyright: Toyo Ito Architects.

23.2 Close-up view of the south face of the Serpentine Pavilion 2002, showing the transparency of the envelope and the depth of the structural façade that articulates spatial pockets, some of which can be inhabited. Copyright: Toyo Ito Architects.

23.3 The interior view of the Serpentine Pavilion 2002 reveals a surprisingly transparent perimeter that contrasts with the exterior impression of a discrete architectural object. Copyright: Toyo Ito Architects.

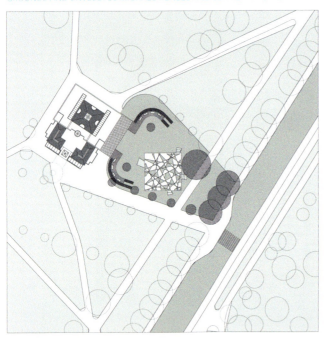 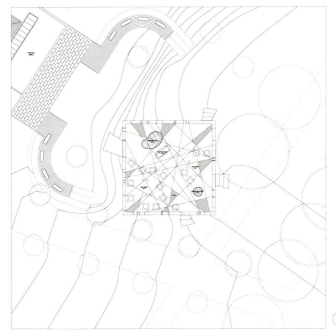

23.4 Plans of the Serpentine Pavilion 2002. *Left*: Site plan of the pavilion, showing its position relative to the Serpentine Gallery to the west and the Serpentine Road to the east. *Right*: Plan showing (1) the layout of the interior with the turf infills, (2) the clustering of furniture arrangements, (3) access to the pavilion in relation to the slight slope of the terrain. Copyright: Toyo Ito Architects.

that is rotated and expanded in size. The off-centred placement of the resulting pattern defies easy comprehension as to how it was generated. Besides the deep structure the envelope consists of opaque and glazed infill, as well as fields that are open to the exterior elements and shifting patterns of weather and life. Even though the exterior of the pavilion appears as a clearly defined box that just hovers above the landscape, the beholder experiences what appears to be an irregular pattern and fragmentation of the building structural envelope. The 550mm depth of the envelope and the steel profiles that deliver structural capacity to it result in spatial pockets that offer more intimate spaces along the perimeter of the 300-square-metre column-free primary space of the pavilion by offering visitors unscripted options of how to inhabit it at areas where the openings meet the floor surface and are large enough to sit within.

The floor of the pavilion acts as a new raised ground plane that extends beyond the envelope in the four entrance areas in the form of a ramp and three stairs. Inscribed on the floor is the pattern of the rotational square that generates the structural envelope that surrounds it. Some patches of the pattern are filled in with turf and grass. The play of light and shadow on the ground that results from the envelope and its infill doubles up the ground pattern and changes over time. The resulting impression is that of a shading tree canopy. Together, these effects blur the distinction between interior and exterior. However, while this is to some extent the design intention, the architecture remains clearly distinguished from the setting. The covert potential of the pavilion design however lies in its capacity to suggest possibilities above and beyond discrete architecture.

It is interesting to imagine how the process that generates the articulating of the envelope and the pattern of the interior raised floor may have been extended to also co-articulate the exterior ground adjacent to the enclosure. The effect could be an intensified blending of architecture and setting by eradicating the seam that separates them. Furthermore, the envelope with its various spatial pockets and related microclimatic modulation could provide for a multitude of different species, an objective that would seem in tune with the setting of the park as a site. As for the provisions of further degrees of interiority, the box-within-a-box section could be employed and combined with the varied infill strategy of the pavilion's envelope.

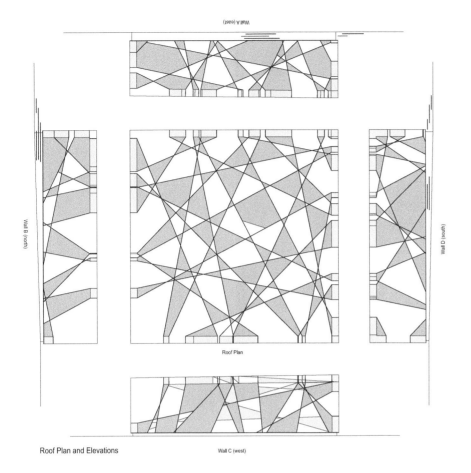

23.5 Diagram drawings of the Serpentine Pavilion 2002. *Top*: Roof plan and northern, southern, eastern and western elevations. *Centre*: Construction phases. *Bottom*: Network of primary beams organized according to beam thickness. Copyright: Toyo Ito Architects.

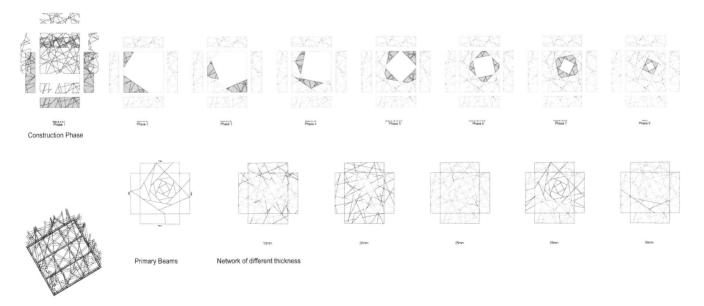

23.6 Diagram drawings of the Serpentine Pavilion 2002. *Top*: Roof plan and northern, southern, eastern and western elevations. *Centre*: Construction phases. *Bottom*: Network of primary beams organized according to beam thickness. Copyright: Toyo Ito Architects.

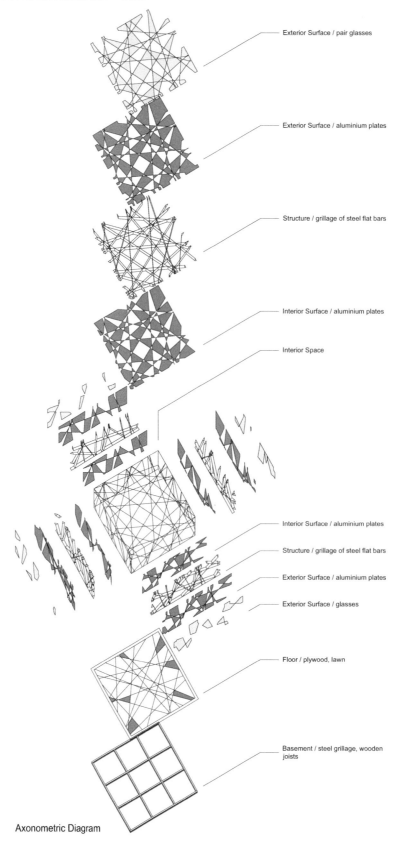

23.6 Expanded axonometric view of the Serpentine Pavilion 2002, showing the tectonic elements that make up the project. Copyright: Toyo Ito Architects.

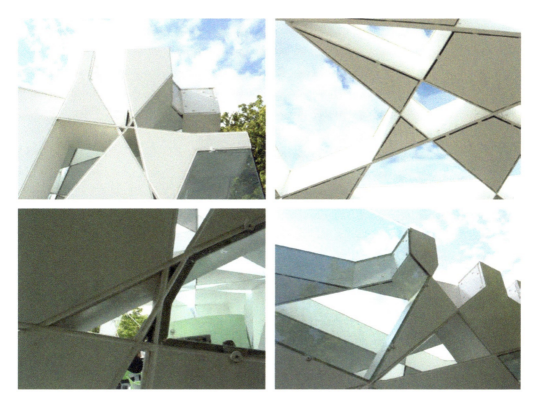

23.7 Detail views of the Serpentine Pavilion 2002 envelope. *Clockwise from top left*: (1) Corner detail of the exterior of the pavilion, showing the opaque and glass infill and the depth of the structural envelope; (2) interior view of the ceiling plane; (3) and (4) close-up details of the structural steel envelope and for the glass fixings. Amos Goldreich

23.8 *Top left*: View of the south-east corner of the pavilion. *Bottom left*: View of the north-west corner of the pavilion. *Right*: View of the interior, showing access from the southern entrance. Amos Goldreich

PROJECT 24
CZECH NATIONAL LIBRARY
Prague, Czech Republic, 2006
OCEAN and Scheffler + Partner

The unbuilt competition entry for the New Czech National Library in Prague designed by OCEAN and Scheffler + Partner aimed to provide both a continuous and gradually differentiated spatial and environmental experience of the building as an extension of the adjacent park landscape of the site.

The ground floor extends the park landscape through the scheme.

Located in the centre of the scheme is the core of the library, containing the national archive, and is articulated as a monolithic extension of the ground. This monolithic volume delivers direction to the connection between Milady Horákové Avenue and Letenské Park, as well as the vertical circulation of the project.

The functional spaces of the library, administration, reading rooms, lecture theatre, restaurant, etc. are set within volumes that are cantilevered from the central monolith volume.

The aim of the project was to facilitate a smooth transition from controlled spaces and interior environmental conditions required for an effective library service to the reading areas that provide for a more flexible use and heterogeneous interior conditioning. This is accomplished by means of a branching structure that envelops the cantilevering volumes.

In an analytic procedure the stress distribution within the envelope is analysed and correlated with the angle of incident of sunlight, viewing directions and spatial characteristics. From this

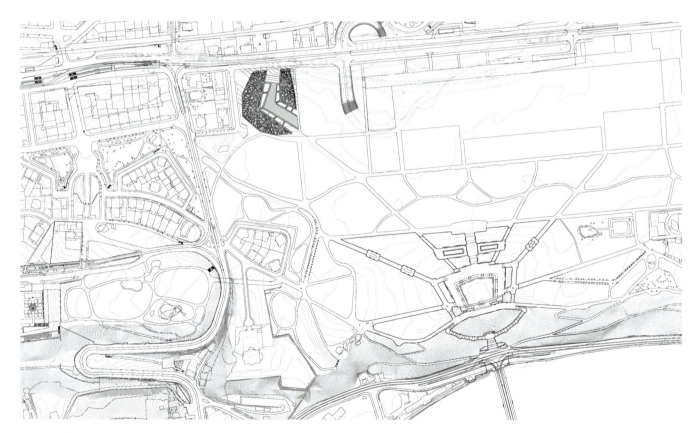

24.1 Site plan showing the Czech National Library set within Letenské Park in Prague and its massing and orientation relative to the adjacent urban fabric terrain form and pedestrian circulation. Copyright: OCEAN Design Research Association and Scheffler + Partner.

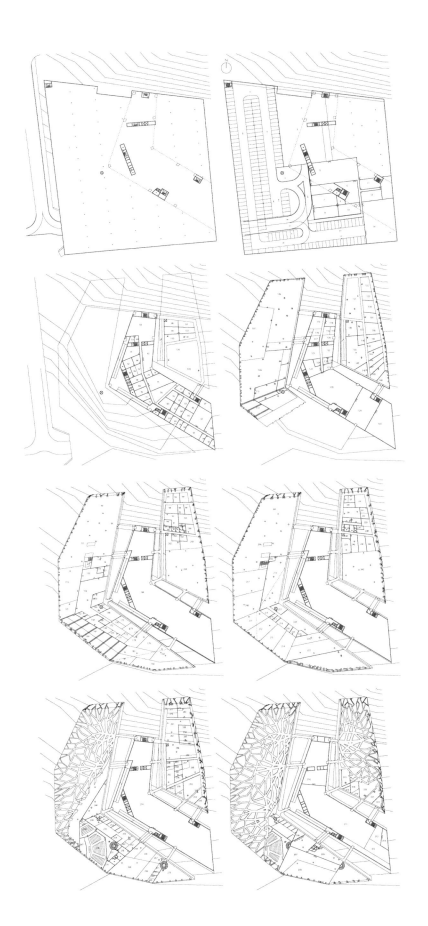

24.2 Plans of the Czech National Library, showing its spatial organization in relation to the local terrain and the extension of the latter into the interior. Copyright: OCEAN Design Research Association and Scheffler + Partner.

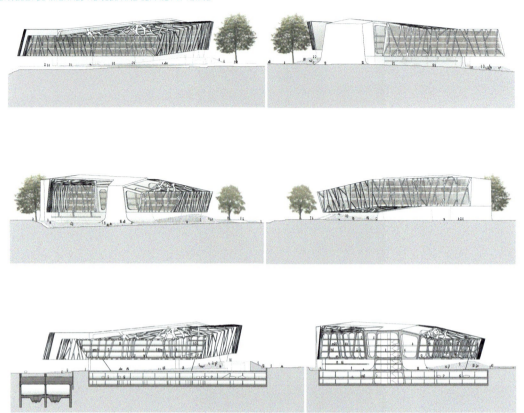

24.3 Elevations (*top*) and sections (*bottom*) of the Czech National Library. The elevations show the central opaque mass of the sensitive library functions and the branching structure of the cantilevering volumes for offices, reading rooms, restaurant, café, etc. Copyright: OCEAN Design Research Association and Scheffler + Partner.

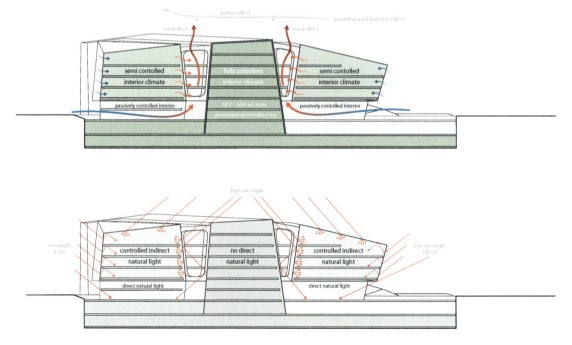

24.4 Sections showing the passive ventilation (*top*) and daylight (*bottom*) modulation strategies of the Czech National Library scheme. Copyright: OCEAN Design Research Association and Scheffler + Partner.

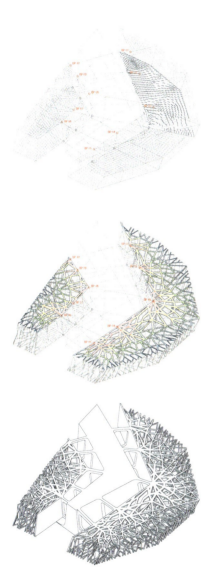

24.5 Process of the development of the branching structure of the cantilevering volumes. *Top*: Vector field describing structural stresses acting on the envelope of the cantilevering volumes. *Centre*: Algorithmic procedure mapping branching pattern to structural stresses. *Bottom*: Resulting tectonic articulation. Copyright: OCEAN Design Research Association and Scheffler + Partner.

the branching structure is generated. Each cantilevering volume is connected at five points to the monolithic core. From there the branching system is initiated and displays its greatest cross-sectional area. Circulation is distributed from these points located within the cross-section of the structure. From here the structure branches increasingly into a merged network that decreases in cross-sectional area towards the perimeter of the cantilevering volumes.

The interstitial space between the central monolithic volume and the cantilevering volumes provides for one of two primary strategies for the passive environmental modulation of areas that do not require highly controlled interior climates. For this the distance and degree of inclination between facing surfaces in relation to the sun-path and angle is critical in order to regulate thermal gain, stack effect and daylight conditions. The second strategy concerns the capacity of the branching network envelope of the cantilevering volumes. The transition from more enclosed to more exposed areas entails also a transition from darker areas closer to the core, to brighter and more transparent ones closer to the perimeter. This is further enhanced by the choice of infill glazing for the branching network envelope. In so doing, the project resonates with Toyo Ito's Serpentine Pavilion (see p. 218) in the way it deploys the envelope to generate varied interior conditions. The combination between branching network density and infill serves to regulate thermal gain, vary daylight conditions and shading, and to provide and direct views. The users of the library are thus able to choose the conditions that suit their individual needs and comfort requirements. Through these strategies it is possible to activate the capacity for larger parts of the building to be climatically free running, a condition not frequently associated with control-intensive building types such as libraries.

24.6 Exterior (*top*) and interior (*bottom*) views of the Czech National Library scheme. The latter shows the increasing transparency and exposure to daylight from the core to the perimeter that results from the branching pattern. Copyright: OCEAN Design Research Association and Scheffler + Partner.

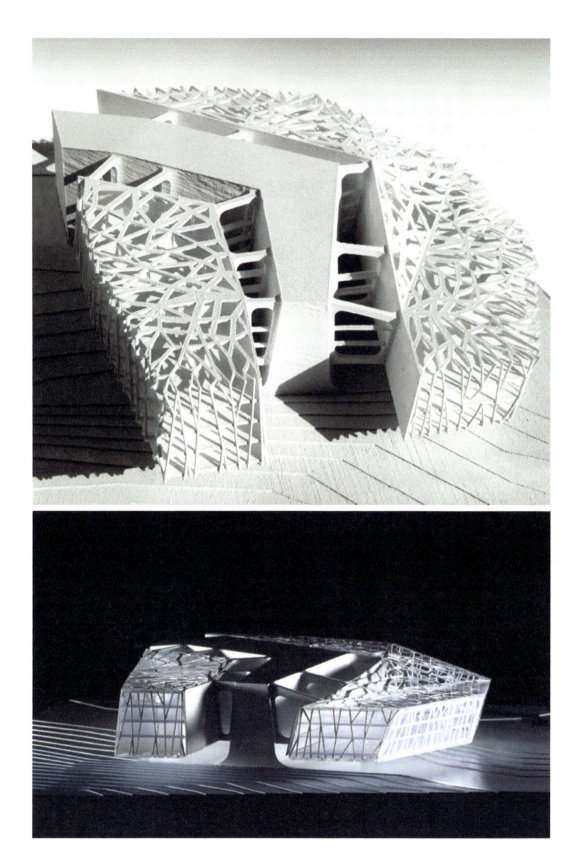

24.7 The photos of the model of the Czech National Library scheme show the filigree branching pattern of the envelope of the cantilevering volumes, as well as the way the ground is continuous through the project and how the central volume rises as an extension of the ground, not unlike a geological ridge. Copyright: OCEAN Design Research Association and Scheffler + Partner.

PROJECT 25
OLYMPIC ARCHERY RANGE
Barcelona, Spain, 1989 to 1991
Enric Miralles and Carme Pinós

The sensibility of architecture and landscape integration that is present in Alvaro Siza's Leça da Palmeira Swimming Pool (see p. 159) may also be discerned in the Olympic Archery Range project designed by Miralles and Pinós for the 1992 summer Olympics. The Olympic Archery Range could therefore also have prominently featured in the grounds section of this book. We chose to include it in the envelopes section, since it is in some way the envelope that constitutes dominant tectonic/stereotomic articulation.

The Olympic Archery Range consisted of both a training ground and a competition ground separated by an access road. Both grounds feature their own buildings and structures

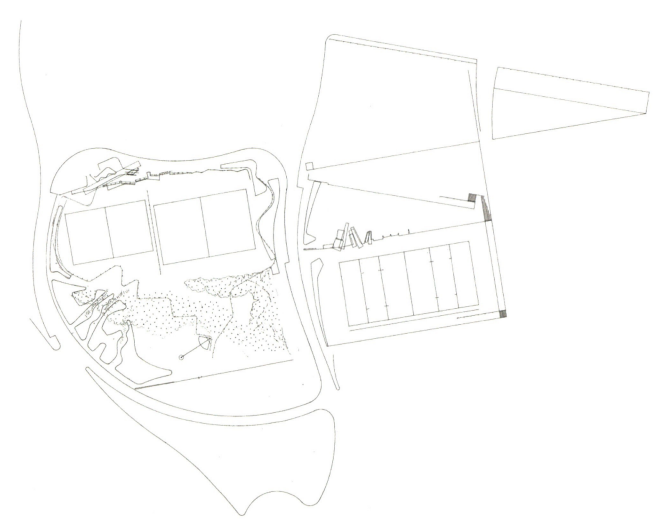

25.1 Site plan drawing of the Olympic Archery Range showing the competition and training buildings located along the western edge of the site, as well as the shooting ranges and the spectator zones that populate the surrounding landscape. Copyright: Enric Miralles and Carme Pinós.

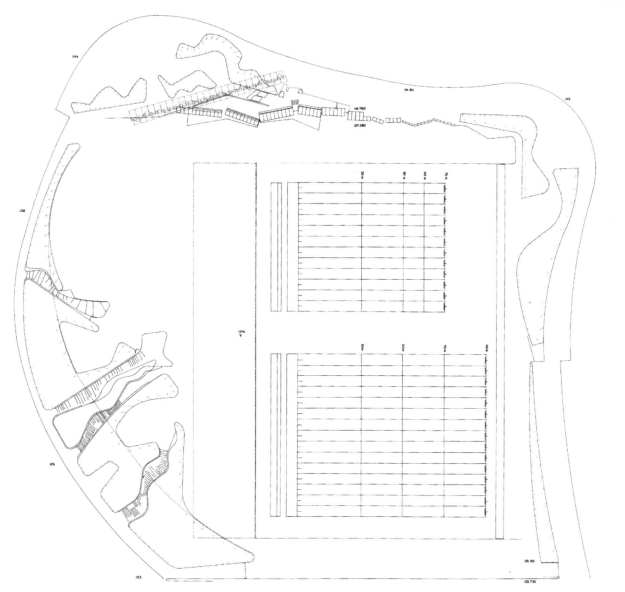

25.2 Site plan of the Olympic Archery Range competition ground. The centrally located shooting ranges are surrounded at the perimeter by landscape and integrated architectures. The competition building and access to the spectator areas inhabit the western edge, leading to viewing areas at the northern perimeter. Copyright: Enric Miralles and Carme Pinós.

characterized by a careful integration of architecture and landscaping that was typical of the work of Enric Miralles and Carme Pinós. The architectures are arranged along an embankment constituting slopes and steps in the terrain with spaces set into the ground. In so doing, this embankment architecture constitutes tectonic landscapes that are designed by deploying serial sections, which are used to articulate a smooth integration of landscape and architecture.

The competition ground provides for 4,000 spectators on the higher level of the terrain. The spaces for the competitors are set against the embankment. The transition from exterior to interior is gradual, changing from open space to a metal screen canopy, to perforated concrete screenwalls that provide for transitional semi-sheltered zones and more enclosed changing and wash-rooms. In some instances the perforated concrete screenwalls are replaced with a metal grid screen that enables greater contact between semi-sheltered zones and the adjacent exterior areas. The perforated concrete screenwalls allow daylight into the screened spaces while at the same providing the necessary privacy. The walls are inclined and fold over to meet the higher level terrain into which the interior spaces are set. Wherever the concrete walls are solely retaining walls the soil meets the concrete; yet, when the concrete walls shelter spaces, a glassed surface separates

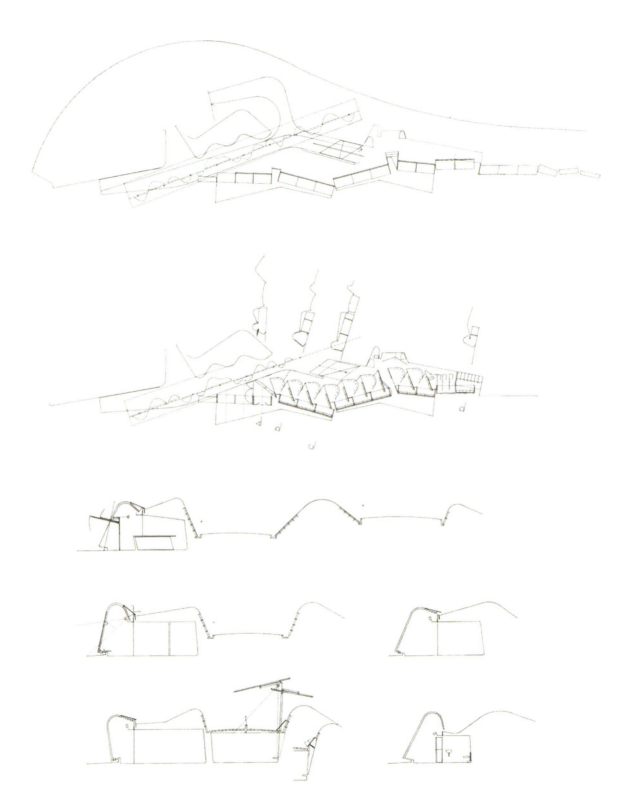

25.3 Plans and section drawings of the Olympic Archery Range competition building. *Top*: Roof plan, showing the access ramps to the areas for spectators. *Centre*: Plan, showing the articulation of the interior spaces and their relation to the steep terrain edge within which they are partly set. *Bottom*: Sectional variation along the north–south axis of the competition building, showing how the ground and architecture are treated as key parts of the enveloping strategy of the scheme. Copyright: Enric Miralles and Carme Pinós.

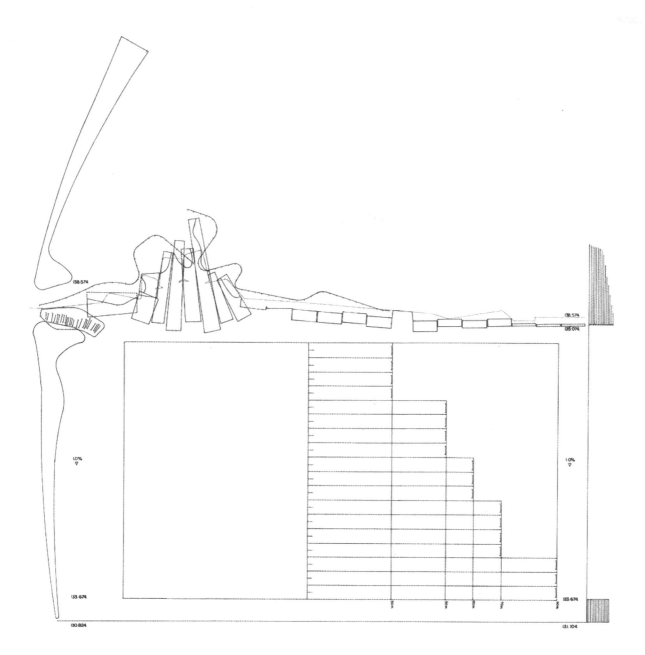

25.4 Site plan of the Olympic Archery Range training ground. The shooting ranges take up most of the site and are positioned to the east. Access to the site is from the south. The training building is positioned along the western edge of the site where it inhabits the embankment as a retaining structure. Copyright: Enric Miralles and Carme Pinós.

concrete and soil to allow daylight into the spaces set into the ground.

The competition building also had to perform as an infrastructure to distribute spectators across its roof surface as an extension of the higher terrain level. The concrete partitioning elements for the spaces below act as the load-bearing structure for the walkable surface above. The walkable spectator surface above is connected via a ramp made of earth that is located at the southern end of the competition building. The steel mesh canopy indicates this transition to the spectator area.

The training building of the archery range is articulated in a different manner.

Miralles and Pinós describe its space as a porch that looks into itself. Along the embankment edge gabion mesh-retaining walls run along most of its length together with a concrete canopy. At the southern end of this embankment wall the porch condition inverts. The gabion mesh wall is exchanged with a concrete retaining wall system that cuts deep into the embankment. This articulated retaining wall, together with a series of free-form masonry walls and the concrete slab canopy, defines the

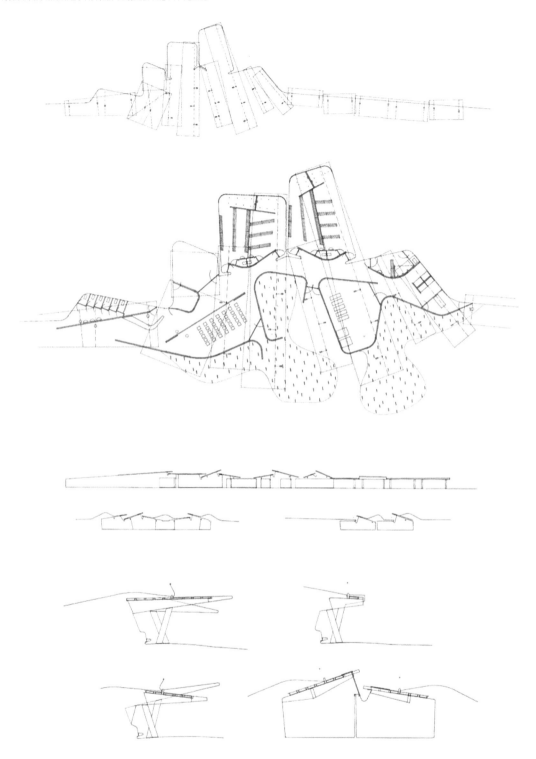

25.5 Plans and section drawings of the Olympic Archery Range training building. *Top*: Roof plan, showing the tessellation of the roof slabs along the north–south axis of the embankment. *Centre*: Plan, showing the changing rooms that are embedded in the embankment as a retaining wall structure, the spaces reserved for circulation, offices and eating that are made of a concrete and masonry partitioning system, and the exterior porch condition that is formed by a free-form partitioning system and the tessellated roof slabs. *Bottom*: Longitudinal and cross-sections along the north–south axis, showing the variation in the porch condition and the spatial coverage provided by the tessellated roof canopy, and detail sections showing how terrain and the tessellated roof slabs are related. Copyright: Enric Miralles and Carme Pinós.

25.6 Views over the Olympic Archery Range training building. *Top*: Looking over the roof towards the shooting range, showing how the roof slabs are articulated in relation to one another, slipping over and under, as well as their relation to the ground of the embankment. *Bottom*: Looking across the roof to the south. The roof becomes an extension of the ground plane of the embankment, making it less of an object and more of a continuation of the landscape. Copyright: Hisao Suzuki.

25.7 Views of the Olympic Archery Range competition building. *Top:* Looking south along the perforated concrete screenwalls from above and how these arch over to meet the retaining walls of the embankment. *Bottom:* Looking north at the entrance of the circulation ramp under the steel mesh canopy from the shooting range level to the spectator level. Here the concrete screenwalls form canopies to offer shelter without interrupting the landscape surface. Copyright: Hisao Suzuki.

extent of the enclosure. The space formed in plan by the free-form masonry walls and concrete retaining walls then becomes enclosed by a system of steel and glass doors that at times are used as a full climate barrier at the perimeter and as partition walls in the interior. The concrete slabs that make up the roof plane and also extend the ground of the embankment are articulated like a paper fan, but instead of a continuous fold the rhythm is broken at the folds. This allows for the provision of daylight into the depth of the plan and also generates a visual relationship with the embankment level above.

Miralles and Pinós pursued the fusion of architecture and landscape in several concurrent projects, most notably their Igualada Cemetery Park scheme from 1991. In this project Miralles and Pinós explored and developed a structural material pallet for the articulation of terrain and containment of earth and, in so doing, produced grounds and ground-related spaces. This pallet includes gabion mesh walls filled with stone and cast in situ or precast concrete elements. The gabions act as retaining walls that facilitate level changes in the terrain in a stereotomic expression and materiality more akin to landscape, whereas the concrete elements provide spaces for urns and coffins, functional spaces for the cemetery and access to adjacent terraced levels.

The way the ground is extended atop of these architectures that cut into it, while articulating a defined tectonic or stereotomic envelope condition, suggests their multiplication in response to more extensive terrain forms.

In utilizing explicit terrain form and in particular embankments and slopes, these works by Miralles and Pinós have the latent potential to be rearticulated as low-rise and high-density architectures for sloped terrains. It is interesting how, for instance, a hill town like Mardin (see Chapter 3) may be rearticulated in a contemporary manner by way of deploying Miralles and Pinós' approach. In so doing, these projects suggest a tectonic/stereotomic resolution to somewhat more diagrammatic urban experimental schemes such as the A Thousand Grounds scheme for Spreebogen, Berlin (see p. 132).

25.8 Views of the interior of the Olympic Archery Range competition building. *Left*: View of the sheltered entrance zone, showing how the perforated concrete and steel mesh screening is used as a secondary enveloping system that enables shade and air to circulate freely through it, keeping it cool during the competition. Glass infill is used as an environmental barrier in areas where more controlled environmental calibrations are needed. *Right*: View of a changing room in the competition building. Here the perforation of the concrete screens provides natural illumination as well as privacy. Copyright: Hisao Suzuki.

PROJECT 26
GC PROSTHO MUSEUM RESEARCH CENTRE
Torii Matsu Machi, Kasugai-shi, Aichi Prefecture, Japan, 2010
Kengo Kuma

Designed by Kengo Kuma and completed in 2010, the GC Prostho Museum Research Centre combines more normative architectural elements with the so-called Chidori system, a traditional Japanese wooden toy with interlocking timber elements that features joints which can be assembled without the aid of fittings such as screws or nails. The Chidori system not only provides a flexible constructional and structural system; it also challenges the understanding and interpretation of the built form in a manner that de-emphasizes the architectural object, a key objective in Kengo Kuma's work.

The GC Prostho Museum however is not Kuma's first foray into this system. He had already experimented with the system for an installation in Milan in 2007. Here too there is an emphasis on the structural system and the spatial architectural effects it produces. Kuma cites in a description of this project another translation of the system as *one thousand birds*, pointing to the effect of birds flying in flocks from which a changing density and transparency results. It is this quality of the system that opens up the question as to what is interior and what is exterior to such form.

The GC Prostho Museum Research Centre is situated in the Aichi Prefecture, Japan, and houses a dental prosthesis research facility. Its primary public space serves the display and exhibition of dental history. The back-of-house architecture is more normative, using concrete walls and floors with glass infill for windows and entrances, and houses the offices, laboratories, etc. The front of house and the public areas are articulated by a dense aggregation of the Chidori system from which the inhabitable spaces are carved out. This deep structure articulates the north-east and south-east perimeter of the building.

The visitor first encounters this deep structure envelope and can catch glimpses of the interior depending on light conditions and viewing angle.

When approaching the building there is at first no indication of the entrance except for a footpath that leads along the length of the volume on the north-eastern edge until the back of the

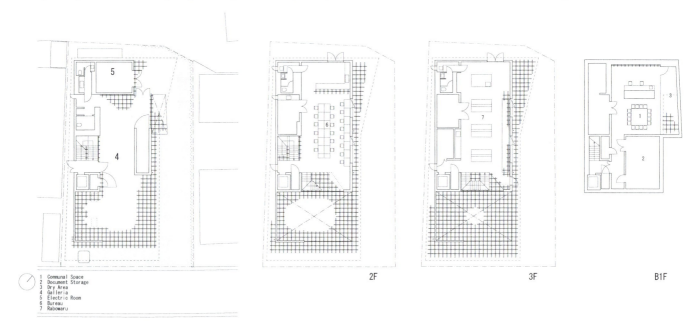

1 Communal Space
2 Document Storage
3 Dry Area
4 Galleria
5 Electric Room
6 Bureau
7 Rabowaru

2F   3F   B1F

26.1 Plans of the GC Prostho Museum Research Centre, showing the arrangement of the Chidori system in relation to the more normative elements of the project. *Left to right*: Ground-floor plan, first-floor plan, second-floor plan and basement plan. Copyright: Kengo Kuma and Associates.

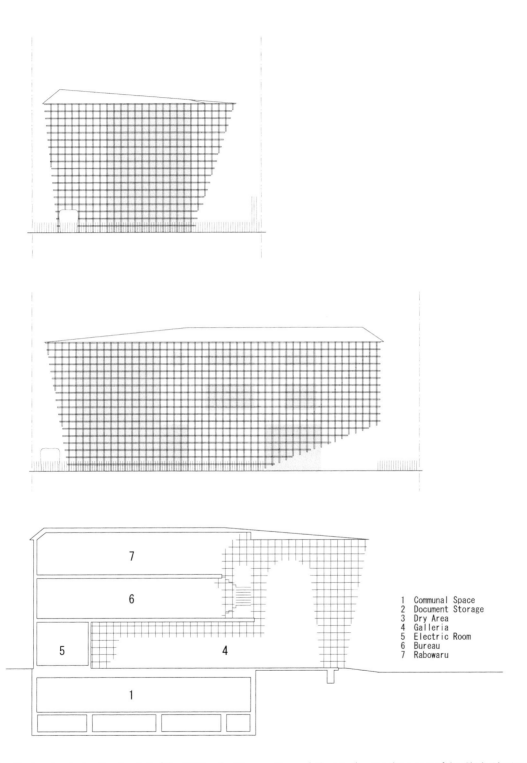

South elevation (*top*) and east elevation (*centre*) of the GC Prostho Museum Research Centre, showing the extent of the Chidori lattice envelope with the environmental barrier areas of glazing highlighted in grey, and section (*bottom*) cut on the north–south axis, showing the depth of the Chidori lattice as it inhabits the interior of the standard floor slabs and how it defines the deep structure building envelope on the southern edge of the building. Copyright: Kengo Kuma and Associates.

26.3 View of the south and east faces of the GC Prostho Museum Research Centre, showing the path along the east façade leading to the entrance of the museum. Here the depth of the Chidori lattice is generally indeterminable. Only at specific viewing angles can the architecture and spaces beyond be seen. Copyright: Kengo Kuma and Associates.

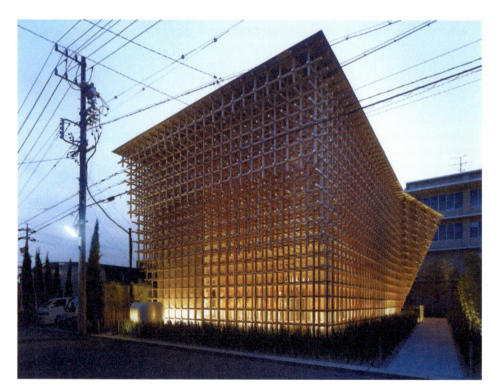

26.4 Night-time view of the south and east faces of the GC Prostho Museum Research Centre. While the interior lighting shows the spaces adjacent to the light source more clearly, the indefinite depth of the deep structure increases with increasing distance from the light source. This effect is accentuated by the change in density of the Chidori system. Copyright: Kengo Kuma and Associates.

26.5 Detail view of the Chidori lattice envelope. Copyright: Kengo Kuma and Associates.

26.6 Interior view of the GC Prostho Museum Research Centre. A direct view of the exterior from the interior is only possible from specific viewing angles. Otherwise the depth of the Chidori lattice renders the depth of the space gradually indeterminable. Copyright: Kengo Kuma and Associates.

26.7 Interior view of the GC Prostho Museum Research Centre vertically up into the atrium space of the main gallery. Copyright: Kengo Kuma and Associates.

26.8 Interior view of the GC Prostho Museum Research Centre's main exhibition space, showing how viewing angle and location of light sources affect the perception of the density of the Chidori lattice. Copyright: Kengo Kuma and Associates.

site is reached where the entrance is located. During daytime the lattice that makes up the building volume seems to hover in places like a heavy shroud that changes over the day, depending on the light conditions. When entering, visitors arrive in a cave-like space carved out of the lattice that is concurrently experienced as connected to the exterior while distanced from it due to the viewing angle densities of the Chidori system. The glass infill that climatically separates the exhibition space from the exterior is barely visible.

In some instances artefacts are displayed within the lattice that become part of the building's envelope. Although the primary spatial experience of the lattice is in the main gallery space on the ground-floor level this lattice expands vertically to form a several-storey-high space and slips below to the basement level, where the stairs connect the first- and second-floor levels and visually connect the carved-out atrium-like space of the gallery below.

The material treatment of the lattice should also be noted. The exterior and interior protruding ends of the lattice are painted white, accentuating where the field of lattice has been cut away to define the interior and exterior geometry. This is a simple treatment but has a great impact upon the readability of the space of the interior and the geometry of the exterior. It defines, as it were, virtual surfaces of the exterior and interior through a cloud of points which changes depending on the beholders' visual relation to the lattice and changing light conditions throughout the day. This move also effaces the lattice, making it less of an object and more of an armature to define space.

PROJECT 27
ENDESA PAVILION
Barcelona, Spain, 2011
IAAC – Institute for Advanced Architecture of Catalonia

Completed in 2011, the 140-square-metre Endesa Pavilion was produced at the IAAC – the Institute for Advanced Architecture of Catalonia – by a team led by architect Rodrigo Rubio. Sited in the marina dock of the Barcelona Olympic Port on Moll de la Marina, the pavilion was produced for the Smart City BCN International Congress Showroom and acted as a control room for testing and monitoring numerous projects that were related to the intelligent management of power sources. The pavilion was designed to be self-sufficient and a prototype for the use of solar energy.

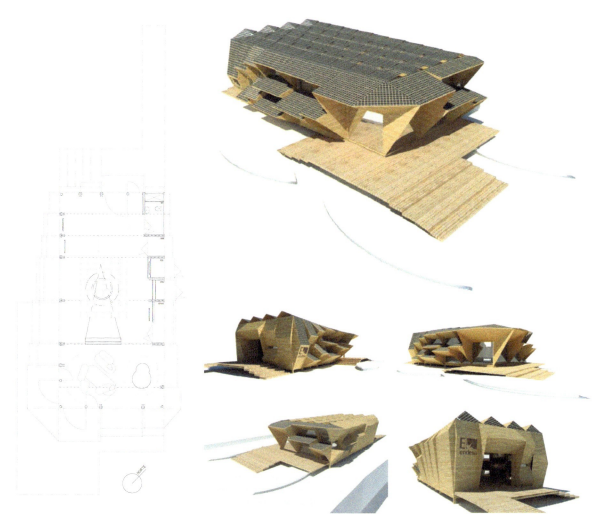

27.1 *Left*: Plan of the Endesa Pavilion, showing the central rectangular space flanked on its perimeter by the spatial pockets of the panelling that folds in and out. *Right*: Rendered views of the scheme, showing the folded articulation of the envelope that generates openings for entrances and windows, as well as inclined surfaces for the placement of photovoltaic panels. Copyright: IAAC – Institute for Advanced Architecture of Catalonia.

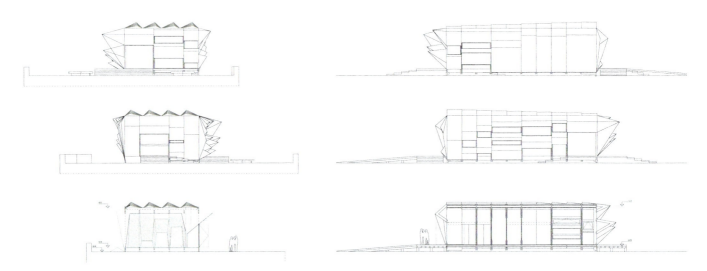

27.2 Elevations and sections of the Endesa Pavilion. *Top, left to right*: South-east and north-east elevations. *Centre, left to right*: North-west and south-west elevations. *Bottom, left to right*: Cross-section and longitudinal section. Copyright: IAAC – Institute for Advanced Architecture of Catalonia.

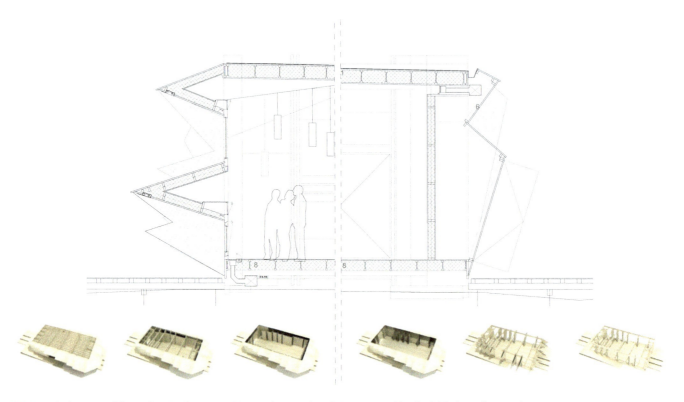

27.3 Detailed section of the Endesa Pavilion (*top*), showing the spatial pockets generated by the folded panelling, and cut-away axonometric sequence (bottom), showing the tectonic elements of the project. Copyright: IAAC – Institute for Advanced Architecture of Catalonia.

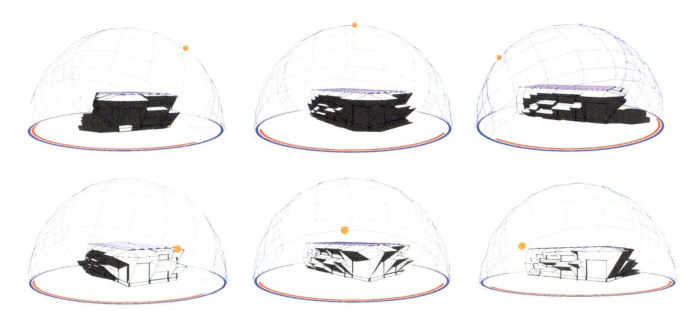

27.4 Location-specific solar analysis of the Endesa Pavilion, showing areas with increased solar gain and self-shading. Copyright: IAAC – Institute for Advanced Architecture of Catalonia.

The project was designed and constructed in three months. The primary material used in its construction is laminated timber: fir for the exterior and birch for the interior. Glazing completed the climate envelope of the pavilion. A further layer of the pavilion's envelope comprises the photovoltaic panels that cover the roof and are also placed on parts of the envelope at the south-west and south-east faces.

The envelope of the pavilion is articulated by way of a modular component called 'parametric solar brick' which folds outward from the perimeter of the interior space of the pavilion. This modular element serves self-shading purposes and the reduction of solar impact and glare upon the interior, as well as for the positioning of the solar panels at a suitable angle for maximum solar gain.

While the modular element is of a set width that follows construction standards, the specific depth and pitch are dependent on the positioning relating to the solar gain and the spatial demand of the interior. In some parts of the envelope a singular element or a set of stacked-up elements with glass infill between them take up the whole segment of the façade, while in others the element is lifted up to allow access into the pavilion. The top face of the modular element is where the photovoltaic patches are placed, making the most of the parametrically positioned surfaces that were angled for maximum solar gain. The bottom face consists of either timber or glass. In this way the modular element results in a series of small spaces that are nested along the perimeter of the rectangular interior space and offer at least latent potential for inhabitation. In so doing, the project resonates with Toyo Ito's Serpentine Pavilion (see p. 218).

The south-facing part of the envelope is more open and permeable, and the articulation of the parametric solar bricks is also at its most extreme in size, with deep extensions outward from the boundary line which defines the rectangular volume. These deep extensions outward make the most of energy gain on the surfaces that are directly impacted by the sun and their depth also offers maximum shading. The northern part of the envelope is more opaque and closed in order to minimize heat and

27.5　Images of the different stages of the construction process of the Endesa Pavilion. Copyright: IAAC – Institute for Advanced Architecture of Catalonia.

27.6 Interior views of the Endesa Pavilion, showing the spatial pockets generated by the folded panelling of the envelope. Copyright: IAAC – Institute for Advanced Architecture of Catalonia.

energy loss. These areas are almost the inverse of the southern-oriented areas. This is particularly notable at the top end of the north-eastern façade, which features a thickening of the modular element on the interior of the scheme that houses the WC and other areas of storage and mechanical infrastructure. The interior consists of two spaces: a control room/lecturing space and a formal/informal meeting area located along the southern face of the scheme and which benefits from the openness of the envelope and the resulting views. The exterior consists of a timber deck, which establishes a raised ground condition for the pavilion and provides access, and to the south it provides a surface for exterior activities. The other provision is a canopy that results from the depth and articulation of the parametric solar brick and which is more prominent on the southern section of the

27.7 Exterior views of the Endesa Pavilion. *Top*: The nesting of the folded panelling of the envelope provides canopies of varied height, width and depth, which articulate the envelope into three spatial zones along the façade. *Bottom*: A larger canopied area in the corner of the pavilion facilitates access to the raised platform. Copyright: IAAC – Institute for Advanced Architecture of Catalonia.

27.8 South-west elevation (*top*) and detail of the north-east elevation (*bottom*) of the Endesa Pavilion. Copyright: IAAC – Institute for Advanced Architecture of Catalonia.

27.9 Night-time view of the Endesa Pavilion, showing how the downward-facing panels of the envelope that are adjacent to windows reflect and accentuate the interior lighting, thus switching from shading during daytime to indirect illumination of the adjacent exterior during the night. Copyright: IAAC – Institute for Advanced Architecture of Catalonia.

envelope, where it forms a large corner window and doors and the main communication space with the exterior deck.

The design team of the Endesa Pavilion also speculated about deploying the parametrically defined envelope system on different building volumes such as multi-storey buildings. The question that arises from these speculative efforts is how to inform the articulation of such an envelope in an increasingly location-specific manner. Clearly this can pertain to a broad pallet of criteria ranging from environmental performance to qualitative aspects of inhabiting the spaces within and adjacent to a given design, both from a human as well as a multi-species perspective. It would seem that such an approach would require well-defined spatial arrangements and hierarchies, ranging from vertically connective spaces, all the way to the spatial pockets generated by the envelope. Thus, it would seem that the latent potential of this design system is considerable.

PROJECT 28
ESTONIAN ACADEMY OF ARTS
Estonia, Tallinn, 2008
Sean Lally WEATHERS in collaboration with Morris Architects

The entry to the Estonian Academy of Arts (EAA) competition design by Sean Lally WEATHERS along with collaborators Morris Architects comprises two primary design strategies: (1) the implementation of a public landscape within the confines of the building, and (2) the implementation of atria that facilitate a range of different interior climates. The interiorized public park programme is intended to be active all the year round and is implemented on the ground and first floor facilitated by a continuous ramped surface.

Given Estonia's cold and dark winters, this aim would not typically be achievable. The park inhabits the continuous ground and is open to the surrounding streetscapes and urban fabrics that meet its edges. Locating specific programmatic infrastructures such as the mechanical rooms and black box theatres within this new ground frees up the subsequent floors above from anything other than studio spaces for the students. This also allows for tapping into the building's excess heat that is produced in order to provide the climatic conditions for garden conditions

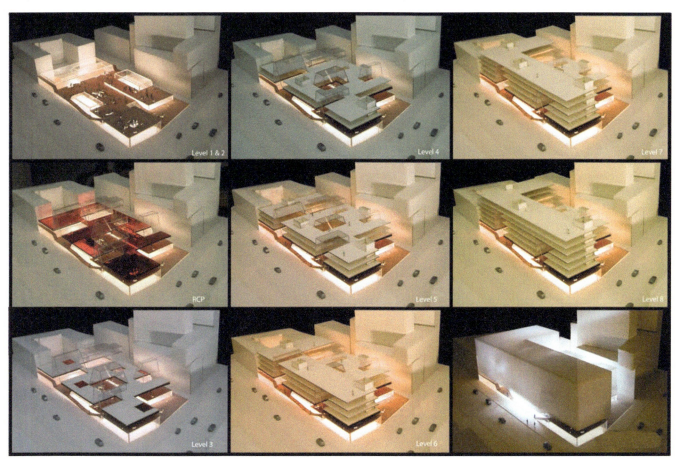

28.1 Cut-away model views of the Estonian Academy of Arts scheme, showing how the ground is continuous and multiplied within the building, as well as the atrium spaces that extend vertically through the volume and serve the interior climate modulation. Copyright: WEATHERS in collaboration with Morris Architects.

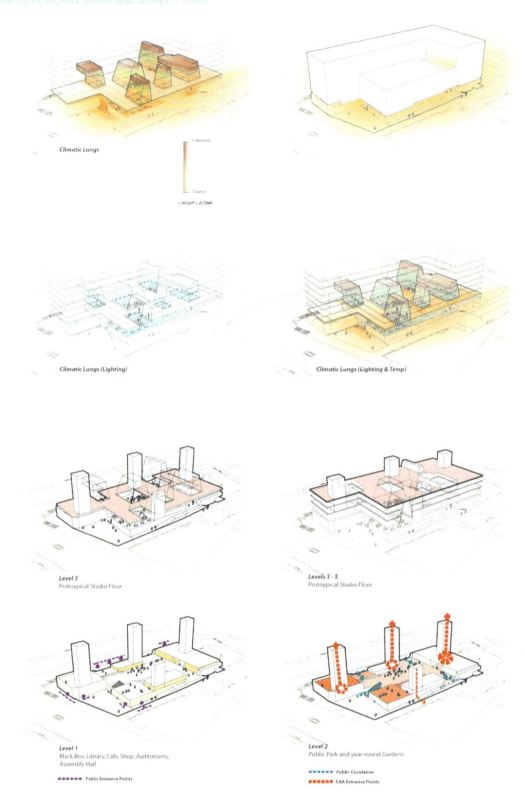

28.2 Diagrams of the Estonian Academy of Arts. *Top row*: Atria for interior climate modulation, showing the gradient of temperature capture and the volume of the scheme. *Upper middle row*: Atria for interior climate modulation, showing the artificial lighting strategy and combined diagram of the lighting and climatic modulation conditions. *Lower middle row*: Levels 3 and 5 arrangements of studio spaces and their adjacency to the atria. *Bottom row*: Spatial and programmatic arrangement of Level 1, which establishes the new ground condition for the scheme and the public park/garden level which provides circulation for the park and entrance points into the EAA. Copyright: WEATHERS in collaboration with Morris Architects.

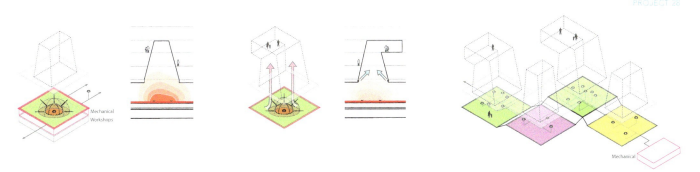

28.3 Diagrams of the Estonian Academy of Arts, showing the role of the atria in the interior climate modulation.
From left to right: (1) Diagram of the point source relationship between the ambient heat source of the workshops and the climatic lungs. (2) Occupation of the climate zones on the upper levels with lighting projected from below to the studios above. (3) Variations in climate-based zoning of the interior. Copyright: WEATHERS in collaboration with Morris Architects.

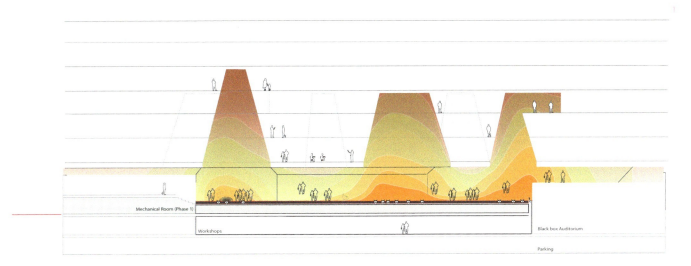

28.4 Diagrammatic section of the Estonian Academy of Arts, showing the vertical gradient of the interior climatic modulation in the public park and climatic lung zones and atria of the scheme. Copyright: WEATHERS in collaboration with Morris Architects.

even during the winter. This use of the inevitable heat sources begins to produce temperature zones as climate barriers. The sandwiched public space is also linked to the studio space floors above by way of the openings in the floor slabs that run vertically and establish the atria known as 'climatic lungs' that capture the heated air and produce a gradient of air temperatures, bringing warmer temperatures into the centre of the building's deep plan, and in so doing, produces an array of distinct climates throughout the building. In addition, the atria also provide the main source of artificial lighting across the spectrum for half of the year when natural daylight is limited during the winter months.

The exterior perimeter of the building that would normally define the primary climate envelope and climate barrier is rendered as an opaque shroud, reminiscent of the Beinecke Rare Book and Manuscript Library at Yale University, designed by Gordon Bunshaft for Skidmore, Owings & Merrill. This scheme by Bunshaft too has a number of envelopes that address specific environmental constraints. The exterior envelope of the library is an opaque translucent cover made of marble that allows the main reading spaces to be illuminated and also acts as a protective screen to the rare materials deep within its interior from direct sunlight. This space has a climate condition that is suitable for both the visitor and reader. The next envelope within this marble box shroud is a glass box envelope that houses the rare books and manuscripts. It seems likely that the scheme for the Estonian Academy of Arts evolved around similar motives. During the summer months the opaque shroud protects the studios from the near-constant sunlight that would affect the comfort of the studio spaces and the varied interior climates in the atria.

During the dark winter months the artificial illumination of the atria would also illuminate the building within the cityscape.

This scheme draws on the articulation of the envelope via the perforation of the floor slabs in a manner reminiscent of projects like MVRDV's Villa VPRO (see p. 178) and Cloud9's MediaTic (see

28.5 Typical floor plans of the Estonian Academy of Arts: Level 4 (*top*) and Level 5 (*bottom*). Copyright: WEATHERS in collaboration with Morris Architects.

28.6 Rendered view of the Estonian Academy of Arts from street level looking into the climate envelope of the public park space and up into one of the atria. Copyright: WEATHERS in collaboration with Morris Architects.

p. 258), yet it internalizes the resulting spaces and emanates from the new ground that houses the new public park. In turn, this inverts the reading as to what is typically exterior and interior.

The new public park and the atria combine to set out the structure for the most dynamic enveloping condition of the scheme: the artificial climate that inhabits this sandwiched space. Similar to the initially intended hot-air curtain of MVRDV's Villa VPRO, the scheme's varied interior climates act as a barrier, yet also facilitate the public park. In this project excess heat, which is commonly seen as a negative condition, becomes an asset due to the way in which the spatial arrangement utilizes it to enable the programmes of the scheme. In so doing, the scheme reveals its affinity with Yves Klein Air-Architecture:

> Air, gases, fire, sound, odours, magnetic forces, electricity, and electronics are materials. They should have two principle functions, specifically: to protect against the elements – rain, wind, and atmospheric conditions in general – and the function of thermal conditioning (heating and cooling).
> (Klein 2013 [1959]: 64)

PROJECT 29
MEDIATIC
Barcelona, Spain, 2007 to 2010
Cloud 9

The MediaTic designed by Cloud 9 was completed in 2010. The project is located in the 22@ district in Barcelona, a former industrial area that has been redeveloped as a technology and innovation hub. The competition brief for the project asked for an architecture that was about technology, information and communication. Cloud 9 was very much suited to take on this task. The studio's previous work boldly experimented with concepts that took on issues of the digital-influencing manufacturing, technologies related to energy efficiencies, intelligent systems and self-sufficiency. Project such as Cloud 9's Villa Nurbs became vehicles for testing these concepts to direct material consequence.

The MediaTic project is a hybrid office building that is conceptualized as a hub for exchanging ideas and communicating across platforms and expertise. Further to this, it is a building that

29.1 View of the south-east and north-east faces of MediaTic, showing the varied articulation of the building envelope depending on orientation. The north-east elevation features a glass curtain wall. In the south-east face the glass curtain wall is set back and partly veiled by a tessellated ETFE cushion surface of varied translucency and coloration. Photography: Michael Hensel.

29.2 View of the south-east and south-west faces of MediaTic. The latter features vertical ETFE channels that can be filled with coloured gas. Photography: Michael Hensel.

addresses public, private, corporate, academic and business in a manner that foregrounds flattening the prevailing hierarchies that currently structure Western city fabrics. It is also a project that addresses how architecture takes a position on energy efficiency, challenging the current approach based on technological means only, through the application of varied and articulated spatial and material solutions.

The MediaTic is an eight-storey block, with an approximately 40m x 40m footprint. The ground floor consists of a large lobby that is column free and open plan, and also houses a mix of public and academic entities such as a multimedia museum and institutes from the local university. The remaining floors above have a mix of shared space, small offices and dedicated open-plan space to incubate young companies and to act as a base for foreign companies in Barcelona. Within the building, 15 per cent of the space is communal. These spaces are delineated by the green coloration of the floor surface.

Structurally, the scheme adopted an approach that would minimize the need for large or numerous columns and would accentuate the varied degrees of transparency aimed for. The primary structure is defined by a series of truss columns and beams. The column trusses delineate the perimeters on the

29.3 Close-up view of the south-west face of MediaTic. A large cut-out of the ETFE channels provides ventilation and daylight for the central atrium of the building. Photography: Michael Hensel.

29.4 Views of the interstitial spaces of the south-east face of the MediaTic, between the ETFE cushion veil and the glass curtain wall. This space is used for circulation and semi-sheltered balconies. Photography: Michael Hensel.

south-eastern and north-western sides of the scheme and are set in place by a tensile triangulated lattice. These support the truss beams which are at a depth of two-storeys, making them inhabitable, and span the 35 metres between the two truss walls. The floors are then suspended on thin tensile supports. The area that gains the greatest impact of the strategy is in the lobby space which has no vertical structure to disrupt the open-plan setting.

The building's enclosure is defined by two materials; on the north-eastern and north-western faces the climatic envelope consists of a glass curtain wall. On the south-eastern and south-western faces the climate envelope is set back to provide an interstitial space that is in parts covered by ETFE cushions. These inflated ETFE cushions enable the building to react to solar impact in two distinctly different ways.

The south-east elevation features tessellated cushion patterns with occasional openings to allow for ventilation and to provide views from the balconies that are set within the interstitial space between the ETFE and glass envelopes. The cushions consist of several layers of ETFE that feature a screen-printed dot pattern. By way of actuators that are linked with sensors on the envelope, the distance between the layers in each cushion may be changed and thus the overlapping dot patterns create greater or lesser shading. The south-west elevation features vertical ETFE channels that can be filled with coloured nitrogen gas which acts as a solar reflector when the solar gains are high.

The MediaTic also provides variations of the façade conditions along the four faces of the building, and also varied articulations of the floor slabs with cut-outs that result in a large semi-sheltered atrium space which faces south-west. The north-east face is a glass curtain wall, and acts as a climate barrier that does not need to address direct solar impact. The south-west face is made of glass curtain walls and ETFE cushions and fulfils the dual role of climate barrier and solar shading device. This face also features an opening that cuts through its centre and deep into the building's interior, providing natural cross-ventilation to the atrium space and the different floors of the building. The thick faces are arranged along the north-west and south-east edges of the building. Both of these faces inhabit the depth of the vertical structural truss. The north-west face is the location for the building's circulation and infrastructure which inhabits the bulk of the structural depth of the truss, housing lifts, stairs and lavatories. The edge along the south-east becomes a transitional zone between exterior and interior. The outer envelope consists of the aforementioned tessellated surface of ETFE cushions that vary in their opacity and transparency, as well as coloration to modulate solar impact. The green-coloured cushions provide constant solar shading of the interior and also act as a solar canopy on the exterior balconies. The tessellation pattern allows for openings in the surface where light penetration is needed or wanted in the interior.

The articulation of the floor slabs is reminiscent of MVRDV's Villa VPRO (see p. 178). A deep horizontal cut across four levels halfway into the plan meets a vertical punch through the slabs from the three levels above. This allows for natural light to reach

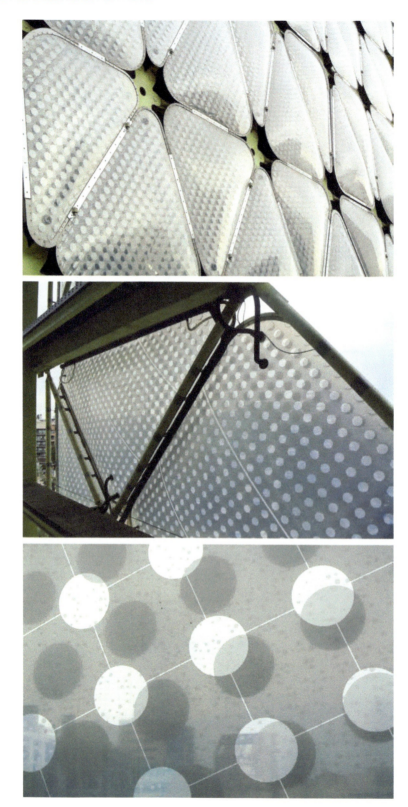

29.5 Detail view of the ETFE cushions of the south-east face of MediaTic. *Top*: Exterior face detail of the tessellation pattern of the ETFE cushions. *Centre*: View of the translucent ETFE cushions from the interstitial space between the cushions and the glass curtain wall, also showing the actuators that modify the cushion cross-section and thus the shading effect on the interior. *Bottom*: Close-up view of the screen-printed solar shading pattern on the ETFE cushions. Photography: Michael Hensel.

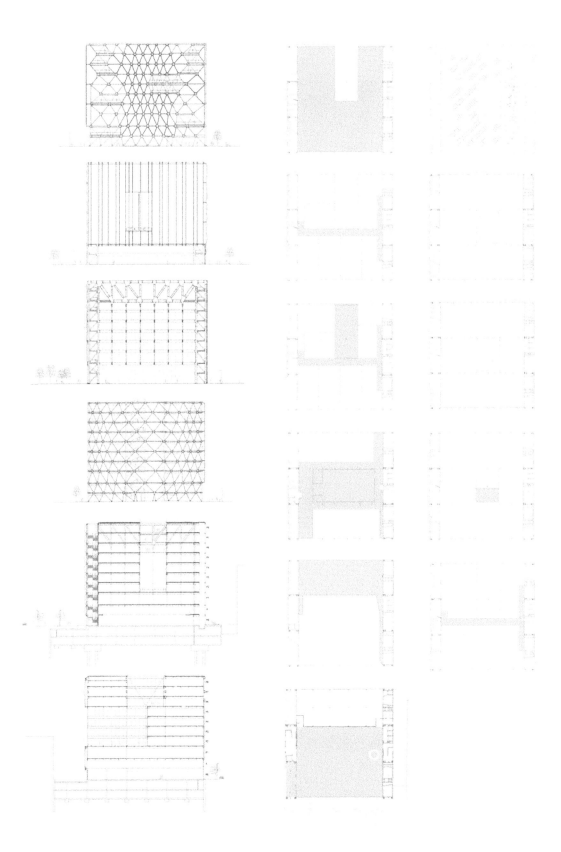

29.6 *Left column, top to bottom*: South-east elevation, south-west elevation, north-east elevation, and north-west elevation and sections. *Centre and right column*: Plans of the MediaTic. Copyright: Cloud 9.

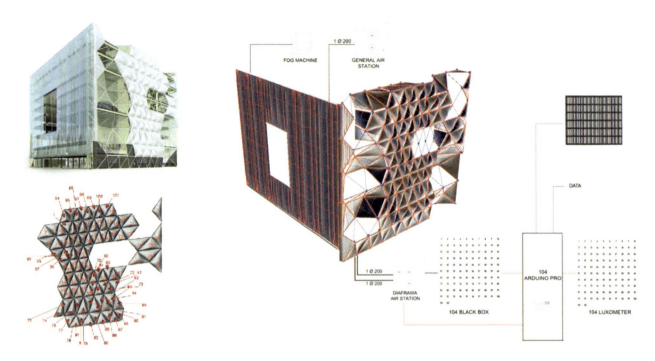

29.7 *Top left*: Rendered view of the south-east and west faces of the MediaTic. *Bottom left*: Diagram of the tessellated ETFE system on the south-east face. *Right*: Diagram showing the set-up of the actuator-driven modulation of the tessellated ETFE cushions of the south-east face and the fog machine and vertical ETFE channels of the south-west face. Copyright: Cloud 9.

into the deep plan of the building as well as effective cross-ventilation. Balconies protrude into the atrium offering semi-sheltered spaces. While it is at first not initially apparent from the exterior, the amount of semi-sheltered transitional space of the building is considerably large and one of the key features of the MediaTic. And while the technical solutions implemented in the building are novel and impressive, these work in tandem with the less obvious and assuming spatial organization of the project.

The MediaTic obviously constitutes a contemporary discrete and distinctive urban architecture, albeit one that stages a range of interesting interactions with the physical environment; the question is whether the design strategies that underlie the project are applicable to non-discrete embedded architecture. One possibility that comes to mind is the use of the light ETFE envelope as a canopy or cover that is not constrained to the volume of the building alone, but that enters into affiliations with the wider setting and with landscape. For this purpose it is possible, for instance, to imagine a hybrid between the MediaTic and RCR's Marquee at Les Cols (see p. 000), with the PVC canopy of the latter being populated with the ETFE cushions of the former. Moreover, it is possible to imagine that the interstitial and atria spaces generated by the envelopes of the MediaTic are linked in section with spaces beyond the footprint of the building, above and beyond the publicly accessible ground plane.

PROJECT 30
BLUR BUILDING
Yverdon-les-Bains, Switzerland, Swiss National Expo 2002
Diller, Scofidio and Renfro

Designed by Diller, Scofidio and Renfro, the Blur Building was completed in 2002 for the sixth Swiss National Exposition in Neuchâtel, Yverdon-les-Bains. The scheme stages architecture as a climatic event, following a lineage of work that commences with Yves Klein's Air-Architectures of the late 1950s and early 1960s, and that spans to interior artworks such as Olafur Elisson's Weather Project at the Tate Modern and Berndnaut Smilde's clouds generated inside buildings. The Blur project evolved from the desire to construct an architecture from the predominant elements of its setting: air and water organized as a climatic event.

The project consists of four distinct elements: (1) the tensegrity structure, (2) decks and catwalks that facilitate visitor circulation, (3) the technology that facilitates the production of water vapour, and (4) the generated water vapour that constitutes the most visible feature of the project. The tensegrity structure is anchored to plies in the bed of the lake and is ellipsoidal in plan, measuring 100 metres in the long axis and 60 metres in

30.1 Aerial view of the Blur Building. Parts of the deck and the tensegrity structure may be discerned through the mist, as well as the bridges that connect the project to the shore of the lake. Copyright: Diller, Scofidio and Renfro.

30.2 View of the Blur Building from the shoreline. The tensegrity structure and the stairs connecting the bridges to the platform may be seen through the mist. Copyright: Diller, Scofidio and Renfro.

30.3 Night-time view of the Blur Building from the shoreline, showing the illuminated bridges and vapour cloud. Copyright: Diller, Scofidio and Renfro.

30.4 This view conveys the spatial perception of the project from within the mist on the main platform. The vapour renders the spatial depth of the project indefinite. There exists no distinctly delineating threshold, but instead a gradient density of mist that changes in response to wind conditions. Copyright: Diller, Scofidio and Renfro.

30.5 This view of the Blur Building from the shoreline shows how the artificially produced vapour cloud of the project blends with the low natural clouds. Copyright: Diller, Scofidio and Renfro.

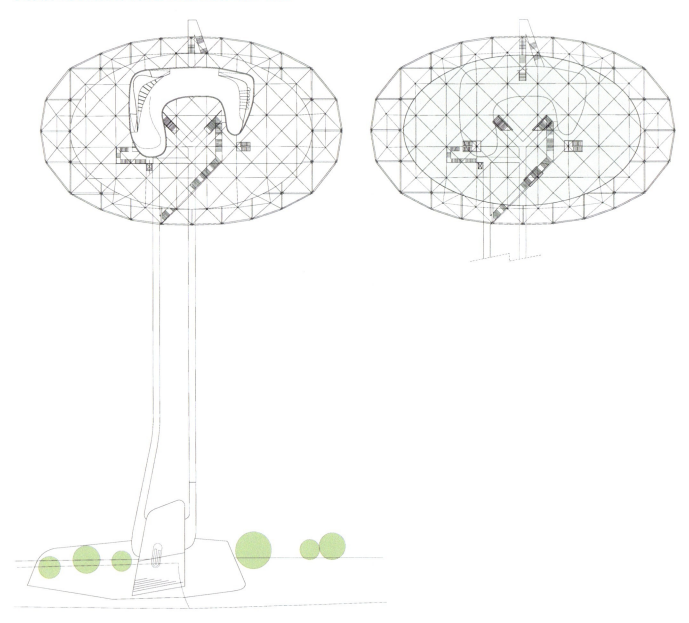

30.6 Plans of the Blur Building. *Left*: Upper deck with the Water Bar and gangway stairs and bridges. *Right*: Media platform level. Copyright: Diller, Scofidio and Renfro.

the short axis. With a vertical height of 23 metres, the structure seems to float above the lake, an impression that is accentuated by the 35-metre cantilevers from the four main columns. The use of the tensegrity system delivers a light and apparently floating structure. Within the section of this tensegrity cloud there are two areas for the public and the display of the pavilion's media exhibitions and events. The first is the media platform at about 11 metres height above the lake surface. The second is the so-called 'Angel Deck', which sits about 19 metres above the lake's surface. All circulation elements are suspended from the main tensegrity structure.

The actual water vapour cloud consists of water pumped directly from the lake which is filtered and shot as a fine mist through an array of densely placed high-pressure nozzles. The array of 31,500 nozzles is placed at 20cm intervals across the structure, computer regulated and adjusted to the local humidity, temperature, wind speed and direction. They also produce an acoustic effect of white noise as they pulse on mass. As visitors move over the bridges out on to the lake and up the catwalks and stairs to the media platform level they become immersed in the cloud to experience a space that lacks form, scale, depth, features, surface or mass. From the first deck the public can

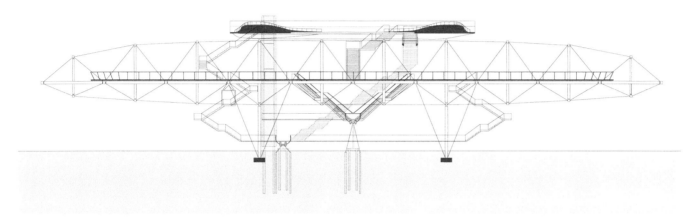

Section of the Blur Building, showing the tensegrity structure anchored to the lake bed, upper and lower decks, and gangway stairs. Copyright: Diller, Scofidio and Renfro.

ascend again to the Angel Deck to emerge to a position of being perched on top of the cloud. From here visitors re-engage with the surrounding context with a view across the lake and the Expo park, as well as being offered sampled waters from around the world in the Water Bar.

The Blur Building poses two interesting possibilities: (1) an architecture that actively engages the local physical environment in its dynamic articulation, and (2) an unconstrained engagement of the visitor in this dynamic. A space that is largely organized as a local climatic event can make provisions both for humans and other species. Here the ability of the pedospheric regime to produce such conditions should not be overlooked, as this offers an expanded range of possibilities to generate localized climatic conditions and effects.

The project's vapour cloud also acts as a direct material index to the prevailing environmental conditions, including wind direction and speed, which immediately impact upon the vapour cloud. Besides affecting its distribution, direction and density wind, humidity and temperature changes also impact upon the height of the cloud above the surface of the lake. Moreover, the technical apparatus enables turning off the whole or parts of the architecture when required or in response to adverse conditions produced by the vapour cloud in interaction with the local physical environment. The Blur Building is simultaneously an exterior and an interior and its threshold is gradient and ultimately permeable. Yet, the question arises as to how to provide differentiated spaces within the cloud. This could be accomplished by the strategic distribution of the high-pressure nozzles in conjunction with hot-air curtains and air valves that impact upon the vapour in a controlled way, as well as a multiple envelope strategy that exteriorizes or interiorizes the vapour cloud locally.

Bibliography

Addington, M. and Schodek, D. (2005) *Smart Materials and Technologies for the Architecture and Design Professions*, Oxford: Architectural Press, Elsevier.

Addington, M., Kienzl, N. and Intrachooto, S. (2001) 'Mat Buildings and the Environment – Examination of a Typology'. In Sarkis, H. (ed.) *Case: Le Corbusier's Venice Hospital*, New York: Prestel, Harvard Design School, pp. 66-79.

Alexander, C. (1964) *Notes on the Synthesis of Form*, Cambridge, MA: Harvard University Press.

Alexander, C., Ishikawa, S., Silverstein, M., Jacobsen, M., Fiksdahl-King, I. and Angel, S. (1977) *A Pattern Language – Towns-Buildings-Constructions*, New York: Oxford University Press.

Allen, S. (1997) 'From Object to Field'. In Bates, D. and Davidson, P. *AD Architecture after Geometry* No. 127, pp. 24–31.

—— (2011) 'Working Concepts: Landform Building. In Allen, S. and McQuade, M. (eds) *Landform Building: Architecture's New Terrain*, Baden, Switzerland: Lars Müller, pp. 32–37.

Banham, R. (1969) *The Architecture of the Well-Tempered Environment*, Chicago, IL: University of Chicago Press.

Bardgett, R.D. and Wardle, D.A. (2010) *Aboveground–Belowground Linkages – Biotic Interactions, Ecosystem Processes and Global Change*, Oxford: Oxford University Press.

Behling, S. and Behling, S. (2000) *Solar Power: The Evolution of Sustainable Architecture*, Munich; London; New York: Prestel.

Berlage, H.P. (1908) *Grundlagen und Entwicklung der Architektur: 4 Vorträge gehalten im Kunstgewerbemuseum zu Zürich*, Berlin: Bard. Reprinted by ULAN Press.

Bettum, J. and Hensel, M. (2000) 'Channelling Systems: Dynamic Processes and Digital Time-based Methods in Urban Design'. In Rahim, A. (ed.) *AD Contemporary Processes in Architecture* No. 145, pp. 36–43.

Blau, E. and Kaufman, E. (ed.) (1989) 'Cities in Plan and Profile'. In Blau, E. and Kaufman, E. (ed.) *Architecture and its Image – Four Centuries of Architectural Representation*, Cambridge, MA: MIT Press, pp. 218–227.

Braathen, M., Kropf, R. and Stangeland, S.H. (eds) (2012) *Helen and Hard – Relational Design*, Ostfildern: Hatje Cantz.

Brandstetter, T. and Harrasser, K. (2010) 'Introduction'. In Brandstetter, T., Harrasser, K. and Friesinger, G. (eds) *Das Leben und seine Räume*, Vienna: Turia+ Kant, pp. 9–22.

Candilis, G. (1957) 'Les Criteres', *L'Architecture d'Aujourd'hui* Vol. 73.

Candilis, G., Josic, A. and Woods, S. (1964) 'Berlin Free University', *Le Carré Bleu* Vol. 1.pp

Canguilhem, G. (1980 [1952]) 'Le vivant et son milieu'. In Canguilhem, G. *La connaissance de la vie*, Paris: J. Vrin, pp. 129–154.

Collins, P. (2003 [1965]) *Changing Ideas in Modern Architecture*, Montreal: McGill-Queens University Press.

Colquhoun, A. (1989) 'The Significance of Le Corbusier'. In Colquhoun, A. *Modernity and the Classical Tradition – Architectural Essays 1980–1987*. Cambridge, MA: MIT Press, p. 187.

—— (2007 [1996]) 'Critique of Regionalism'. In Canizaro, V.B. (ed.) *Architectural Regionalism – Collected Writings on Place, Identity, Modernity, and Tradition*, New York: Princeton Architectural Press, pp. 141–155.

—— (2009) 'The Significance of Le Corbusier'. In Colquhoun, A., *Collected Essays in Architectural Criticism*, London: Black: pp. 193–200.

Corner, J. (2006) 'Terra Fluxus'. In: Waldheim, C. (ed.) *The Landscape Urbanism Reader*, New York: Princeton Architectural Press.

Cressey, G.B. (1955) *Land of the 500 Million: A Geography of China*. New York: McGraw-Hill.

Curtis, W.J.R. (2011) 'A Conversation with RCR Aranda Pigem Vilalta Arquitectes'. *RCR Arquitectes 2007–2012 – Poetic Abstractions – El Croquis 162*, pp.16–35.

Da Rocha, P. (2007) *Paulo Mendes da Rocha – Fifty Years*, New York: Rizzoli.

Deleuze, G. and Guattari, F. (1988 [1980]) *A Thousand Plateaus – Capitalism and Schizophrenia*, London: Athlone.

Derrida, J. (1989 [1962]) *Edmund Husserl's Origin of Geometry – An Introduction*, Lincoln; London: University of Nebraska Press.

Eisenman, P. (1992) 'Unfolding Events'. In Crary, J. and Kwinter, S. (eds) *Zone 6 Incorporations*, New York: Urzone, pp. 423–426.

—— (2003) Interview by Vladimir Belogolovsky, online: http://www.curatorialproject.com/interviews/petereisenmani.html (accessed 1 July 2013).

—— (2004) 'Cannaregio Town Square'. In Noever, P. (ed.) *Barefoot on White Hot Walls*, Ostfildern-Ruit: Hatje Cantz, pp. 104–107.

Fathy, H. (1986) *Natural Energy and Vernacular Architecture: Principles and Examples with Reference to Hot Arid Climates*, Chicago, IL: University of Chicago Press.

Frampton, K. (1983) 'Towards a Critical Regionalism: Six Points for an Architecture of Resistance'. In Foster, H. (ed.) *The Anti-aesthetic – Essays on Post-modern Culture*, Seattle: Bay Press, pp. 16–30.

—— (2007 [1987]) 'Ten Points on an Architecture of Regionalism: A Provisional Polemic'. In Canizaro, V.B. (ed.) *Architectural Regionalism – Collected Writings on Place, Identity, Modernity, and Tradition*, New York: Princeton Architectural Press, pp. 375–385.

—— (1996) *Studies in Tectonic Culture*, Cambridge, MA: MIT Press.

Gates, C. (2003) *Ancient Cities – The Archaeology of Urban Life in the Ancient Near East and Egypt, Greece, and Rome*, London: Routledge.

Golany, G.S. (1992) *Chinese Earth-sheltered Dwellings – Indigenous Lessons for Modern Urban Design*, Honolulu: University of Hawaii Press.

Gray, M. (2004) *Geodiversity: Valuing and Conserving Abiotic Nature*, London: John Wiley & Sons.

Hamann, H. and Moro, J.L. (1984) 'Toldos'. In Krause-Valdovinos, G. (ed.) *Schattenzelte: Sun and Shade – Toldos, Vela* (IL series, Vol. 30), Stuttgart: Institute for Lightweight Structures, pp. 93–103.

Harper, J.L. and Hawksworth, D.L. (1995) *Biodiversity – Measurement and Estimation*. Oxford: Chapman and Hall.

Hensel, M. (2013) *AD Primer: Performance-oriented Architecture – Rethinking Architectural Design and the Built Environment*, London: AD Wiley.

Hensel, M. and Sunguroğlu Hensel, D. (2010) 'Extended Thresholds III: Auxiliary Architectures'. *Turkey: At the Threshold*, AD Architectural Design Vol. 80(1): 76–83.

Hensel, M. and Verebes, T. (1999) *Urbanisations*, London: Black Dog.

Hildebrand, A.v. (1893) *Das Problem der Form in der Bildenden Kunst*, Strasbourg: Heitz.

Hertzberger, H. (1996) 'Shell and Crystal'. In Strauven, F. *Aldo Van Eck's Orphanage – A Modern Monument*, Amsterdam: NAi Publishers.

Holl, S. (1993) 'Palazzo del Cinema'. In *GA Architect 11 – Steven Holl*, Tokyo: A.D.A. Edita, pp. 136–139.

Husserl, E. (1939) 'Der Ursprung der Geometrie als intentional-historisches Problem', *Revue international de philosophie* Vol.1(2), pp 203–225.

Jencks, C. (1984) *The Language of Post-modern Architecture*, New York: Rizzoli.

—— (2013 ([1997]) 'Landform Architecture: Emergent in the Nineties'. In Carpo, M. (ed.) *AD Reader: The Digital Turn in Architecture 1992–2012*, London: Wiley, pp. 88–107. Originally published in *AD 67* September–October 1997, pp. 15–31.

Kipnis, J. (1993) 'Towards a New Architecture'. In Lynn, G. (ed.) *Folding in Architecture – AD* 63(3–4): 40–49.

Klein, Y. (2004 [1958]) 'Fire, or The Future Without Forgetting The Past'. In Noever, P. and Perrin, F. (eds) *Air Architecture – Yves Klein*. Ostfildern-Ruit: Hatje Cantz.

—— (2013) [1959] 'The Evolution of Art Towards the Immaterial'. In Yves *Klein/Claude Parent – The Memorial, an Architectural Project*, Paris: Éditions Dilecta.

Koolhaas, R. (1994) *Delirious New York*, Rotterdam: 010 Publishers.

—— (2013 [2001]) 'Junkspace'. In Koolhaas, R. and Foster, H. *Junkspace with Running Room*, London: Notting Hill Editions, pp. 3–37.

Kuma, K. (2008) *Anti-object: The Dissolution and Disintegration of Architecture*, London: AA Publications.

Kwinter, S. (2001) *Architectures of Time – Towards a Theory of the Event in Modernist Culture*, Cambridge, MA: MIT Press.

Lang, F. (1984) 'Projects and Ideas'. In: Krause-Valdovinos, G. (ed.) *Schattenzelte: Sun and Shade – Toldos, Vela* (IL series, Vol. 30), Stuttgart: Institute for Lightweight Structures, pp. 124–131.

Larsen, C.T. and Lönberg-Holm, K. (1936) 'Design for Environmental Control'. *Architectural Record* August: 157–159.

Leatherbarrow, D. (2002) *Uncommon Grounds – Architecture, Technology, and Topography*, Cambridge, MA: MIT Press.

—— (2004) *Topographical Stories – Studies in Landscape and Architecture*, Philadelphia: University of Pennsylvania Press.

—— (2009) *Architecture Oriented Otherwise*, New York: Princeton Architectural Press.

Le Corbusier (1991 [1930]) *Precisions: On the State of Architecture and City Planning*, trans. Aujame, E.S., Cambridge, MA: MIT Press.

Lynn, G. (1998 [1993]) 'Probable Geometries'. In Lachowsky, M. and Benzakin, J. (eds) *Folds, Bodies and Blobs – Collected Essays*, Brussels: La Lettre Volée, pp. 79–94.

—— (1998 [1994]) 'Differential Gravities'. In Lachowsky, M. and Benzakin, J. (eds) *Folds, Bodies and Blobs – Collected Essays*, Brussels: La Lettre Volée, pp. 95–108.

Moussavi, F. and Zaera Polo, A. (1995) 'Yokohama International Port Terminal', *AA Files* Vol. 29: 14–21.

Mumford, E. (2001) 'The Emergence of Mat or Field Buildings'. In Sarkis, H. (ed.) *Le Corbusier's Venice Hospital*, Munich; London; New York: Prestel, pp. 48–65.

Oke, T.R. (1987) *Boundary Layer Climate*, 2nd edn, London: Routledge.

Parent, C. and Virilio, P. (1996) *Architecture Principe 1966 et 1996*, Les editions de l'imprimeur, Verdier edition.

Rajchman, J. (1998) *Constructions*, Cambridge, MA: MIT Press.

Reichholf, J.H. (2008) *Stabile Ungleichgewichte – Die Ökologie der Zukunft*. Franfurt a. M.: Suhrkamp.

Ricoeur, P. (2007 [1965]) 'Universal Civilisation and National Cultures'. In Canizaro, V.B. (ed.) *Architectural Regionalism – Collected Writings on Place, Identity, Modernity, and Tradition*, New York: Princeton Architectural Press, pp. 43–53.

Roche, F. (2004) '(Science) Fiction and Mass Culture Crisis'. *Corrupted Territories _ R&Sie(n) Architects DD Design Document Series* Vol. 5, pp. 5–11.

Rosenberg, N.J, Blad, B.L. and Verma, S.B. (1983) *Microclimate – The Biological Environment*, Chichester: John Wiley & Sons.

Rudofsky, B. (1964) *Architecture without Architects – A Short Introduction to Non-pedigreed Architecture*, New York: Museum of Modern Art.

Schmarsow, A. (1894) *Das Wesen der architektonischen Schöpfung*, Leipzig: Hiersemann.

Semper, G. (1989 [1851]) *The Four Elements of Architecture and Other Writings*, Cambridge: Cambridge University Press.

Spitzer, L. (1942) 'Milieu and Ambience – An Essay in Historical Semantics', *Philosophy and Phenomenological Research* Vol. 3: 1–42 and 169–218.

Torroja, E. (1958) *Philosophy of Structures*, Berkley and Los Angeles: University of California Press.

Tschumi, B. (1990 [1977]) 'The Pleasure of Architecture'. In Tschumi, B. *Questions of Space*. London: Architectural Association, p. 51.

Ulrich, W. (2002) 'Boundary Critique'. In Daellenbach, H.G. and Flood, R.L. (eds) *The Informed Student Guide to Management Science*, London: Thomson, pp. 41–42.

Vandermeer, J., van Nordwijk, M., Anderson, J., Ong, C. and Perfecto, I. (1998) 'Global Change and Multi-species Agroecosystems: Concepts and Issues'. *Agricultures, Ecosystems and Environment* Vol. 67: 1–22.

Vellinga, M., Oliver, P. and Bridge, A. (2007) *Atlas of Vernacular Architecture of the World*, London: Routledge.

Wagner, G. (1999) 'Looking Back Towards the Free University, Berlin'. In *Free University Berlin – Candilis, Josic, Woods, Schiedhelm – Exemplary Projects 3*, London: AA Publications.

Wall, A. (1999) 'Programming the Urban Surface'. In Corner, J. (ed.) *Recovering Landscape – Essays in Contemporary Landscape Architecture*, New York: Princeton Architectural Press, pp. 232–249.

Wolfe, C. (2010) *What is Posthumanism?*, Minneapolis; London: University of Minnesota Press.

Wölfflin, H. (1886) *Prolegomena zu einer Psychologie der Architektur*, Philosophische Dissertation, Universität München.

—— (1894) 'Rezension zu August Schmarsow "Das Wesen der architektonischen Schöpfung"'. *Repertorium für Kunstwissenschaft* Vol. 17(2): 141-following.

Wright, F.L. (1932) *An Autobiography*, London; New York; Toronto: Longmans, Green.

—— (1955 [1914]) In Kaufman, E. (ed.) *An American Architecture*, New York: Horizon Press.

Zaera Polo, A. (2008) 'The Politics of the Envelope – A Political Critique of Materialism'. *Log* Vol. 13: 193–207.

Zago, A. (1993) 'A New Federal Capital for Germany'. *OZ Journal* Vol. 15: 8–13.

Author Biographies

Michael U. Hensel (Dipl. Ing. Grad Dipl Des AA Ph.D. Reading) is an architect, researcher, educator and writer. Currently he is tenured Professor for Architecture at AHO the Oslo School of Architecture and Design where he directs the Research Centre for Architecture and Tectonics (www.rcat.no) and co-founded the Advanced Computational Design Laboratory (www.acdl.no). From 1993 to 2009 he taught at the Architectural Association School of Architecture in London. In his academic work he integrates research and education along a research-by-design trajectory with a strong emphasis on the development of non-discrete, performance-oriented and intensely local architectures (www.performanceorienteddesign.net), proof of concept through design-and-build efforts (www.scls.no), interdisciplinarity, and critical and projective abilities. He is a founding member of OCEAN (1994), and founding and current Chairman of the OCEAN Design Research Association (www.ocean-designresearch.net) and the Sustainable Environment Association (www.sustainableenvironmentassociation). From 2007 to 2012 he was a board member of BIONIS – The Biomimetics Network for Industrial Sustainability. He has been an editorial board member of the International Journal of Design Sciences and Technology since 2013. From 2007 to 2009 he was an editorial board member of the Journal for Bionic Engineering (JBE), Elsevier Scientific Press and from 2007 to 2014 of AD Wiley. He has authored, co-authored and edited numerous books and journals.

Jeffrey P. Turko (AA Dipl. RIBA II) hails from New Jersey, USA, and received his architectural education at the Architectural Association, London. He began practicing in 1999 under the name Urban-Office and has been a registered architect in The Netherlands since 2000. Before launching NEKTON STUDIO (www.nekton.org) in 2010 he was founding partner of the design practice NEKTON DESIGN in the early 2000's. A practice whose project work ranged in scales from urban design and private houses to art installations. A design practice which has received awards in international competitions and participated in expos such as the 2008 Beijing Biennial and has been published and exhibited widely. Most recent published work appears in, Performance – Oriented Architecture [AD WileY 2013] and Mobility of the Line [Birkhauser 2013]. Jeffrey is an educator and researcher currently based in the UK. He is a Senior Lecturer of Architecture at the University of Brighton where he teaches design, fabrication and technology. He has previously taught at the University of East London and at the Architectural Association School where he has acted as Director of the AA Global Visiting School in Sydney, Australia and most recently as the Director of the AA Global Visiting School Melbourne. He is also a member of the OCEAN Design Research Association (www.ocean-designresearch.net). In OCEAN he directs the Grounds and Envelopes research area and co-directs the Auxiliary Architectures research area.

Index

Page numbers in *italics* denotes an illustration/figure
Page numbers in **bold** denotes a chapter devoted to subject

AAGDG: Chiangliu City masterplan 16, *17*, 20–1, *21*
abiotic processes 58
Addington, Michelle 52
Agadir Convention Centre 15, 31, 179
agroecology 58, *60*
agroecosystems management 58–9
Ahmedabad: Mill Owners' Association Building 41, *41*
Air Architectures 38, 50, 180, 257, 265
air curtains 50
Alexander, Christopher 6, 51, 64; *A Pattern Language* 78
Allen, Stan 2, 6, 7, 122
Anatolia (Turkey) 61; underground cities of 29
animal species: provision of in architectures 59–62, *60*
animated envelopes 7
Anomalous Gallery project (Oslo) *40*
Aranda, Rafael 100
Archery Range (Barcelona Olympics) 14, **230—7**
Architectural Association: Graduate Design Program 132
architecture: Frampton's four elements of 66; Le Corbusier's five points of 138
articulated envelopes 7, 38, 41, 46–7
Arup: Advanced Geometry Unit 218
Asphalt Spot (Tokamashi, Japan) **167–71**
auxiliary architectures 7, 42, 43, 43–4, 49, 53
awnings 43

Baghdad Kiosk (Istanbul) 39, *40*, 41, 47
Balmond, Cecil 218
Banham, Reyner 47
Barcelona: Endesa Pavilion **245–52**; MediaTic 38, 199, 255, **258–64**
Barcelona Olympics (1992) 230; Archery Range 14, **230–7**
Barcode project (Oslo) 9
Barer, George *37*
Bates, Donald 132
Behling, S. and Behling, S. 39
Beinecke Rare Book and Manuscript Library (Yale University) 255
Berlage, H.P. 38
Berlin: Free University Building 15, 30; International Urban Planning Competition for Spreebogen area (1992) **94–8**; 'A Thousand Grounds' project - Spreebogen **132–7**, 236
biodiversity 8, 54, 57; planned and associated 58–9
biotic interactions 54
Blur Building (Yverdon-les-Bains, Switzerland) 22, 38, 50, **265–9**
boundaries 52
boundary problem 64
box-within-box section 19–20, *20*, 42, 111, *132*, 184, 190
Braga Municipal Stadium (Portugal) **152–8**
Brazilian Museum of Sculpture (MuBE) (Sao Paulo) 14, 31, 84, **87–93**, 98, 122
Brazilian Pavilion for the Osaka World Expo 14, 32, **83–6**, 100

Bunshaft, Gordon 255
Burle Marx, Roberto 90, 91–2

Caetano de Campos Education Institute 84
campfire 47
Catalhöyük (Turkey): Neolithic settlement 25–6
Chan, Mark 48
channelling systems strategy 15
Chiangliu City masterplan 16, *17*, 20—1, *21*
Chidori system 238, *238*, 244
Chile: *Las Piedras del Cielo* 32, 44, 45, 67, 71, 72; Pumanque community centre 46, 54, 70, 71, 75–8; Wall House 20, 41, 194, **200–6**, 210
China: underground dwellings (*yaodong*) 26
Church of the Holy Sepulchre (Jerusalem) 42
Church of San Martin de Porres (San Juan, Puerto Rico) 41
cinematic section 16
City of Culture of Galicia (Spain) **117–24**
climate, local 52–3
climatic events: staging of as part of an architecture 47, 50
closed outer envelope projects 20
Cloud 9 39; MediaTic (Barcelona, Spain) 38, 199, 255, **258–64**; Villa Nurbs 258
Collins, Peter 12
Cologne: apartment block 38, *39*, 41
Colquhoun, Alan 41, 63–4

column-slab system 1, 2–3, 4
Community Centre (Pumanque, Chile) 46, *46*, 54, 70, 71, 75—*8*
complex geometry 16
computer-aided design 66
continuous surface schemes 14–15, *18*, 21, 24, 31, 87, 145
Corner, James 32–3
Cressey, George B. 28
critical regionalism 9, 63–5; objective of 65
Czech National Library (Prague) 199, **224–9**

deep structures 41, 42
DeFormation 19
Deleuze, Gilles 16, 23
Derinkuya (Turkey) 29
Derrida, Jacques 16
design process 4
difference: and region 64
Diller, Scofidio and Renfro: Blur Building (Yverdon-les-Bains, Switzerland) 22, 38, 50, **265–9**
discrete architecture 1, 2, 5, 24
dovecotes 61–2
Down River Town project 37
Downsview Park competition (Toronto) 13–14
Downtown Athletics Club 3, 13

ecology 56
economic developments: impact of on architectural production 4
ecosystems 54, 54–9, *56*; and dynamic equilibrium 59; and stabile disequilibria 59
Eisenman, Peter 2, 5, 19; City of Culture of Galicia (Spain) **117–24**; Nördliches Derendorf masterplan (Düsseldorf) 117; Rebstock masterplan (Frankfurt) 117
Elisson, Olafur 265
embedded architectures 6
Endesa Pavilion (Barcelona, Spain) **245–52**
environments 51–62; provision for animal species in architectures 59–62
Estonian Academy of Arts (Tallinn) 199, **253–7**
'everyman's right' 25
Extended Threshold Studio (Oslo School of Architecture) 46, *47*, 54, *55*

FAR (Frohn and Rojas): Wall House (Santiago de Chile) 20, 41, 194, **200–6**, 210
Fathy, Hassan 38, 53
feather shades 43
Fernando Millan house (Sao Paulo) 31
field: shift from architectural object to 6
field-like spatial organization 2
figure-ground arrangement 1, 2, 7, *8*, 9, 23–4
Flamego Park (Rio de Janeiro) 116
floors: disjunction between stacked 3
Foreign Office Architects (FOA): Meydan-Umraniye Retail Complex & Multiplex (Istanbul) 14, 16, 20, 21, *22*, 47, **111–16**, 132, 137, 210; Yokohama International Passenger Terminal (Japan) 14, 16, *19*, **138–44**
Frampton, Kenneth 3, 4, 38, 52, 64, 66; 'Six Points for an Architecture of Resistance' 65
France: Jussieu Library scheme (Paris) 14, 17, 183; Le Fresnoy Art Centre (Tourcoing) 19, 20, 42, **189–94**, 210; Spidernethewood project (Nimes) 12, 21, 41, 53, 81, 206, **212–17**
Free University Building (Berlin) 15, 30
free-running buildings 8
'freedom to roam' 25
Fresnoy Art Centre, Le (Tourcoing, France) 19, 20, 42, **189–94**, 210
Frohn & Rojas *see* FAR
Future Vision for Kyoto competition 15

GAMMA 15, 30
gardens 12, 87, 90, 91
Gates, Charles 25
GC Prostho Museum Research Centre (Japan) 41, 214, **238–44**
geodiversity 57
geometry 16
Geopark Playground (Stavanger, Norway) 33, 98, 137, **172–7**, 201
Golany, Gideon 26
green roofs 54, *57*, *58*
greening of architecture 54
ground and membrane system 44, 46
Guattari, Félix 16, 23

Hadid, Zaha 218
Hamann, H. 42–3
heat islands, urban 52
Heatherwick, Thomas 214
Helen & Hard: Geopark Playground (Stavanger, Norway) 33, 98, 137, **172–7**, 201
Hensel, Michael 36
Hertzberger, Herman 31
Hi Res Lo Rise Scheme *49*

Hoen, Joakim: Seaside Second Homes 20, 38, 41, 53, 66, 194, **207–11**
Holl, Stephen 41; Palazzo del Cinema (Venice, Italy) 19, 20, 41, **184–8**, 194, 210
homogenization, global 63, 66
horizontal surface: preoccupation with by landscape urbanists 32–3
Husserl, Edmund 16

IAAC (Institute for Advanced Architecture of Catalonia): Endesa Pavilion (Barcelona, Spain) **245–52**
idiosyncratic architecture 2, 4, 66
Igualada Cemetery Park scheme 14, 236
Immaterial Dwellings 50
immersion 6
in-between space 19, 190
InFormation 19–20
informed non-standard architecture 207
Institute for Advanced Architecture of Catalonia see IAAC
International Urban Planning Competition: Spreebogen (Berlin) **94–8**, 103
interstitial space 19
Islamic screenwalls 38, 39, 53
Istanbul: Baghdad Kiosk 39, *40*, 41, 47; Meydan-Umraniye Retail Complex & Multiplex 14, 16, 20, 21, *22*, 47, **111–16**, 132, 137, 210
Italian Renaissance 39
Ito, Toyo: Serpentine Pavilion (London) **218–23**, 227, 247

Japan: Asphalt Spot (Tokamashi) **167–71**; GC Prostho Museum Research Centre 41, 214, **238–44**; Marquee for Les Cols Restaurant (Olot) 22, 32, 98, **99—103**, 137, 154, 264; Nexus World housing project (Fukuoka) 15, *28*, 31, 179; sun roofs 42; Yokohama International Passenger Terminal 14, 16, *19*, **138–44**
Jencks, Charles *8*, 16
Jerusalem: bazaar 25; Church of the Holy Sepulchre 42
junkspace 4, 15–16, 111
Jussieu Library scheme (Paris) 14, 17, 183

Kehne, Holger 46
Khaju Bridge *53*
Kipnis, Jeffrey 12, 19, 41–2, 132; 'Towards a New Architecture' 18–19
Klein, Yves 50, 257, 265
Koolhaas, Rem 1, 4, 13, 14, 15; *Delirious New York* 3, 13
Kropf, Reinhard 175
Ku-ring-gai National Park (Australia) 56
Kuma, Kengo 1, 5, 12; GC Prostho Museum Research Centre (Japan) 41, 214, **238–44**
Kwinter, Sanford 1, 6, 51

landform buildings 2, 7, 122
landscape: relationship between architecture and 12–14
landscape-oriented approach 6, 7, 13–16
landscape urbanism 13, 15, 16, 24
Landsc[r]aper Ringbridge project (Düsseldorf) 16, *18*
Lang, Fritz 43
Lasipalatsi Media Square competition (Helsinki) 15

Lautner, John 50
Le Corbusier 41, 63; five points of architecture 138; Maison Domino 2, 179; Villa Savoye 138
Leatherbarrow, David 6, 12, 13, 41, 51
Leça da Palmeira Swimming Pool (Portugal) 152, 154, **159–66**, 230
Libera, Adalberto *46*, 71
Libeskind, Daniel 218
lines 23
livestock: integration of into buildings 62
local climate 52–4
locality 8–9, 63–81; and critical regionalism 63; experimental small-scale projects 67; relationship between stereotomics and tectonics 65–6
Los Angeles: re-envisioning project *48*
louvre walls 41, *41*
Luminous Veil textile membrane screenwall (Izmir University of Economy) 44, *44*
Lynn, Greg 6, 16, 23, 24, 168

M-Velope project (New York City) 44, *45*
Macedo Soares, Lota de 116
map: importance of 23–4
Mardin (Turkey) 26, *27*, 236
Marquee for Les Cols Restaurant (Olot) (Japan) 22, 32, 98, **99–103**, 137, 154, 264
marquee tents 100
mashrabiyas 38, 53
mat-building typology 15, 30–1
MediaTic (Barcelona) 38, 199, 255, **258–64**

membrane systems 44, *45*, 47, 53–4
Mendas da Rocha, Paulo: Brazilian Museum of Sculpture 14, 31, 84, **87–93**, 98, 122; Brazilian Pavilion 14, 32, **83–6**, 100
Meydan-Umraniye Retail Complex & Multiplex (Istanbul) 14, 16, 20, 21, *22*, 47, **111–16**, 132, 137, 210
microclimate 52–5
Mill Owners' Association Building (Ahmedabad) 41, *41*
Miralles, Enric 16
Miralles, Enric (and Carme Pinós): Igualada Cemetery Park scheme 14, 236; Olympic Archery Range (Barcelona) 14, **230–7**
Moghul *jaalis* 38, 53
Moro, J.L. 42–3
Morocco 30
Morris Architects 253
Mostafavi, Mohssen *18*
multiple envelopes 7, 21, 38, 39–41, 42, 47
multiple grounds 7, 15, 25–6
Mumford, Eric 30
Museum of Sculpture (Sao Paulo) *see* Brazilian Museum of Sculpture
museums 87
MVRDV: Villa VPRO (Hilversum, Netherlands) 14, 50, **178–83**, 255, 261

nature conservation 59
Nekton Design 15; Turf City (Reykjavik, Iceland) 15, 31, 116, **145–51**, 158
Neolithic settlement (Catalhoyuk) 25–6
nestedness 7
NETSCAPE SCI-Arc Graduation Pavilion *80*

Neutra, Richard 13
New National Theatre (Tokyo) *20*
New York City: M-Velope project 44, *45*; World Centre for Human Concerns **195–9**
Nexus World housing project (Fukuoka, Japan) 15, *28*, 31, 179
Nolli, Giambattista: map of Rome 23, *24*
non-discrete architecture 1, 2, 5–6, 12, 16, 20, 59
non-standard architectures 66
Non-standard Architectures exhibition (2003/04) (Paris) 66
Nördliches Derendorf masterplan (Düsseldorf) 117
North African towns 30
Norway 25; Geopark Playground (Stavanger) 33, 98, 137, **172–7**, 201; Seaside Second Homes 20, 38, 41, 53, 66, 194, **207–11**
Novel, Jean *20*

oblique 14, 15, 171, 209
OCEAN: apartment block in Cologne 38, *39*, 41; Czech National Library (Prague) 199, **224–9**; Jyväskylä Music and Art Centre in (Finland) 16, *18*; Landsc[r]aper Ringbridge project (Düsseldorf) 16, *18*; Luminous Veil project 44, *44*; M-Velope project 44, *45*; Synthetic Landscape project 14, *15*; World Centre for Human Concerns (New York City) **195–9**
Oke, Tim 52, 53–4
Olympic Archery Range (Barcelona) 14, **230–7**
Olympic Sculpture Park (Seattle) 15, **104–10**

OMA *28*; Agadir Convention Centre 15, 31, 179; Jussieu Library scheme (Paris) 14, 17, 183; Nexus World Housing project (Fukuoka) 15, *28*, 31, 179
Open City (Ritoque, Chile) 64, 67, 71, 73, 74; *Las Piedras del Cielo* 32, *33*, 44, *45*, 67, 71, *72*–4
open outer envelope projects 20
Osaka World Expo: Brazilian Pavilion 14, 32, **83–6**, 100
Oslo: Anomalous Gallery project *40*; Barcode project *9*; Opera House *10*, 183
Oslo School of Architecture and Design 46, *47*, *see also* Scarcity and Creativity Studio
Otto, Frei 42
Oyler Wu Collaborative: Hi Res Lo Rise Scheme *49*; *NETSCAPE* SCI-Arc Graduation Pavilion *80*
Özkonak (Turkey) *29*

Palazzo de Cinema (Venice) 19, 20, 41, **184–8**, 194, 210
paper architectures 4
parametric architecture 3–4, 31
Parc de la Villette competition (Paris) 13–14
Parent, Claude 14, 171
parks, urban 13
partitioning of space 6
Persian Empire 61
Piedras del Cielo, Las project (Chile) 32, *32*, 44, *45*, 67, *72*–4
pigeon towers 61, *61*
Pinós, Carme *see* Miralles, Enric and Pinós, Carme
Piranesi 2, 19

pit cave dwellings 26, 28
plans 24
Plasma Studio and GroundLab: Xi'an Horticultural Expo (Longgang, China) **125–31**
Polo, Alejandro Zaera 3, 4, 42
Portugal: Braga Municipal Stadium **152–8**; Leça da Palmeira Swimming Pool 152, 154, **159–66**, 230
postmodernism 2–3, 4
privately-owned land: right of public use of 25
Protetch, Max 195
provisional grounds 7
Pruitt-Igoe project (St Louis, Missouri) 8
Puerto Rico: Church of San Martin de Porres (San Juan) 41
Pumanque community centre (Chile) 46, 54, 70, 71, 75–8

R&Sie(n): Asphalt Spot (Tokamashi, Japan) **167–71**; Spidernethewood project (Nimes, France) 12, 21, 41, 53, 81, 206, **212–17**
Rajchman, J. 23
RCR Arquitectes: Marquee for Les Cols Restaurant (Olot, Japan) 22, 32, 98, **99–103**, 137, 154, 264
Rebstock masterplan (Frankfurt) 117
regionalism 63
region(s): and boundary problem 64; and difference 64; institutional role of 64
Reichholf, Josef Helmut 59
Research Centre of Architecture and Tectonics (RCAT) 32
Reykjavik: airport 15; Turf City 15, 31, 116, **145–51**, 158

Ricoeur, P. 63
Roche, François 167
Roland, Conrad 197
romantic gardens 12
Rome: Giambattista's map of 23, *24*
Rosenberg, N.J. 54
Rubio, Rodrigo 245
Rudofsky, Bernard 26, 28

Sami people 195, 197
Scarcity and Creativity Studio 67–74; 2x2 Bathing Platform (Nusfjord, Norway) 32, *33*, *34*, 67, *68*, *69*; *Las Piedras del Cielo* project (Chile) 32, *32*, *44*, *45*, 67, *70–2*; Pumanque community centre (Chile) 46, 54, 71, 75–8; Sørenga Bridge Event Space 32, *35*
Scheffler + Partner 224
Schindler, Rudolph 13
Schodek, Daniel 52
School of Architecture and Design (Valparaiso) 64
Schouwburgplein (Rotterdam) 33
screenwalls 38, 46, 74; Islamic 38, *39*, 53; Luminous Veil textile membrane 44, *44*
Seaside Second Homes (Norway) 20, 38, 41, 53, 66, 194, **207–11**
Seattle Art Museum 14–15, **104–10**
sectional design methods 15–22, *18*
Semper, Gottfried: *The Four Elements of Architecture* 65, 66
serial sectional technique 16–18, *18*, 20
Serpentine Pavilion (London) **218–23**, 227, 247
Shanghai Expo (2010): British Pavilion 21

Sheats Goldstein Residence 50
Siza, Alvaro: Swimming Pool (Leça da Palmeira, Portugal) 152, 154, **159–66**, 230
Smilde, Berndnaut 265
Snøhetta: Oslo Opera House *10*, 183
Sørenga Bridge Event Space 32, 35
Sørensen, Soren S. 46
Souto de Moura, Eduardo, Braga Municipal Stadium (Portugal) **152–8**
Spain: City of Culture of Galicia **117–24**; *see also* Barcelona
Spanish toldos 42–3
spatial organization 6–7, 12–22; and continuous surface schemes 14–15; and gardens 12; landscape-oriented approach 6, 12–15; and mat-building typology 15; and sectional design methods 16–18, *18*, 20; and Wright 12–13
Spidernethewood project (Nimes, France) 12, 21, 41, 53, 81, 206, **212–17**
Spreebogen (Berlin): 'A Thousand Grounds' project **132–7**, 236; International Urban Planning Competition **94–8**, 103
stacking floors 3, 4, 7
'standing out' 4
Stangeland, Siv 175
star fort (trace atalienne) 23–4, *24*
Starck, Philippe *20*
stereotomics: and tectonics 65–6, *66*, 81
sun breaker 41
sun sails 42, 43
sustainability 7

Swimming Pool (Leça da Palmeira, Portugal) *see* Leça da Palmeira Swimming Pool
Switzerland: Blur Building (Yverdon-les-Bains) 22, 38, 50, **265–9**
Synthetic Landscape project 14, 15

Taipei: Zhonghua Road 16, *18*
Team X 15, 30
tectonics: and stereotomics 65–6, 66, 81
tents 43
textile membrane systems 43–4, *44*, *45*, 46, 53–4
theoretical projects 4
thick structures/screens 7, 38
Thousand Grounds project (Spreebogen) **132–7**, 236
thresholds: transition between interior and exterior as extended 7, 15, 18
Timberlake, Kieran 54
toldos, Spanish 42–3
topography 13
Torroja, Eduardo 2
Trans-Canada Highway (Alberta, Canada): wildlife crossing *60*
Tschumi, Bernard 12, 13; Le Fresnoy Art Centre (Tourcoing, France) 19, 20, 42, **189–94**, 210
Tunisia: cliff-cave and pit-cave dwellings 29, *29*, *30*
Turf City (Reykjavik, Iceland) 15, 31, 116, **145–51**, 158

Turko, Jeffrey 15, 46
2x2 Bathing Platform (Nusfjord, Norway) 32, *33*, *34*, 67, *68*, *69*

Ulrich, W. 64
unbuilt projects 4
underground dwellings 26–9; Tunisian cliff-cave and pit-cave dwellings 29, *29*, *30*; underground cities in Anatolia (Turkey) 29; *yaodong* (China) 26, 28–9, 32, 33
Urban Anomaly project *17*
urban climatology 52
urban ecology 8, 54
urban heat islands 52
Urban Office 15, *18*, *40*; Urban Anomaly project *17*
urban parks 13
urbanism, landscape 13, 15, 16, 24

Vandermeer, J. 58
vastness 18–19, 41–2
vegetation 53–4, 214–15
Vellinga, M.: *Atlas of Vernacular Architecture of the World* 64
Venice: Palazzo del Cinema 19, 20, 41, **184–8**, 194, 210
Villa Malaparte (Capri) 71
Villa Nurbs 258
Villa VPRO (Hilversum, Netherlands) 14, 50, **178–83**, 255, 261
Virilio, Paul 14, 171

Wagner, George 30
Wall, Alex 13, 24, 33
Wall House (Santiago de Chile) 20, 41, 194, **200–6**, 210
Weathers, Sean Lally: Estonian Academy of Arts (Tallinn) 199, **253–7**
Weiss/Manfredi: Olympic Sculpture Park (Seattle) 15, **104–10**
West 8 33
wilderness urbanism 217
Wolfe, Cary 14
World Centre for Human Concerns (New York City) **195–9**
World Expos 83
Wright, Frank Lloyd 12–13, 166

Xanthorrhoea (Australian grass-tree) *56*
Xi'an Horticultural Expo (Longgang, China) **125–31**

Yamasaki, Minoru *8*, 197
yaodong 26, 28–9
Yokohama International Passenger Terminal (Japan) 14, 16, *19*, **138–44**

Zaera Polo 38
Zago, Andrew: International Urban Planning Competition Spreebogen entry **94–8**, 103
ZKM Centre for Art and Media Karlsruhe 20

T - #0082 - 230323 - C294 - 276/216/15 - PB - 9780415639170 - Gloss Lamination